Insurance Law in Bosnia and Herzegovina

Insurance Law in Bosnia and Herzegovina

Dina Bajraktarević Pajević

This book was originally published as a monograph in the International Encyclopaedia of Laws/Insurance Law.

Founding Editor: Roger Blanpain
General Editor: Frank Hendrickx
Volume Editor: Herman Cousy

Wolters Kluwer

Published by:
Kluwer Law International B.V.
PO Box 316
2400 AH Alphen aan den Rijn
The Netherlands
E-mail: lrs-sales@wolterskluwer.com
Website: www.wolterskluwer.com/en/solutions/kluwerlawinternational

Sold and distributed by:
Wolters Kluwer Legal & Regulatory U.S.
920 Links Avenue
Landisville, PA 17538
United States of America
E-mail: customer.service@wolterskluwer.com

ISBN 978-94-035-2807-6

e-Book: ISBN 978-94-035-2817-5
web-PDF: ISBN 978-94-035-2827-4

The Author

Dr Dina Bajraktarević Pajević is a Full Professor at the Faculty of Criminal Justice, Criminology and Security Studies, University of Sarajevo, Bosnia and Herzegovina (B&H). She was born in Sarajevo, B&H, where she obtained her academic degrees in Law – Bachelor of Law (2006), Master of Law (2009) and her PhD from the Law Faculty, University of Sarajevo. Her research interests include the protection of consumers of insurance services and the investigation and prevention of insurance fraud.

The Author

Table of Contents

Table of Contents

List of Abbreviations

B&H	Bosnia and Herzegovina
BD B&H	Brcko District of Bosnia and Herzegovina
EU	European Union
FB&H	Federation of Bosnia and Herzegovina
HC B&H	High Court of Bosnia and Herzegovina
HC FB&H	High Court of Federation of Bosnia and Herzegovina
HCC	High Court of Croatia
IA B&H	Insurance Agency of Bosnia and Herzegovina
IAS	International Accounting Standards
IFRS	International Financial Reporting Standards
ISA	International Standards on Auditing
LAA B&H	Law on Accounting and Auditing of Bosnia and Herzegovina
LCIT	Law on Compulsory Insurance in Traffic
LCP	Law on Consumer Protection
LEMRDU	Law on Employment Mediation and Rights During Unemployment
LERDU	Law on Employment and Rights During Unemployment
LHP	Law on Health Protection
LI	Law on Insurance
LIC	Law on insurance Companies
LIM	Law on Insurance Mediation
LIML	Law on Insurance against Motor Liability
LMESSUP	Law on Mediation in Employment and Social Security of Unemployed Persons
LPDI	Law on Pension and Disability Insurance
LPIT	Law on Personal Income Tax
LRMIR RS	Law on Representation and Mediation in Insurance and Reinsurance
LVAT	Law on Value Added Tax

List of Abbreviations

LVPF	Law on Voluntary Pension Funds
LVPFPP	Law on Voluntary Pension Funds and Pension Plans
LVPFPS	Law on Voluntary Pension Funds and Pension Schemes
OJ	Official Journal
RS	Republic of Srpska
VAT	Value Added Tax
B&H	Bosnia and Herzegovina

Preface

This monograph has been prepared on the basis of the present legal framework for insurance activity in Bosnia and Herzegovina (B&H). Due to the specific state organization of B&H and its position as a potential candidate for accession to the European Union (EU), the insurance legal regime is in a process of constant reform that includes internal harmonization of the Entity – level insurance legislation, on one side, and the harmonization of the state – level legislation with the EU insurance legislation and international standards in order to ensure implementation of European rules, on the other. Because of this, important pieces of contemporary insurance legislation are yet to be adopted.

This monograph presents some of the key characteristics of B&H's complex legal regime regarding insurance companies and practices. The reader should have in mind that the reinsurance company is not separately elaborated within the monograph and that references are made within the segments dedicated to insurance companies and reinsurance. Finally, it should be noted that the insurance sector in B&H is underdeveloped in comparison to the other countries in the region and the EU, which is strongly reflected in the characteristics of the legal regime as presented in the monograph.

The author would like to thank Mrs Božana Šljivar and Mr Mladen Jovanović from the Insurance Agency of the Republic of Srpska and Mr Zlatan Filipović from the Bosna Reinsurance Company for their assistance in the preparation of this work.

General Introduction

1. Bosnia and Herzegovina (B&H) is a developing European country, situated on the western part of the Balkan Peninsula. It is a complex state that consists of two Entities – the Federation of Bosnia and Herzegovina (FB&H) and the Republic of Srpska (RS). Bosnia and Herzegovina was one of the six constituent republics of the Socialist Federal Republic of Yugoslavia. B&H declared its independence in 1992.

§1. General Background Information

I. The Political System

2. B&H has a complicated, multi-layered political system that is characterized by the division of sovereign power between the state and the two Entities: the FB&H and the RS. Both Entities are governed as federal units. State-level institutions are mostly located in Sarajevo, the capital of B&H.

3. The uniqueness of the Constitution of B&H is enshrined due to the fact that it is part of the General Framework Agreement for Peace in B&H. More precisely, it is contained in Annex 4 of the Agreement. The provision of the Constitution of B&H relevant to this monograph refers to the prohibition of impediments to the freedom of movement of persons, goods, services and capital throughout B&H. This provision is contained in Article I(4) of the Constitution of B&H. Article III(3)(a) of the Constitution of B&H stipulates the presumption of competences in favour of the Entities. Namely, it specifies that all governmental functions and powers not expressly assigned in the Constitution of B&H to the institutions of B&H shall belong to the Entities. Furthermore, the Constitution of B&H in Article III(5)(a) provides for additional state's competences regarding the matters: agreed upon by the Entities; provided for in Annexes 5 through 8 to the General Agreement; or necessary to preserve the sovereignty, territorial integrity, political independence and international personality of B&H in accordance with the division of responsibilities between the institutions of B&H. However, exclusive competence for the regulation of financial services markets belongs to the Entities (the Constitution of FB&H and the Constitution of the RS). Although the Constitution of B&H does not explicitly mention the principle of the division of power, the analysis of relevant provisions of the Constitution indicates that tripartite division is applied: legislative, executive and judicial. One of the key constitutional principles is the principle of constituency of peoples, i.e., three ethnic groups (Bosniacs, Serbs and Croats), which is strongly reflected in the formation of the legislative, executive and judicial authority at every level of state organization.

4. The legislative power of state government is vested in the Parliamentary Assembly, which consists of two chambers: the House of Peoples and the House of Representatives. The Parliament assembly has the power to: enact legislation, decide upon the sources and amounts of revenues for the operations of the institutions of B&H and international obligations, approve a budget for the institutions of B&H, give consent to the ratification of treaties and other matters that are necessary to carry out its duties or that are assigned to it by mutual agreement of the Entities. All legislation must be approved by both chambers. The House of Peoples comprises fifteen delegates. Two-thirds of the delegates are from the FB&H (five Croats and five Bosniacs) and one-third from the RS (five Serbs). Delegates from the FB&H are elected by the delegates of the House of Peoples of the Federation. Similarly, delegates from the second Entity, the RS are chosen by the National Assembly of the RS. The House of Representatives is comprised of forty-two members, two-thirds elected from the territory of the FB&H and one-third from the territory of the other Entity. Members of the House of Representatives are directly elected from their Entity in accordance with election law.

5. The executive power at state level is exercised by the Presidency and the Council of Ministers. B&H's Presidency consists of three members: two members elected from the territory of the FB&H (one Bosniac and one Croat) and one member elected from the territory of the RS. The members of the state Presidency are directly elected in each Entity (with each voter voting to fill one seat of the Presidency).[1] The term of this collective head of the state is four years. According to the constitutional rule set in Article V(1)(b), members of the state Presidency can serve two terms and thereafter are ineligible for four years.

6. The state Presidency's members appoint a chair. For the first term of the Presidency, the chair becomes the member with the highest number of votes. Afterwards, the chairing of the new convocation of the Presidency is automatically determined in accordance with the rotation of the previous convocation, unless the members reach a different decision by consensus. The Presidency chairmanship is changed every eight months. The general rule is that the Presidency adopts all decisions by consensus. Such decisions may be adopted by two members when all efforts to reach a consensus have failed. The dissenting member of the Presidency may declare such a decision to be detrimental to the interests of the Entity from the territory in which he/she was elected, provided that he/she does so within three days of its adoption. However, such a decision shall be referred immediately to the National Assembly of the RS, if the declaration was made by the member from that territory; to the Bosniac delegates of the House of Peoples of the Federation, if the declaration was made by the Bosniac member; or to the Croat delegates of that

1. *See* the Constitution of B&H, Art. V(1)(a).

body, if the declaration was made by the Croat member.[2] If the declaration is confirmed by a two-thirds vote within ten days of the referral, the challenged Presidency decision does not take effect.[3]

7. The second executive authority at state level is the Council of Ministers. The Presidency nominates the Chair of the Council of Ministers, who assumes office upon the approval of the second chamber of the Parliament Assembly. If the new Chairman is not confirmed by the House of Representatives, the Presidency must appoint a new candidate within eight days and submit this decision for approval to the House of Representatives. Immediately after assuming office, the Chair of the Council of Ministers is required to appoint ministers and deputy ministers.[4] The ministerial appointments then have to be promptly approved by the House of Representatives. If the House of Representatives decides to reject the decision of the Chairman of the Council of Ministers, the Chairman must then appoint another member to assume the position in question within a period of eight days and resubmit that decision for approval to the second chamber, or resign. The Chair and the ministers together constitute the Council of Ministers, with the responsibility for carrying out the policies and decisions of B&H in the fields referred to in Article III(1), (4) and (5) and reporting to the Parliamentary Assembly (including, at least annually, on expenditures by B&H). No more than two-thirds of all ministers may be appointed from the territory of the Federation. The Chair is also required to nominate deputy ministers (who may not be of the same constituent people as their ministers), and who may assume office upon the approval of the House of Representatives.[5]

8. The Chairman of the Council of Ministers, ministers and deputy of ministers can resign without explanation. If the Chair resigns or is permanently unable to perform his/her duties, the Council of Ministers is required to resign as a whole. The Presidency of B&H may propose the dismissal of the Chairman of the Council of Ministers. If the Chairman obtains a vote of no confidence by the Parliament Assembly, the Council of Ministers is obligated to resign as a whole, but may continue to perform its duties until the new Chairman and members of the Council of Ministers are confirmed. Furthermore, the Council of Ministers are required to resign if at any time there is a vote of no confidence by the Parliamentary Assembly.

9. The Constitutional Court of B&H represents the form of institutionalized protection of constitutionality traditionally present in the legal system of B&H. It is the only judicial institution on state level that is regulated by the Constitution of B&H[6] since the Constitution delegates the organization of the judicial system to the Entities and the Brcko District of B&H.[7] The Constitutional Court consists of nine members. Four members are selected by the House of Representatives of the Federation,

2. *See ibid.*, Art. V(2)(d).
3. *Ibid.*
4. *See ibid.*, Art. V(4).
5. *See ibid.*, Art. V(4)(b).
6. *See ibid.*, Art. VI.
7. *See ibid.*, Art. III(3)(a).

and two members by the Assembly of the RS. The remaining three members are selected by the President of the European Court of Human Rights following a consultation with the Presidency. These judges cannot be citizens of B&H or citizens of any neighbouring state. All appointed judges serve until the age of 70 unless they resign or are removed for cause by consensus of other judges. Due to the influence of the German legal tradition, the position of the Constitutional Court of B&H entails exclusive jurisdiction regarding the disputes that arise under the Constitution between the Entities or between B&H and the Entity or Entities, or between institutions of B&H.[8] Furthermore, the jurisdiction of this Court extends to determine the consistency with the Constitution of the Entity's special parallel relationship with a neighbouring state and provisions in the Entity's constitution or laws. Disputes can only be referred by a member of the Presidency, the Chairman of the Council of Ministers, one-fourth of the members of either chamber of the Parliament Assembly, or one-fourth of either chamber of the legislature of an Entity.[9] The Constitutional Court also has appellate jurisdiction over issues under this Constitution arising out of a judgment of any other court in B&H and over issues referred by any court in B&H concerning whether a law, on whose validity its decision depends, is compatible with the Constitution of B&H, with the European Convention for Human Rights and Fundamental Freedoms and its Protocols, or with the laws of B&H; or concerning the existence of or the scope of a general rule of public international law pertaining to the court's decision. Decisions of the Constitutional Court are final and binding.[10]

10. The judicial system of the FB&H includes the municipal, the cantonal and the Supreme Court as the highest judicial authority. Abstract and concrete normative control is performed by the Constitutional Court of FB&H. It is not included in the court system as a court of last instance. Similarly, the judicial system of the RS consists of general courts, district courts, the Supreme Court and the Constitutional Court of the RS. The Brcko District of Bosnia and Herzegovina (BD B&H) also has its own judicial organization that includes the General Court and the Court of Appeal.

11. A particularity of B&H's judicial system is the establishment of a special state-level judicial institutional Court of B&H in order to guarantee the effective application of human rights and the rule of law.[11] This state Court has criminal, administrative and appellate jurisdiction, but unfortunately, the highest judicial power is not vested in it. To be precise, the Court of B&H is powerless with respect to the harmonization of law application in distinct jurisdictions: the state, the FB&H, the RS and the BD B&H.

8. *See ibid.*, Art. VI(3).
9. *See ibid.*, Art. VI(3)(a).
10. *See ibid.*, Art. VI(4).
11. *See* the Law on Court of B&H (OJ B&H, 49/2009), Art. 1(1).

12. In order to ensure the independence, impartiality and professionalism of the judiciary, judges in all courts at the state, Entity, cantonal, district, basic and municipal levels (including the BD B&H) in B&H are appointed by an independent state organ – the High Judicial and Prosecutorial Council of B&H.[12] This appointment process does not include the judges of the constitutional courts of the state and the Entities. The Council also appoints prosecutors at all mentioned levels of the judicial organization. Besides appointments of judges and prosecutors, the Council also: receives complaints against judges and prosecutors, conducts disciplinary proceedings, determines disciplinary liability, imposes disciplinary measures on judges and prosecutors, supervises the advanced professional training of judges and prosecutors, etc.[13]

13. The two Entities of B&H are organized differently. While the FB&H is highly decentralized into ten cantons with extensive competences resembling federal states, the RS is greatly centralized. The BD B&H has a special status as a self-governing administrative unit within the complex territorial organization of B&H. Separated from both Entities, it is subjected only to the control of the state. Governments of both Entities as well as the government of the BD B&H are in general organized along the same tripartite lines as the state government.

II. Commerce and Industry

14. The economic system of B&H has been strongly influenced by political conditions that shaped and directed its development. Change from a centrally planned economy to a market-oriented economy, which started at the end of the eighties is ongoing. This lengthy transition process is due to the slow process of post-war reconstruction. Due to this and a still complex political situation, the economy of B&H is characterized by stagnation. Although there is continuous development of economic activity, economic growth is still modest.[14]

15. Large quantities of water, forest wealth, land and mineral wealth make the country relatively rich in natural resources. Those natural resources represent B&H's comparative advantage. Furthermore, the comparative advantage of B&H also lies in the production of hydropower, coal and thermal energy, iron ores and ferrous metallurgy, bauxite and the aluminium industry as well as the processing of other important metals, non-metals (rock salt, pyrophyllite, barite, asbestos, kaolin and gypsum) and building materials (decorative stone, limestone, dolomite, clay, sand and gravel). Other dominant branches of industry also include the wood industry, chemical industry, textile industry and machine industry.

12. *See* the Law on High Judicial and Prosecutorial Council of B&H (OJ 25/04, 93/05, 48/07, 15/08), Art. 17(1).
13. *See* the Law on High Judicial and Prosecutorial Council of B&H, Art. 17(2).
14. Directorate for Economic planning (2021), *Bosnia and Herzegovina Economic Trends, Annual Report 2020*. http://www.dep.gov.ba/razvojni_dokumenti/izvjestaji/Archive.aspx?langTag=bs-BA&template_id=140&pageIndex=1 (accessed: 15. Dec. 2022).

16. Confinement of the monetary policy of B&H by the currency board arrangement is characterized by the impossibility to utilize the basic instruments of monetary policy. The Central Bank of B&H cannot give credit to the state in order to cover the budgetary deficit, nor can it grant credit to the commercial banks in order to protect liquidity of the banking system (it is not the lender of last resort).[15] Given that it does not grant credit, it cannot determine the discount rate or in any other way influence the level of interest rates. Also, the Law on Central Bank of B&H explicitly forbids the involvement of the Central Bank in any operations on the money markets including securities of any kind.[16] As a result, the only instrument of monetary policy available to the Central Bank is the required reserve. This sole instrument of monetary policy is maintained by keeping cash or money deposits with the Central Bank and it is calculated in the form of average daily reserves in a ten-day period.[17]

III. Financial Institutions

17. The first forms of organized securities trading within the territory of B&H were performed after B&H became part of the Austro-Hungarian Empire. The shares of B&H's companies appeared on advanced stock exchanges in Vienna and Budapest at the time. In addition to these stock exchanges, other important stock markets in the region were established in Belgrade and Zagreb, which initially only traded securities that large stock exchanges, such as the above-mentioned, refused to enlist. In the mid-1930s, new single regulation on stock markets was adopted, which gave equal basis for operations to all stock exchanges established in the Kingdom of Serbs, Croats and Slovenes. In the socialist state organization, the operation of stock exchanges ceased. The commencement of comprehensive social and economic reforms only occurred at the end of the 1980s after the adoption of the Law on the Money Market and Capital Market created the conditions for the reestablishment of the capital market. The Yugoslav capital market was founded in 1989 by the largest banks from the territory of the former Yugoslavia.

18. The development of the capital market in B&H, after its declaration of independence was discontinued due to the war. Today the capital market of B&H is organized and regulated in the form of two capital markets with separate legislative and institutional frameworks. Securities are traded on the two stock exchanges established in 2001: the Sarajevo Stock Exchange and the Banja Luka Stock Exchange. Both officially began to operate in 2002. The functioning of the capital market is under administration of the Entities' securities commissions (Securities

15. *See* the Law on Central Bank of B&H, OJ 1/1997, 29/2002, 8/2003, 13/2003, 14/2003, 9/2005, 76/2006.
16. *See* the Law on Central Bank of B&H, Art. 37.
17. *See ibid.*, Art. 36(2).

Commission of the FB&H and Securities Commission of the RS) that act as supervisors and regulators.[18] Both Entities have established institutions of the registries of securities (Registry of Securities of FB&H and Registry of Securities of RS)[19] that perform important operations that include, *inter alia*: the registration and storage of data on securities and all transactions relating to the transfer of ownership or change of status; the opening and management of accounts of securities and the list of shareholders and reports on issuing, certification and verification on the status of and changes on these accounts; calculations, settlements and transfer of securities based on transactions on the stock exchange or other regulated public markets, etc.

19. The beginnings of organized banking in the territory of B&H appeared at the end of the nineteenth century under the rule of the Austro-Hungarian Empire. Initially, foreign monetary institutions were founded as forerunners of banking institutions. After World War I, these monetary institutions were formally nationalized. Although the number of institutions increased, their capital never reached half the amount of its pre-war state. The prosperity that followed the end of World War I did not bring a capital boost, but only its rapid circulation and high profitability. Most of these monetary institutions dealt purely with credit operations. After World War II, nationalization of all banking institutions was enforced and transferred to the administrative – central planning in accordance with the socialist state occurred. The banking system in this respect was characterized by the absence of capital markets and frequent changes: the phase of organization in accordance with the territorial principle on federal, republican and local banks (i.e., municipal banks and savings banks) was replaced with the phase of administrative management and absolute concentration of the banking system – a system of one single bank. The phase of gradual decentralization followed, when in addition to the National bank, specialized banks, local banks such as municipal and communal thrift institutions as well as city and local savings institutions began to operate; the next phase saw the establishment of commercial banks whose operations were relatively independent; and finally, the phase of reorganization of the National bank – a System of central banks was introduced instead of a single Central Bank, which included the National bank of Yugoslavia and central banks of republics and provinces. The concentration of financial assets and their circulation was achieved through the organization of the banking sector in a manner that included banks, specialized financial institutions and savings and credit organizations. The banking system established in the socialist state system assigned an important role to the Service of Social Accounting (*Služba društvenog knjigovodstva*) entrusted with the management of social accounting, control, statistical analysis and keeping a record of cash flow.

20. Following the Declaration of Independence, B&H's banking sector went through reform with the aim of financial liberalization. More intensive development

18. *See* the Law on Securities Commission of FB&H, OJ FB&H, 39/1998, 39/1999, 33/2004, 92/2013, 6/2017; and the Law on the Securities Market of RS, OJ RS, 92/2006, 34/2009, 30/2012, 59/2013, 108/2013, 04/2017, 63/2021.
19. *See* the Law on Securities Registry in FB&H, OJ FB&H, 39/1998, 36/1999, 33/2004; and the Law on the Securities Market of RS, OJ RS, 92/2006, 34/2009, 30/2012, 59/2013108/2013, 04/2017, 63/2021.

of the banking sector occurred after the adoption of the Law on Politics of Direct Investments in B&H, the establishment of the Central Bank of B&H and the introduction of a single currency in cash and non-cash payment operations. Today, commercial banking dominates the financial system of B&H, which is organized into two banking sectors within the Entities. Banking sectors are under supervision of Entities' banking agencies (Banking Agency of the FB&H and Banking Agency of the RS). The complex legal framework in the banking sector includes the Entities' laws: on banks,[20] banking agencies,[21] microcredit organizations[22] and leasing,[23] the FB&H Law on the Development Bank of FB&H,[24] the Foreign Exchange Operations Act,[25] the Law on National Payment Transactions in RS,[26] the Law on Saving-Credit Organizations in RS,[27] the Law on Deposit Insurance in Banks of B&H[28] and a number of various secondary regulations adopted by competent banking agencies.

IV. Currency Legislation and Monetary Regulations

21. The monetary policy regime applied in B&H is the arrangement known as the currency board, based on the fixed exchange rate and rules determined by the Law on the Central Bank of B&H.[29] The exchange rate of the national currency convertible mark (*konvertibilna marka* – KM; currency code is BAM) is pegged to the Euro (EUR) in the ratio of 1 EUR=BAM 1.95583. Full convertibility of the domestic currency into the Euro as the reserve currency (and vice versa) and thus in other currencies is guaranteed. The Central Bank of B&H emissions and withdraws money by purchasing and selling the convertible marks in exchange for foreign currencies. The purchasing and selling of the convertible mark is done with commercial banks and state institutions that have deposits with the Central Bank of B&H while the other economic agents obtain the funds in domestic currency via commercial banks. Net foreign currency reserves of the Central Bank must, at all times, fully cover its monetary liabilities in convertible marks, which include: all the banknotes and coins in circulation, balances of reserve accounts of commercial banks with the Central Bank of B&H and other demand deposits (sight deposits) with the Central Bank of B&H. One of the key prerequisites for sustainability of the established currency board arrangement is the absence of the possibility of the Central Bank of B&H to monetize the fiscal deficit as well as the possibility of crediting

20. The Law on Banks of FB&H, OJ FB&H, 27/2017; and the Law on Banks of RS, OJ RS, 4/2017, 19/2018, 54/2019.
21. The Law on the Banking Agency of FB&H, OJ FB&H, 75/2017; the Law on the Banking Agency of RS, OJ RS, 59/2013, 4/2017.
22. The Law on Microcredit Organizations in FB&H, OJ FB&H, 59/06; the Law on Microcredit Organizations in RS, OJ RS, 64/2006, 116/2011.
23. The Law on Leasing in FB&H, OJ FB&H, 85/2008, 39/2009, 65/2013, 104/2016; and the Law on Leasing in RS, OJ RS, 70/2007, 116/2011.
24. OJ FB&H, 37/2008.
25. *Ibid.*, 47/2010.
26. OJ RS, 52/2012, 92/2012, 58/2019, 38/2022.
27. *Ibid.*, 93/2006.
28. OJ B&H, 32/2020.
29. *Ibid.*, 1/1997, 29/2002, 8/2003, 13/2003, 14/2003, 9/2005, 76/2006.

any economic agent. Furthermore, the Central Bank of B&H is deprived of the function of bank supervisor having in mind that it can only coordinate the functioning of the agencies that are responsible for chartering and supervising the banks at the Entities level.

22. The Constitution of B&H stipulates that the Central Bank of B&H is the sole authority for issuing currency and for monetary policy in B&H.[30] The vital objective of the Central Bank of B&H is to achieve and maintain stability of domestic currency (the convertible mark) by issuing the domestic currency under the currency board arrangement. The basic unit of currency in B&H is the convertible mark (KM), which is after the withdrawal of 1 KM banknotes from circulation in 2009 issued only in coins. On the banknotes are presented portraits of famous writers from B&H: Mehmedalija Mak Dizdar and Aleksa Šantić on the 10 convertible mark banknotes, Antun Branko Šimić and Filip Višnjić on the 20 convertible mark banknotes, Musa Cazim Catić and Jovan Dučić on the 50 convertible mark banknotes, Nikola Šop and Petar Kočić on the 100 convertible mark banknotes and Ivo Andrić on the 200 convertible mark banknotes. Convertible mark coins are minted in the denomination of 1, 2 and 5 convertible marks. The lowest denomination coin in circulation is the 5 fening which is one-twentieth of a convertible mark.

23. The monetary policy of B&H is limited by the currency board arrangement which is manifested in the form of the inability to use the basic instruments of monetary policy. As previously mentioned, the Central Bank cannot give credit to the state in order to cover the budgetary deficit nor can it grant credit to commercial banks in order to protect liquidity of the banking system (it is not the lender of last resort). Given that it does not grant credit, it cannot determine the discount rate or in any other way influence the level of interest rates. Also, the Law explicitly excludes the engagement of the Central Bank in any operation on the money market including securities of any kind.[31] The required reserve is therefore the only instrument of monetary policy available to the Central Bank. This sole instrument of monetary policy is maintained by keeping cash or money deposits with the Central Bank, and it is calculated in the form of average daily reserves in a ten-day period.[32]

V. Insurance Business, General Organization and Special Features

24. In the financial services sector, largely dominated by banking services (88.35%), insurance services represent only a small share of total assets (5.47%). Despite the continuous growth in the last two decades, the insurance industry in B&H is relatively underdeveloped. This is strongly confirmed by the following: only 2.12% of the achieved insurance premium in GDP and the prevalence of the

30. *See* the Constitution of B&H, Art. VII.
31. *See* the Law on Central Bank of B&H, Art. 37.
32. *See ibid.*, Art. 36(2).

compulsory automobile third-party liability insurance sector (49.96%).[33] Another characteristic of the insurance business in B&H is a low level of development of the life assurance market (21.36%) with a prevalence of non-life insurance (78.64%).[34] Nevertheless, life insurance shows continuous but modest growth. To be precise, in the last four years, the annual growth rate of life assurance was 7.52%.[35] According to the ownership structure of the insurance companies in B&H, domestic insurance companies still prevail (fifteen domestic insurance companies versus ten foreign insurance companies). However, the share of companies with the majority of foreign capital in total premiums in 2021 amounted to 54.62%.[36] The share of these companies was much larger in the life assurance market and amounted to 98.16%.[37] The share of companies with the majority foreign capital in the non-life insurance market in 2021 was 42.80%.[38]

25. Particularities of the political system have strongly influenced the organization of the insurance business in B&H. Consequently, there are two insurance markets with separate legislative and institutional frameworks. Companies with the intention to engage in providing insurance services must obtain an Entity licence issued by the relevant supervisory and regulatory agency. A company registered for the provision of insurance in one Entity (FB&H or RS), can provide insurance services in the other Entity only through registered subsidiaries.

26. The insurance business is not equally developed in both Entities. The total gross written premium in B&H was BAM 818,406,451 and the share of the companies with the office in the FB&H in total premium was 69.99%, whereas the share of the companies from the RS was 30.01%.[39]

§2. Historical Background of Insurance and Insurance Legislation

27. Insurance activities in their contemporary form have been present in B&H since the second half of the nineteenth century in accordance with the Commercial Law for B&H from 1883. The development of the insurance business in the territory of B&H closely followed the development of the insurance business in the region, where the first insurance policies were offered primarily by foreign insurance companies. This Law did not stipulate particular rules on the subject of insurance, so the general provisions on commercial transactions were applicable. However, the Order given in the 1907 edition of Commercial Law for B&H, which

33. *See* the Insurance Agency of B&H (2022), *2021 Annual Report of the Insurance Agency of B&H*, http://www.azobih.gov.ba/dokumenti/publikacija-en-21.pdf (accessed: 22 Dec. 2022).
34. *See* the Insurance Agency of B&H (2022), *2021 Annual Report of the Insurance Agency of B&H*, 46, 64.
35. *See ibid.*, 40.
36. *See ibid.*, 33.
37. *Ibid.*
38. *Ibid.*
39. *See ibid.*, 35.

approved business transactions of Austrian and Hungarian joint-stock and commercial companies, explicitly mentioned insurance companies. Conducting business was conditioned on the appointment of a representative with a permanent residence in the territory of B&H. Furthermore, under this Law, foreign companies were required to duly prove their legitimate existence in their country of origin to the Common Ministry, the ruling authority at the time.

28. During the period of the Kingdom of Serbs, Croats, and Slovenes and the Kingdom of Yugoslavia, the concession system was applicable to the insurance sector. Under this system, in order for insurance companies to offer their services, it was not sufficient to establish an insurance company in the form of a joint-stock company or cooperative because the state held the discretionary right to grant concessions, that is to give permission to carry out operations. The involvement of the state transformed this concessional, i.e., discretional system into a normative system under which a concession is automatically obtained following the satisfaction of the stipulated requirements. The collapse of a number of insurance companies eventually resulted in a general lack of confidence in the insurance business. This prompted the adoption of the Regulation of the insurance sector and placed all insurance companies under the strict control of the Ministry of Commerce and Industry, the national supervisory authority. Adoption of this Regulation marked a turning point in the development of insurance in the Kingdom of Yugoslavia. Some of the basic conditions, which this Regulation stipulated, were that insurance businesses could operate only in the form of joint-stock companies, paid-up capital had to be at least 3 million dinars, every insurance company performing life assurance operations had to appoint its actuary to verify the accuracy of the calculation of the mathematical reserves. The type and amount of investment from the mathematical reserve had to be accurately determined. The funds from savings premiums were not permitted to be used for other types of insurance.

29. After World War II, the organization of the established insurance system was thoroughly altered. The State Insurance Bureau (*Državni osiguravajući zavod*) was established in 1946 and transitioned to the system of insurance bureaus and communities in 1961. It decentralized the organization and business of the insurance sector and introduced social management in insurance. In 1967, the system was replaced with a system of insurance and reinsurance bureaus and thus significantly equalized the insurance organizations with other commercial organizations in the legal system. However, 1971 was the year that marked the beginning of the insurance system that was officially founded in the 1974 Constitution and Law on Fundamentals of Property and Person Insurance. Constitutional amendments from 1988 established the new system which was shaped in accordance with the Law on Fundamentals of Property and Person Insurance from 1990. This new system transformed organizations for property and person insurance into new financial organizations that had the character of market economy subjects and at the same time harmonized the relevant republic and provincial laws.

30. After the independence of B&H in 1992, the Collective Presidency of the Republic of B&H issued a Regulation on taking over the federal legislation including the federal Law on Fundamentals of System Insurance of Property and Person. Additionally, in the territory of B&H a former republican Law, the Law on Insurance of Property and Person in the FB&H was introduced in 1995. This Law was in force for a decade until the new reform of insurance law replaced it with three new laws: the Law on Insurance Companies in Private Insurance, the Law on Motor Vehicle Liability Insurance and Other Provisions on Compulsory Liability Insurance, and the Law on Mediation in Private Insurance.

31. The reform process has progressed simultaneously in the RS, the other B&H Entity, where the old republican Law on Property and Person Insurance was also replaced in 2005 by three new laws: the Law on Insurance Companies, the Law on Motor Vehicle Liability Insurance and Other Compulsory Liability Insurances, and the Law on Mediation in Insurance.

§3. Sources of Insurance Law

I. Legislation

32. Due to the specific structure of the political system of B&H and the continuous changes in its legislation, there are plenty of legal provisions in place to regulate the insurance industry. However, at state level there is only one law: the Law of the Insurance Agency of B&H.[40] The main purpose of this Law is to ensure the necessary approximation of the Entities' insurance legislation and to regulate the legal position and competencies of the state Insurance Agency. Having in mind that supervisory government agencies are situated at the Entities' level, the role of this Agency has been reduced to the fulfilment of duties to provide: uniform implementation of the Entities' insurance legislation; efficient cooperation between insurance supervisory agencies of the FB&H and the RS; and implementation and interpretation of the Entities' legal provisions on fair and uniform grounds. Furthermore, the Agency has to ensure equal treatment of all insurance companies in both Entities and in the BD B&H and to provide equal legal protection to policyholders and third parties, i.e., claimants. Also, one of the key duties of the Agency is to ensure harmonization of the insurance legislation with pertinent legislation of the EU.

33. The main legal sources of law regarding insurance are the Entities' laws: the Law on Insurance,[41] the Law on Compulsory Traffic Insurance,[42] the Law on

40. OJ B&H, 12/2004.
41. OJ FB&H, 23/2017, 103/2021.
42. *Ibid.*, 57/2020, 103/2021.

Mediation in Private Insurance,[43] the Law on Insurance Companies,[44] the Law on Compulsory Traffic Insurance,[45] and the Law on Mediation Insurance and Reinsurance.[46]

34. The Entities' laws on insurance (FB&H) and insurance companies (RS) provide comprehensive regulation on the issues that affect the establishment/incorporation, management, business operations, supervision and termination of insurance and reinsurance companies. Furthermore, these laws regulate: conditions for performing insurance and reinsurance activities, laws applicable to insurance contracts, supervision of insurance activities and protection of consumers. Attention is given to the terms and avenues of conducting business activities of companies that perform life and non-life insurance services – authorization, types of insurance, separation of life and non-life insurance, establishment of the subsidiaries between the Entities, business operations of foreign insurance companies, risk management system, solvency margins and guarantee funds, technical and mathematical reserves, investing, secrecy, financial statements and auditing, and insurance portfolio transfer. Within these laws, special attention is given to insurance companies in the form of joint-stock companies (FB&H and/or RS). These laws also contain provisions, which prescribe measures for the reorganization and the winding down of insurance and reinsurance companies.

35. Compulsory insurance, primarily regulated by the Entities' general legislation on insurance and compulsory insurance in traffic, includes a set of rules that are crucial for the most common types of compulsory insurance.

36. The Entities' laws on insurance mediation regulate the activity of intermediaries (insurance brokers and insurance agents in the insurance industry), the types and conditions for conducting these activities, and insurance mediation supervision.

37. Provisions of substantive law that are enshrined in the Entities' laws on obligations that regulate the content of contractual relations constitute an important source of insurance. Insurance contract law in B&H is regulated by the Law on Obligations of the former Socialist Federal Republic of Yugoslavia[47] that was taken over into the legal system of B&H in 1992 and only slightly adjusted to the new circumstances.[48] Provisions relating to insurance are contained in Articles 897–965. The insurance contract is governed by general provisions applicable to all types of insurance (section 1) and special provisions relating to property insurance (section

43. *Ibid.*, 22/2005, 8/2010, 30/2016.
44. OJ RS, 17/2005, 01/2006, 64/2006, 74/2010, 47/2017, 58/19.
45. *Ibid.*, 82/2015, 78/2020.
46. *Ibid.*, 4/2017.
47. OJ SFRY, 29/1978, 39/1985, 45/1989.
48. Ordinance on Accepting of the Law on Obligations (OJ R B&H 2/1992, 13/1994) and the Law on Obligations (OJ RS, 17/1993 and 3/1996).

2) and insurance of persons (section 3). Although this type of legislation is dispositive, provisions relating to insurance have a predominantly imperative character. Therefore, derogation from legal provisions is possible only when it is explicitly allowed.

II. Governmental Regulations

38. Besides these laws, the legal framework of the insurance sector in B&H is also regulated by subordinate legislation adopted by the regulation and supervision agencies on the Entities level: the Insurance Supervisory Agency of FB&H and the Insurance Agency of the RS. The Entities' legislation as a basic source of insurance law is usually further elaborated through various by-laws, such as rulebooks, decisions, instructions, regulations, orders and criteria.

III. Private International Law

39. The law applicable to insurance contracts in B&H is determined by provisions contained in general law on international private law (the Law on Conflict of Laws with Regulations of Other Countries in Certain Relations)[49] as well as in the Entities' insurance legislation (laws on insurance and insurance companies).[50] The former law in relation to the latter special insurance laws of Entities has the status of *lex generalis.*

40. According to the general Law on Conflict of Laws with Regulations of Other Countries in Certain Relations, contracting parties choose the applicable law for contracts, unless otherwise specified by this Law or an international treaty. If the applicable law is not determined by the parties and the particular circumstances of the case do not indicate another law, then the law applicable to the insurance contract is the law of the place of residence of the insurer at the time of the receipt of the offer.[51] The Entities' insurance legislation provides rules on the choice of applicable laws for insurance contracts that cover the risks situated in the Entities.[52] Provisions of the Entities' laws stipulate the fundamental rule that the applicable law is the law of the Entity in which the residence or seat of the insured person is situated. And only in exceptional circumstances, parties have the possibility to choose the law of the other Entity and the other country where the policyholder has a residence or a seat (the Law on Insurance Companies in Private Insurance in the FB&H). Laws in both Entities stipulate that regardless of previously mentioned rules in cases

49. OJ SFRY, 43/82, 72/82, OJ RB&H, 2/1992-5,13/1994-189.
50. *See* the Law on insurance, OJ FB&H, 23/2017, 103/2021; and Law on Insurance Companies in Private Insurance, OJ RS, 17/2005, 01/2006, 64/2006, 74/2010.
51. *See* the Law on Conflict of Laws with Regulations of Other Countries in Certain Relations, Art. 20(1) and (13).
52. *See* the Law on Insurance FB&H, Art. 215 and the Law on Insurance Companies RS, Art. 4.

when risk covered with the insurance contract is limited to the events that take place in the RS or the FB&H, contracting parties can always choose the law of that Entity.[53]

§4. Dispute Settlement and Arbitration

41. Insurance disputes in B&H can be settled judicially and extrajudicially. Ordinarily, they are settled in regular judicial proceedings since the application of extrajudicial procedures in insurance still does not represent a genuine alternative. The judicial system of B&H briefly described earlier is used to settle insurance disputes. If an insurance dispute is to be settled in court, the procedure takes place within the ordinary courts of law. These judicial courts are organized in the Entities as a tripartite hierarchy consisting of: first instance or municipal courts, higher courts or district courts and Supreme Courts (the Supreme Court of FB&H and the Supreme Court of RS). Insurance disputes are usually brought to the municipal courts of the FB&H and the RS as courts of first instance, and appeals against the pronounced judgment can eventually be logged with the higher cantonal or district court and afterwards with the Supreme Courts of the FB&H and the RS.

42. If a dispute relating to the insurance matter is to be settled extrajudicially, several alternative actions may occur. Normally it is settled directly between the insurer and the insured or by methods of mediation or arbitration as the two main extrajudicial methods of dispute resolution in the legal system of B&H. Although both of these methods represent alternative dispute resolution, the court still has a significant role given that it suggests mediation procedures to the parties and solves issues that can arise in arbitration procedures. The changes in procedural laws at the Entity level in 2003 made it possible for judges to direct parties in a dispute to mediation proceedings or to allow them to opt for mediation during the judicial process. The Law on Mediation in B&H[54] stipulates obligatory extrajudicial mediation. This entails that the parties involved in a dispute may agree to try to solve the dispute in a mediation procedure before bringing it to court. This is also possible in disputes tried before the courts if both parties reach an agreement to solve a dispute by mediation before the conclusion of a main hearing, or if following the judge's proposal of a preliminary hearing they decide that this kind of alternative dispute resolution is appropriate for that particular case. Unlike mediation procedures, arbitration procedures are prescribed by the law of civil procedure at the lower state organization level (the FB&H, the RS and the BD B&H).[55] These laws allow for the parties to reach an agreement to resolve their dispute by arbitration in all cases unless the parties cannot dispose of claims, or if claims are contrary to the mandatory provisions.

53. *See* the Law on Insurance FB&H, Art. 215(1)(d)) and Law on Insurance Companies RS, Art. 4(1)(d).
54. OJ B&H, 37/2004.
55. The Law on Civil Procedure in the FB&H, OJ FB&H, 53/03, 73/05, 19/06; the Law on Civil Procedure in the RS, OJ RS, 58/03, 85/03, 74/05, 63/07; and the Law on Civil Procedure in the BD B&H, OJ BD B&H, 08/2009.

43. Insurance policies in B&H usually do not contain arbitration clauses or suggest other alternative dispute resolution. Typically, they only indicate judicial dispute resolution and the competent court. The reason for not using arbitration in the insurance business may lie in the fact that B&H has no established courts of arbitration or arbitrators specializing in insurance contracts.

44. Disputes relating to consumer insurance can be brought to the state Institution of Consumer Ombudsman and to the institutions of insurance ombudsman established within the supervisor agencies for insurance at the Entities level. Recent establishment of these specialized bodies was a result of the introduction of the EU's standards for consumer protection in the domestic legal system. The Insurance Ombudsman mediate in order to peacefully resolve disputes between consumers (policyholders, the insured, beneficiaries of the insurance contract and third injured parties from the basis of insurance against civil liability for damage) and providers of insurance services (insurers and intermediaries). Both parties have to accept mediation of the Insurance Ombudsman. Consumers submit complaints relating to providers of insurance services to the Insurance Ombudsman. The complaint meets the requirements for handling by Insurance Ombudsman if it relates to violations of consumer rights or omissions done by the provider of insurance services when concluding and executing the insurance contract and if the consumer had previously submitted a complaint to the provider of the insurance service and did not receive a satisfactory response or any response at all. However, Insurance Ombudsman will not accept a complaint if a consumer had not previously exhausted a remedy or filed a claim to the insurance company in internal appeals procedures. In the FB&H, the Insurance Ombudsman is not authorized for deciding in cases where there is already ongoing litigation before the competent court. Also, a precondition for initiation of proceedings before the Insurance Ombudsman is that proceedings with the provider of insurance services relating to the subject of dispute had already been conducted.

45. The Insurance Ombudsman applies state regulations governing the mediation proceedings and also may engage other authorized persons with specialized knowledge or mediators. During the mediation procedure, the Ombudsman can suggest a partial or complete solution to a dispute to the parties, but it cannot make the final decision on an agreement. Proceedings before the Insurance Ombudsman are free for consumers, but every party involved in proceedings bears the material costs that occur in relation to proceedings (e.g., the expertise and the evidence process). In the first semi-annual report of the Agency for Insurance of the RS for 2022, it was stated that the Insurance Ombudsman received thirty-nine written submissions where claims regarding the procedure of payment of damages on the basis of motor vehicle liability insurance were predominant.[56] There is no available data on performance of the institution of Insurance Ombudsman in the FB&H.

56. *See* Insurance Agency of RS, *Annual Report on Work of Insurance Agency of RS for Period 01.01. – 30.06.2022.* https://www.azors.rs.ba/azors/lat/podaci/Izvjestaj_R2022PG.pdf (accessed 3 Dec. 2022).

§5. Consumer Protection (In General, and with Regard to Insurance)

46. B&H is currently in the process of developing a more efficient system of consumer protection. Efforts to create a unified legal framework of consumer protection have been predominately motivated by aspirations to integrate its market model based on the EU's internal market and thus facilitate its eventual integration into the EU market. The creation of a unified legal framework represents a substantial leap forward since the previous legal system protected consumers merely by a limited number of provisions, prescribed by various regulations, which resulted in a fragmented, inconsistent and unsystematic consumer protection system.

47. Although consumer protection was primarily provided by provisions of the law on obligation (rules on liability for violation of equivalence in contracts), the position of the consumer in B&H's legal system was also strongly regulated with provisions of commercial law, administrative law, criminal and misdemeanour law. Significant changes in social, political and economic settings that happened two decades ago incited comprehensive alterations in the legal system. The most intensive changes, however, have occurred as previously stated under the influence of legal harmonization within the process of European integration.

48. The primary source of consumer protection in B&H is provided by the Law on Consumer Protection (LCP B&H)[57] adopted at state level in 2006 as a result of continuous efforts to harmonize national legislation with European and international consumer protection standards. This Law regulates the relationships between consumers, manufacturers or producers and traders. It regulates the relationships between the natural persons who buy, acquire or use products and services for their personal needs or the needs of their household, and the legal or natural persons, who produce or provide, entirely or partly, those services and products, as well as those persons that directly or through mediation sell products or give services to consumers.[58]

49. In the LCP B&H, a consumer is defined as any natural person who purchases, acquires or uses products and services for their personal needs and the needs of their household.[59] This narrow interpretation of the notion of a consumer follows the concept of the consumer that prevails in EU law.

50. Regarding financial services, the Law focuses on consumer credit while insurance is only sparsely mentioned. Namely, only two provisions directly related to insurance. The first provision[60] mandates that insurance contracts concluded with or offered to consumers must be in accordance with the legislation on obligations and special insurance regulations. The second provision[61] establishes the right of the

57. OJ B&H, 25/2006, 88/2015.
58. *See* the LCP B&H, Art. 1(3), (4) and (5).
59. *See ibid.*, Art. 1(3).
60. *See ibid.*, Art. 68.
61. *See ibid.*, Art. 69.

consumer to withdraw from the insurance contract. According to this provision, a consumer may terminate a contract without specifying any particular reason, provided that he/she notifies the insurer in written form within fifteen days of signing the insurance contract. In addition to the previously mentioned provisions, provisions regulating contracts concluded away from business premises, distance contracts, unfair terms and advertising of products and services may also apply to insurance contracts.

51. Besides the state-level legislation (LCP B&H), the RS has also adopted legislation on consumer protection.[62]

52. A specific law aimed solely at the protection of financial services users was adopted in 2014 in the FB&H.[63] However, this Law governs the rights of users of financial services that are provided by banks, microcredit organizations, providers of financial leasing and merchants as well as the requirements for the application and protection of these rights. Insurance services are not covered by this Law.

53. Furthermore, due to the specific nature of financial services, the market position of consumers in B&H is governed directly and indirectly, apart from the LCP B&H, the LCP RS and the Law on Protection of Financial Services Users, by a whole range of states and Entities' laws. The laws that regulate financial services include: two laws on obligatory relations (FB&H and RS), the Law on Competition B&H, two laws on banking (FB&H and RS), the Law on Deposit Insurance in Banks of B&H, the Law on Capital Markets RS, the Law on the Securities Market FB&H, the Law on the Banking Agency of FB&H, the Law on the Banking Agency of RS, the Law on the Securities Commission of FB&H, the Law on Insurance FB&H, the Law on Compulsory Traffic Insurance FB&H, the Law on Mediation in Private Insurance FB&H, the Law on Insurance Companies RS, the Law on Compulsory Traffic Insurance RS and the Law on Insurance Mediation (LIM) RS.

54. The current institutional framework for the protection of consumers of financial services is intricately constructed. There are two categories of competent authorities that are responsible for the protection of consumers of financial services. The first category, defined by the LPC B&H encompasses: the Institution of Ombudsman for consumer protection in B&H, the Ministry of Foreign Trade and Economic Relations of B&H, the Council of Competition of B&H, the competent authorities of the Entities and the District of Brcko, the bureaus for competition and consumer protection in the FB&H and the RS, consumers' associations, educational institutions, the media, inspection panels and other bodies.

55. This complex institutional framework was intended to ensure a comprehensive consumer protection mechanism on all levels of government. The crucial institution in this first category is the Ombudsman for Consumer Protection. It was established as an independent body with the aim of promoting good and efficient

62. OJ RS, 6/2012, 63/2014, 18/2017, 90/2021.
63. The Law on Protection of Financial Services Users, OJ FB&H, 31/2014.

enforcement of consumer protection policy in B&H. The duties of the Ombudsman are broadly formulated and include: informing on consumer rights and responsibilities, proposing and initiating consumer dispute resolution by applying mechanisms for alternative dispute resolution, decision-making and undertaking other measures in case of consumer complaints or infringement of good business practice. These duties make the Institution of the Ombudsman the key driver, supervisor and implementer of consumer protection activities.

56. In order to provide efficient protection of consumers in the field of financial services, it was necessary to include institutions that have the role of regulators and supervisors of financial markets. Therefore, the second category of authorities responsible for consumer protection consists of: banking agencies (FB&H and RS), securities commissions (FB&H and RS), insurance supervisory agencies (FB&H and RS), the Insurance Agency of B&H and the Deposit Insurance Agency of B&H. These institutions contribute to the protection of consumers through amendments to existing legislation and the creation of new legislation. They also play a role in the establishment of institutional forms of consumer protection and as a mediator in proceedings for the resolution of consumer complaints. The result has been increased transparency. The consumers are better informed about financial services and provided assistance in terms of understanding how to use them and how to exercise their rights arising from specific financial service contracts.

57. Under the influence of consumer protection law, institutions of the Ombudsman in insurance and banking were recently established within organizational units of insurance and banking agencies dedicated to the protection of consumers. The Ombudsman in the banking system is only established in one Entity (FB&H) with the goal of promoting and protecting the interests and rights of consumers. This Ombudsman mediates in dispute resolutions between institutions of the banking system and users of financial services in a fair, quick and peaceful manner with minimum formality. However, institutions of ombudsman in insurance are established in both Entities. Similarly, to the concept of the Ombudsman in banking, the Ombudsman in insurance operates in order to protect consumers of insurance services in alternative, extrajudicial resolution of disputes related to the insurance contract. The Ombudsman mediates between the consumers (natural persons: policyholders, the insured, beneficiaries from insurance contracts and third damaged parties on the basis of the contract against civil liability for damage) and providers of insurance services (insurance companies and insurance intermediaries). The scope of work of the Ombudsman is very broad and encompasses a variety of activities such as: providing information on the rights and duties of consumers and providers of insurance services; monitoring and proposal of activities for improvement of relations between consumers and insurance services providers; mediating in peaceful dispute resolutions between consumers and insurance services providers; investigating activities on the insurance market ex officio or on the basis of complaints, notifications and other submissions in order to protect the rights and interests of consumers and users of insurance services, etc. Insurance services providers are obliged to cooperate with the Ombudsman.

§6. COMPULSORY INSURANCE

58. Classification of insurance as compulsory or voluntary is based on the origination of obligation; to be precise it derives from the essence of the incentive to conclude the insurance contract. While voluntary insurance contracting is underlined by free will, compulsory insurance is required by state laws and regulations.

59. In former SFRJ Yugoslavia, the concept of social property and related economy organization based on a five-year planning period, combined with general underdevelopment of insurance, resulted in the predominance of compulsory insurance. After radical changes in social, economic, political and legal conditions, this comprehensive and inadequate system of compulsory insurance was abandoned.

60. The legal framework of compulsory insurance in B&H was characterized by complexity and fragmentation for a long time. Namely, it was comprised of numerous provisions enshrined in different laws that were in force at the Entities' level. While the compulsory insurance of owners or users of motor vehicles against liability for damages caused to third parties and the compulsory insurance against liability were minutely regulated by Entities' laws,[64] important provisions on compulsory insurance[65] are also contained in former Entities' laws on property and persons' insurance. Thus, although the set of new insurance laws was adopted in 2005, certain provisions of former legislation remained in force in order to avoid legal gaps. These provisions of former laws remained in force until new legislation on these forms of compulsory insurance was adopted.[66] This happened in the RS in 2015 when the Law on Compulsory Insurances in Traffic[67] was adopted and replaced the Law on Insurance Against Motor Vehicle Liability and other Provisions on Compulsory Insurance against Liability.[68] In 2020 FB&H adopted the Law on Compulsory Insurances in Traffic and with the entry into force of this new Law, previous FB&H's legislation on insurance against motor vehicle liability and other provisions on mandatory liability insurance as well as Articles 69–72 and 93–95 of the Law on Property and Personal Insurance[69] ceased to be in force.[70]

64. The Law on Insurance Against Motor Vehicle Liability and other Provisions on Compulsory Insurance against Liability, OJ FB&H, 24/2005; and the Law on Compulsory Insurances in Traffic, OJ RS, 85/2015.
65. For example, provision that regulates the fundamental division of compulsory insurance on: compulsory insurance of passengers in public transport from consequences of accidents; compulsory insurance of owners or users of a motor vehicle against liability for damages caused to third persons; compulsory insurance of owners or users of an aircraft from liability for damages caused to third parties; and compulsory insurance of owners or users of a motor boat from liability for damages caused to third parties.
66. *See* the Law on Insurance Against Motor Vehicle Liability and Other Provisions on Compulsory Insurance Against Liability in RS, Art. 34; the RS Law on Insurance Companies, Art. 83; and the FB&H Law on Insurance Against Motor Vehicle Liability and other Provisions on Compulsory Insurance Against Liability, Art. 27.
67. OJ RS, 85/2015.
68. OJ RS, 102/2009.
69. OJ FB&H, 2/1995, 7/1995, 6/1998 and 41/1998.
70. *See* the Law on Compulsory Insurances in Traffic FB&H, Art. 80.

61. Furthermore, various laws contain provisions on obligatory liability insurance, such as laws on notaries,[71] laws on advocacy,[72] laws on security guards,[73] laws on insurance intermediaries,[74] etc. Insurance of natural and legal persons' deposits in financial institutions in case of their insolvency is also a form of compulsory insurance present in B&H's legal system.[75]

62. Since compulsory insurance represents a form of governmental (coercive) involvement, it inevitably deviates from the principle of voluntary conclusion of insurance contracts. Therefore, even though compulsory insurance has a contractual nature, it is characterized by substantial limitation of autonomy by the will of the contractual parties because of the legal requirement to conclude such contracts under the conditions which are predetermined by the relevant law. Obligation of the insured to conclude an insurance contract corresponds with the duty of the insurer specialized in this type of insurance, to accept his/her offer to conclude the contract if this offer includes the existing insurance conditions.

63. In the law of the FB&H, there are exceptions from the general rule that compulsory insurance is based on a contract. In certain cases, compulsory insurance relations can be formed without the contract and established entirely on the law if certain conditions are met. For instance, if the owner of the vehicle that is used for transport of passengers in public transportation has not concluded the insurance contract (on insurance of passengers from consequences of accident), in the event of an accident passenger or person that would be the beneficiary in case of the death of passenger, is entitled to demand payment from the Protection fund.[76]

64. The above-mentioned also illustrates the essence of compulsory insurance which is the protection of persons outside the contractual relationship. This protection exists in the form of specific legal devices, such as direct action of victim against insurer, prohibition of objections of the victim although those objections can be submitted to the insured, etc.

65. Another important aspect of compulsory insurance is that protected interests demand continuous risk coverage. This is evident when a vehicle owner changes during the insurance period. In this situation, the new owner of the vehicle is obligated to conclude an insurance contract with regard to his/her liability for the use of

71. The Law on Notaries in FB&H, OJ FB&H, 45/2002; the Law on Notaries in RS, OJ RS, 86/2004, 02/2005, 74/2005,76/2005, 91/2006, 37/2007, 50/2010, 78/2011; the Law on Notaries in Brcko District B&H, OJ BD B&H, 1/2000.
72. The Law on Advocacy in FB&H, OJ FB&H, 40/2002, 29/2003, 18/2005 68/2005; Law on Advocacy in RS, OJ 80/2015.
73. The Law on Agencies and Internal Services for Protection of People and Property, OJ FB&H, 78/2008, 67/2013; the Law on Agencies for Ensuring of Persons and Property and Private Detective Activity (OJ RS, 42/2012, 85/2012).
74. The Law on Mediation in Private Insurance, OJ F&H 22/2005, 8/2010, 30/2016; and the Law on Mediation in Insurance, OJ RS, 17/2005, 64/2006, 106/2009.
75. The Law on Insurance of Deposit in Banks of B&H, OJ B&H, 32/2020.
76. The Law on Compulsory Insurance in Traffic FB&H, Art. 21(3).

the vehicle on which he/she acquired ownership.[77] The insurance contract concluded with the previous owner of vehicle is terminated at the moment when the new owner of the vehicle has concluded the motor vehicle liability insurance contract in his/her own name.[78] Exceptionally, the motor vehicle liability insurance contract concluded with the previous owner remains in force until the expiration of the insurance period if the new owner, within that period, has not concluded an insurance contract in his/her own name, the rights and obligations, as well as liability for the use of the motor vehicle are transferred to the new owner of the vehicle on the day of conclusion of the contract on the transfer of ownership of the vehicle.[79]

66. The available figures on the insurance sector in B&H show that compulsory insurance in the insurance sector of B&H prevails.[80] Unfortunately, this data also indicates a general underdevelopment of the insurance sector in the financial system of B&H resulting from a low level of awareness of the need for insurance protection.

77. The Law on Compulsory Insurances in Traffic FB&H, Art. 45(1).
78. *Ibid.*, Art. 45(3).
79. *Ibid.*, Art. 45(5).
80. *See* the Insurance Agency of B&H (2022), *2021 Annual Report of the Insurance Agency of B&H*, http://www.azobih.gov.ba/dokumenti/publikacija-en-21.pdf (accessed: 22 Dec. 2022).

Part I. The Insurance Company

Chapter 1. The Insurance Company: Its Form

67. Insurance activity in the law of B&H has been defined as an activity of concluding and executing insurance and reinsurance contracts, as well as taking measures of prevention and suppression of risks that endanger insured property and persons.[81] According to relevant law, insurance activity also includes directly related activities, such as identification and assessment of risks and damages, intermediation for the sale and sale of the remains of insured damaged items and provision of other intellectual and technical services related to insurance business.[82] Therefore, in B&H's insurance law, insurance activity is performed by insurance companies, reinsurance companies, insurance agents, insurance brokers, insurance agencies, brokerage companies, as well as specialized public bodies established by special laws to perform certain types of insurance of special interest. However, insurance activity in its narrow sense is performed exclusively by insurance companies which have obtained adequate operating authorization from competent Entity agencies. According to the LI FB&H and the LIC RS, the term 'insurance company' refers to joint-stock companies[83] and mutual insurance companies registered in the territory of the Entity.[84]

§1. Mutual Insurance, Premium, and Other

68. B&H's law regulates two key forms of insurance: premium insurance, which is more prevalent on the market, and mutual insurance. Due to their specificities, different types of companies provide different forms of insurance. Premium insurance is performed by joint-stock insurance companies, while mutual insurance is performed by mutual insurance companies. The main difference between the two is the purpose of their business. The mutual insurance company does not have the purpose of generating profit. The specificities of these special forms of companies are the reflection of insurance features. The prevailing form of insurance companies on B&H's insurance market is the joint-stock insurance company that provides life and

81. *See* the Law on Insurance FB&H, Art. 3(1)&(2).
82. *See ibid.*, Art. 3(4) and the Law on Insurance Companies RS, Art. 2(1).
83. *See* the Law on Insurance FB&H, Art. 2(1).
84. *See* the Law on Insurance Companies FB&H, Art. 2(1) and the Law on Insurance Companies RS, Art. 2(1).

non-life insurance services. The lack of mutual insurance companies on B&H's insurance market can be explained by the non-profit nature of this type of insurance company which makes it unattractive to potential founders. Namely, the goal of the mutual insurance company is risk coverage and compensation in case of damages, not profit.

69. The new legislation adopted in FB&H stipulates a joint-stock company as an exclusive form of insurance company.[85] Therefore, since 2017, insurance companies can have a form of mutual insurance company only in one Entity (RS).

70. A joint-stock company is a legal person performing insurance activities with the purpose of generating profit. This basic form of insurance companies may perform insurance activity as a specialized entity (performing just one type of insurance) or a general entity (performing several types of insurance). In addition, B&H's legal system provides that only joint-stock companies may perform the activity of reinsurance.[86] Joint-stock companies can be established by domestic or foreign natural or legal persons as well as persons from EU Member States.[87]

71. There are two ways to establish a joint-stock company: the first is when the joint-stock company's founders establish a joint-stock company by purchasing all shares upon the establishment (simultaneous establishment) and the second is when the founders purchase the agreed number of shares and the remaining ones are purchased by other persons based on a public call for subscription and payment (successive establishment).[88] As in other joint-stock companies in B&H's legal system, joint-stock insurance companies have management, a supervisory board and an assembly. The management and the supervisory board play an important role and therefore require high-level expertise and competence of their members to perform insurance activities. The management of a joint-stock insurance company comprises a steering board and a director.

72. The mutual insurance company is another form of insurance company in B&H's legal system which performs the activity of property and persons' insurance on behalf of their members – policyholders. As previously mentioned, the specificity of the mutual insurance company is that it does not have a lucrative nature; it is established to meet the needs of its members who jointly guarantee that they shall finance and compensate upon the occurrence of the agreed insured event based on the principle of reciprocity and solidarity.[89] The exclusive goal of a mutual insurance company is to perform the activity of direct insurance. The liability of members for company obligations is limited. Funds necessary to cover the insurance

85. *See* the Law on Insurance FB&H, Arts 2(1) and 5(3).
86. *See ibid.*, Art. 5(4) and the Law on Insurance Companies RS, Art. 3(3).
87. *See* the Law on Insurance FB&H, Art. 5(2) and the Law on Insurance Companies RS, Art. 26(1).
88. *See* the FB&H Company Law (OJ FB&H, 81/2015, 75/2021), Art. 109; and the RS Company Law (OJ RS, 127/2008, 58/2009, 100/2011, 67/2013, 100/2017, 82/2019), Art. 188.
89. *See* the Law on Insurance Companies FB&H, Art. 51(1); and the Law on Insurance Companies RS, Art. 50(1).

amount to be paid when a risk occurs are collected through payment of contributions not premiums and only in the scope necessary to meet the liabilities of the company to the insured and to create reserves.[90] Membership in mutual insurance companies is open to all persons permanently residing in B&H.[91]

73. There are two types of mutual insurance companies that differ in the manner of loss coverage at the end of the year: companies operating on the basis of limited contribution and those operating of the unlimited contribution of their members.[92] Mutual insurance companies with unlimited contribution may request from each member payment of additional amounts without limitation that may be necessary to settle the outstanding insurance claims. However, if the revenue and reserves of a mutual insurance company with limited contribution are insufficient to settle the outstanding claims in a given financial year, the mutual insurance company with limited contribution may request from each insured member to pay additional amounts that may not exceed the sum equal or less to the total previous contribution paid for that financial year.[93] In case mutual insurance is established to provide several types of insurance, an obligation to pay additional contribution for each type of insurance individually at the end of the business year may be expected.

74. The management of any mutual insurance company must consist of at least three members elected by the assembly of members.[94] At least two-thirds of management members must be members of the mutual insurance company, and the number of members who are members of the company may not be less than two.[95] The management appoints one or several executive officers to manage the affairs of the company who have adequate experience and competencies.[96] These persons do not have to be company members. The assembly of the mutual insurance company comprises both founders and members.

§2. Public or Private Nature

75. The forms of insurance companies presented above are mostly private companies. In the early 1990s, the insurance organizations which have been organized as Property and Persons Insurance Communities (*Zajednice osiguranja imovine i lica*) in line with the legislation of the former state were transformed into shareholders' companies which then underwent a process of conversion (i.e., privatization of companies as the exclusive right of their workers) and the majority are nowadays privatized.

90. *See* the Law on Insurance Companies RS, Art. 50(2).
91. *See ibid.*, Art. 50(3).
92. *See ibid.*, Art. 51(1).
93. *See ibid.*, Art. 51(3).
94. *See ibid.*, Art. 51(6).
95. *See* the Law on Insurance Companies FB&H, Art. 52(6); and the Law on Insurance Companies RS, Art. 51(6).
96. *See* the Law on Insurance Companies RS, Art. 51(7).

76. In addition to companies, there are also public bodies that provide certain types of insurance of special interest. The FB&H's Law on the Organization of Pension and Disability Insurance[97] and the RS Law on Pension and Disability Insurance (LPDI)[98] have established the Federal Institute for Pension and Disability Insurance and the RS Pension and Disability Insurance Fund that deal with pension and disability insurance. Entities' laws on health insurance[99] have established the FB&H Health Insurance and Reinsurance Institute and the RS Health Insurance Fund which provide mandatory health insurance. Mandatory health insurance in the FB&H is provided by cantonal institutes as legal persons for each canton, established pursuant to cantonal laws on health insurance institutes. These types of insurance will be elaborated on in more detail in the following chapter (Part VI – Social Security).

77. Also, the B&H's Law on Deposit Insurance in Banks[100] established a state-level Deposit Insurance Agency of B&H that insures all eligible deposits (the aggregate of all assets deriving from deposits, savings accounts or bank certificates deposited by a depositor in a member bank) of natural and legal persons in member banks in B&H.

§3. Factual Data

78. The Insurance Agency of Bosnia and Herzegovina (IA B&H) is entrusted with the obligation to record and publish all relevant data about the overall insurance market in B&H.

79. According to the 2021 Annual Report,[101] twenty-five insurance companies and one reinsurance company operated on the insurance market of B&H in 2021. Of all insurance companies, sixteen companies provide exclusively non-life insurance, no company deals exclusively with life insurance, and nine insurance companies provide services of both life and non-life insurance. In terms of the ownership structure and type of insurance, the companies in B&H deal with, a total of fourteen insurance companies are in domestic ownership, and eleven are foreign. The only reinsurance company in B&H is in domestic ownership. Furthermore, 1,502 intermediaries are registered on the market – 1,408 natural persons and ninety-four legal persons. Out of the total number of registered intermediaries –

97. OJ FB&H, 32/2001.
98. OJ RS, 134/2011, 82/2013.
99. The Law on Health Insurance, OJ FB&H, 30/1997, 7/2002, 70/2008, 48/2011, 100/2014 – Decision of Constitutional Court, 36/2018, 61/2022 and the Law on Mandatory Health Insurance of RS, (OJ RS, 93/2022 i 132/2022).
100. OJ B&H, 32/2020.
101. *See* the Insurance Agency of B&H (2022), *2021 Annual Report of the Insurance Agency of B&H.* It presents data collected from the competent entity insurance agencies: FB&H Insurance Supervisory Agency, RS Insurance Agency, as well as from the Central Bank of B&H and the B&H Statistics Agency. The Report is available at, http://www.azobih.gov.ba/dokumenti/publikacija-en-21.pdf.

natural persons, 1,379 are insurance agents and twenty-nine are insurance brokers. Out of the total number of registered intermediaries – legal persons, sixty-seven are insurance agencies and twenty-seven are registered brokerage companies. Companies with the majority of foreign capital in the total premium participate with 52.71%. The share of companies with the majority foreign capital on the life insurance market in 2021 was 98.16% and on the non-life insurance market 42.80%. The total premium in B&H in 2021 amounted to BAM 818,406,451, which shows a growth of 8.27% in relation to 2020. The share of companies with a seat based in FB&H from the total premium is 69.99%, while the share of companies with a seat based in RS is 30.01%. Out of the total realized insurance premium in 2020, BAM 174,794,673 (21.36%) refers to life insurance and BAM 643,611,778 (78.64%) to non-life insurance business. In the structure of the total insurance portfolio in B&H in 2020 that comprised of nineteen types of insurance, motor third-party liability insurance was the most common at 49.96%. Motor third-party liability insurance represented more than half of the non-life insurance premium at 78.64%; motor hull insurance share was 9.73%; and accident insurance 6.18%.

80. The insurance premium share in our country's GDP was 2.12%, *per capita* premium amounts to USD 137,[102] and insurance and reinsurance companies have a BAM 2.20 billion, i.e., 5.47% share in the overall financial sector.[103]

102. *Ibid.*, 63.
103. *Ibid.*, 15.

Chapter 2. Access to Business

§1. General Overview

81. The requirements for the performance of insurance activities are entirely regulated by the Entities' regulations: the FB&H Law on Insurance[104] (LI FB&H)[105] and the RS Law on Insurance Companies (LIC RS)[106] in accordance with provisions of the Constitution of the FB&H[107] and the Constitution of the RS.[108] Direct insurance and reinsurance activities may be performed only by a company that has obtained an operating authorization from the Entities' insurance agencies (RS Insurance Agency and FB&H Insurance Supervisory Agency).[109]

82. The establishment of insurance companies in both forms (the joint-stock insurance company and the mutual insurance company) is subject to the same authorization regime administered by Entity-level insurance agencies.[110] Once an authorization is issued, it is valid on the overall territory of B&H. The issuance of the authorization is conditioned by requirements referred to in Articles 18 and 22 LI FB&H and Articles 34, 49, and 50 LIC RS and the decisions on types of insurance adopted by the insurance agencies.[111] The authorizations entitle insurance companies to perform insurance activity in both Entities according to the right of establishment.

83. All insurance companies, with the exemption of mutual insurance companies, may perform reinsurance business with the approval of the competent Agency. Every joint-stock company performing or intending to perform reinsurance activities must obtain a prior approval from the Agency which covers all types of reinsurance.[112] A company with the authorization issued by the Agency from either Entity may provide reinsurance coverage on the overall territory of B&H.[113] Reinsurance companies are established as joint-stock companies performing reinsurance affairs as their sole activity.[114]

104. Which replaced the previous FB&H's legislation: the Law on Insurance Companies in Private Insurance.
105. *See* the LI FB&H, Arts 5, 12, 17, etc.
106. *See* the LIC RS, Art. 26, etc.
107. *See* III. Division of Competence between the Federal Government and Cantonal Governments of FB&H Constitution, Art. 1(1).
108. *See* the Constitution of RS, Art. 68(1).
109. *See* the LI FB&H, Art. 5 and LIC RS, Art. 3.
110. *See* the LI FB&H, Art. 17 and LIC RS, Art. 26.
111. FB&H Insurance Supervisory Agency: Decision on the distribution of risk types by groups and types of insurance (OJ FB&H, 82/2017); RS Insurance Agency: Decision on Types of Insurance (OJ RS, 57/2006) and Implementing Instructions for the Decision on Types of Insurance.
112. *See* the LIC FB&H/LIC RS, Art. 3(4).
113. *See* the LI FB&H, Art. 12(10) and LIC RS, Art. 3(8).
114. *See* the LI FB&H, Art. 12(8) and LIC RS, Art. 3(4).

84. An insurance company without a seat in B&H may obtain a branch authorization at the territory of an Entity, provided the requirements stipulated by special provisions of Articles 55 and 56 of the LI FB&H and Article 46 of the LIC RS are met.

85. Insurance companies established in B&H are issued a special, separate authorization to perform life insurance business or non-life insurance business.[115] Exceptionally, the insurance company may also perform operations that are directly or indirectly related to insurance operations,[116] such as mediation of the sale, i.e., the sale of items that belong to the insurance company based on the performance of insurance businesses; taking measures to prevent and eliminate threats that endanger insured property and persons; assessment of the degree of risk exposure of the insured object and damage assessment, as well as performance of other intellectual and technical services in connection with insurance businesses.[117] Insurance companies may perform reinsurance operations in relation to risks of both life and non-life insurance.[118]

86. Insurance companies which had their seats in one of B&H's Entities and which at the time the LI FB&H and the LIC RS entered into force performed both life and non-life insurance business had to separate non-life insurance from life insurance activity. Both types of insurance could be combined, provided that each category has its separate management and administration.[119]

87. Notion of separate administration indicates separation of non-life insurance activities from life insurance activities in order to prevent: harm to the interests of life insurance policyholders and non-life insurance policyholders by the simultaneous management of non-life and life insurance activities; burdening the life insurance activities with the creation of minimum financial guarantees, especially the solvency margin required for non-life insurance business and vice versa.[120] Furthermore, separate administration allows the mixed company, if it has covered the necessary financial guarantees as stated in the legal provisions and after notifying the competent supervisory Agency, to use certain solvency margin funds that are still available for both non-life and life insurance activities.[121] Competent supervisory Agency analyses the results of the two activities and makes sure that the provisions regulating separate administration are respected.[122] Balance sheets must be prepared in such a way as to show the sources of income and expenses for each of these two activities, separately for non-life insurance and separately for life insurance. In this way, all income (especially premiums, payments from reinsurers, investment income) and expenses (especially insurance premiums, additions to technical

---

115. *See* the LI FB&H, Art. 12 and the LIC RS, Art. 31.
116. *See* the LI FB&H, Art. 12(5).
117. *See ibid.*, Art. 12(6).
118. *See ibid.*, Art. 12(8) and the LIC RS, Art. 31(1).
119. *See* the LI FB&H, Art. 226(1) and the LIC RS, Art. 31(2).
120. *See* the LI FB&H, Art. 226(3) (a) and (b).
121. *See ibid.*, Art. 226(3) (c).
122. *See ibid.*, Art. 226(3) (d).

reserves, reinsurance premiums, business expenses related to insurance business) will be distributed according to their origin.[123]

88. An insurance company with a seat in one of the Entities and an authorization to perform insurance business form the group of life insurance may also perform insurance businesses of accident insurance and health insurance if it obtains authorization for it from the competent Entity Agency.[124] Furthermore, in FB&H, an insurance company that performs insurance businesses from the group of life insurances can also perform supplementary insurances, which, first, include disability insurance in the event of an accident or illness, insurance in the event of death due to an accident and insurances in the event of an injury, including insurances for inability to work due to an injury, provided that these forms of insurance are contracted as a supplement to life insurance.[125] An insurance company that has received authorization from a competent Agency to perform businesses of one or more types of non-life insurance may accept risks from a type of non-life insurance for which it has not received authorization if the following conditions are met: (a) insurance covers the risk: (1) associated with the main risk, (2) in connection with the subject of the main risk, and (3) covered by the same insurance contract; (b) the risk is not included in the types of insurance from the Article 9(2) n) and o); (c) the risk is of secondary importance in relation to the main risk.[126]

§2. Authorization: Requirements and Procedures

89. Authorizations for insurance companies issued by Entity supervisory bodies are valid on the overall territory of B&H and are issued by types of insurance, for all or a number of insured cases included in the type, or for a group of insurance types.[127] Insurance agencies limit the authorization to the type of insurance that the insurance company is registered for and for which it secured the necessary founding assets.

90. The LIC RS prescribes that mutual insurance companies shall not cover tasks in the following types of insurance: liability of the owner or user of a motor vehicle, aircraft or vessel; general civil liability insurance unless it constitutes accompanying, or secondary risks as laid down in the decision of the Agency on the types of insurance; or credit insurance and suretyship insurance.[128]

---

123. *See ibid.*, Art. 226(4).
124. *See ibid.*, Art. 12 and the LIC RS, Art. 32. Under the same conditions, in Entity of RS company performing non-life insurance with the approval to perform only non-life accident insurance or insurance against illness may get the approval to provide life insurance. *See* the LIC RS, Art. 32(2).
125. *See* the LI FB&H, Art. 12(3).
126. *See ibid.*, Art. 12(4).
127. *See ibid.*, Art. 12 and LIC RS, Art. 26.
128. *See* the LIC RS, Art. 50(6).

91. Authorization of the insurance company is a condition for its entry into the registry of the competent court. Issuance of authorization is conditioned by the requirements referred to in Articles 18 and 22 of the LI FB&H and Articles 34, 49, and 50 of the LIC RS and the decisions on types of insurance adopted by the insurance agencies.[129] The requirements primarily refer to: the company being established in a legal form of an insurance company (joint-stock insurance company or mutual insurance company); and the minimum founding capital being paid in the amount that depends on the type of life or non-life insurance or reinsurance.[130] The minimum capital required for the establishment of an insurance company varies (for both its forms): BAM 4,000,000.00 (3,000.000.00 in RS) liability insurance for usage of motor vehicle, aircraft and vessel, other liability insurance, credit insurance, suretyship insurance; BAM 4,000,000.00 for accident insurance, health insurance, passenger vehicle insurance – hull, railway rolling stock insurance (hull), aircraft insurance (hull), marine, river and hull on inland waters, goods in transit insurance, fire and other hazards insurance; BAM 2,000,000.00 for a company performing one or several of the following types of insurance: other property insurance, legal protection cost insurance, assistance insurance; BAM 6,000,000.00 for a company providing life insurance; and BAM 6,000,000.00 for a company providing reinsurance exclusively. Founding capital must be paid in money upon establishment and the LIC RS in Article 49(3) stipulates that the share capital may not derive from: loan funds approved by a company to whose capital the payment is made; loans approved by a bank or a financing institution for a different purpose; or funds the return of which is guaranteed by the company to whose capital the payment is made. Similarly, the LI FB&H in Article 25(2) states that the assets of the share capital of insurance or reinsurance company may not originate from loans or credits or be encumbered in any way.

92. In addition to the above requirements, other criteria that have to be met refer to: transparency of data relating to the shareholder's identity or associated legal persons having a qualifying holding, as well as data on the amounts of qualifying holdings;[131] eligibility of persons at important functions in the company (their general and professional qualifications and experience);[132] stable and solid management of the insurance company[133] and eligibility of shareholders or partners;[134] and the financial standing (eligibility) of legal persons having qualifying holdings in the insurance companies that have become their affiliates.[135]

---

129. *See*: FB&H Insurance Supervisory Agency: Decision on the distribution of risk types by groups and types of insurance (OJ FB&H, 82/2017); RS Insurance Agency: Decision on Types of Insurance (OJ RS, 57/2006) and Implementing Instructions for the Decision on Types of Insurance.
130. *See* the LI FB&H, Art. 50 and the LIC RS, Art. 49.
131. *See* the LI FB&H, Arts 2 and 18 and the LIC RS, Arts 2 and 61.
132. *See* the LIC RS, Art. 60.
133. *See ibid.*, Art. 61.
134. *See ibid.*, Art. 28.
135. *See ibid.*.

93. To obtain the authorization, insurance company founders must submit a request for its issuance to the competent Entity insurance agency along with a number of documents stipulated by Article 18 of the LI FB&H and Articles 34(2), 49 and 50 of the LIC RS and the decisions of the supervisory agencies.[136] Request for authorization must be accompanied by: the founding act; business plan; insurance company statute in form of the notarial document; proof of payment of share capital and secured funds for cost of establishment, organizational cost and operating cost; list of shareholders with their personal information or company names and seats, number and total nominal value of shares and percentage of the share in the share capital of the insurance company; for shareholders – legal persons and holders of qualifying holdings: an extract from the court registry, where the shareholder is a joint-stock company, also the extract relating to the shareholder from the shareholders' register, financial statements for the past two business years; a list of persons (natural and/or legal) who are closely related to the holders of qualified shares; for shareholders – natural persons holders of qualifying shares: their personal information; statement and evidence of origin of the funds for the qualified share in insurance company; a list of persons (natural or legal) who are closely related to the holders of qualifying holdings along with the description of their relationship; document on personal and technical qualifications, and additional documentation in accordance with the by-laws of competent Agency.[137] Along with the request for authorization to perform insurance business, founders of insurance company must submit the opinion of the authorized actuary on whether the insurance company is capable of ensuring the adequacy of the capital given the types of insurance and the scope of business, which will be performed, as well as the opinion of the authorized actuary on the design of the premium price list and technical insurance reserves in accordance with the provisions of the laws and adopted by-laws.[138]

94. In addition to the documents mentioned above, the request for authorization should also be supported by a three-year business plan of the insurance company. The plan must include at least: basics of business policy; types of insurance that the company will work with; the reinsurance programme with tables of maximum retention by types of insurance; calculation of the solvency margin, assessment of liquidity and financial resources available to cover liabilities and ensure capital adequacy; a detailed projection of expected operating results for a period of at least three years, including in particular the expected premium income, expected insurance premiums and claims, expected commission expenses and other expenses, as well as estimated levels of technical provisions and other reserves in accordance

136. Decision on additional documentation, type and content of business policy documents, which should be submitted with the request for authorization (OJ FB&H, 84/2017, 15/2019) and Decision on Documents to be Submitted with the Request for Authorization from the RS Insurance Agency (OJ RS, 116/2006).

137. *See* Decision on Documents to be Submitted with the Request for Authorization from the Insurance Supervisory Agency of FB&H, Arts 4–11 and Decision on Documents to be Submitted with the Request for Authorization of the RS Insurance Agency, Art. 3.

138. *See* the LI FB&H, Art. 18(2).

with the laws.[139] Furthermore, in addition to the mandatory content prescribed by law, company's business plan should also contain the following: plan of necessary personnel with a proposal of organization and systematization of workplaces, necessary qualifications and work experience; evidence of the company's technical capability to perform activities: evidence of the method of securing business premises, documents of the competent authority that the business premises are suitable for the purpose of carrying out insurance business operations.[140] If the insurance company intends to perform business activities with regard to assistance insurance, the business plan must also contain a description of the funds that the company has at its disposal, which are necessary for the performance of non-monetary obligations – providing of assistance by the company from these insurances.[141]

95. The competent Insurance Agency shall decide on a duly submitted request no later than sixty days from the day of its submission together with supporting documents or shall require amendments of the request if needed.[142] The procedure to issue the authorization by the competent Insurance Agency for an insurance company may, in addition to the documentation, also include an interview with representatives of the company or founders, on-site control and request for verification and/or confirmation of financial data based on the current and previous state.[143] In case when all required documents or information have not been submitted with the request, the Agency may ask the applicant to submit the additional documents or information within the set time limit.[144]

96. Article 20 of the LI FB&H and Article 28 LIC RS stipulate situations when the request for authorization may be rejected. The competent Agency shall revoke the issued authorization in the cases explicitly laid down in Article 21 of the LIC FB&H and Article 29 LIC RS. Once the authorization is revoked, the Agency shall commence the procedure to liquidate the insurance company.[145] In the case of revocation of the authorization, the competent Agency performs supervision until the end of the liquidation procedure of the insurance company.[146] Revocation (or termination) of the authorization does not release the insurance company from obligations founded on concluded insurance contracts.[147]

---

139. *See* LI FB&H, Art. 22 and Decision on additional documentation, type and content of business policy documents, which should be submitted with the request for authorization, Art. 5, and Decision on Documents to be Submitted with the Request for Authorization of the RS Insurance Agency, Art. 7.
140. *See* Decision on additional documentation, type and content of business policy documents, which should be submitted with the request for authorization, Art. 5(1).
141. *Ibid.*, Art. 5(2).
142. *See* the LI FB&H, Art. 19(6) and LIC RS, Art. 27(2).
143. *See* Decision on Documents to be Submitted with the Request for Authorization of the RS Insurance Agency, Art. 19.
144. *See* the LI FB&H, Art. 19(6) and LIC RS, Art. 27(2), as well as Decision on Documents to be Submitted with the Request for Authorization of the RS Insurance Agency, Art. 21.
145. *See* the LI FB&H, Art. 21(10) and Decision on Documents to be Submitted with the Request for Authorization of the RS Insurance Agency, Art. 21.
146. *See* the LI FB&H, Art. 21(11).
147. *See ibid.*, Art. 21(12).

97. Just as the joint-stock insurance companies, mutual insurance companies[148] must obtain an authorization from the competent Agency to perform direct insurance activity. The procedure to issue the authorization to this type of insurance company follows to a great extent the one described above for the establishment of joint-stock insurance companies. The mutual insurance companies must thus have a minimum capital equal to the joint-stock company capital, classified according to the types of insurance.[149] However, there are some other specific criteria that apply: a mutual insurance company must have at least 250 members if the company is authorized to cover just one type of risk, and at least 300 members if it is authorized to cover more than one type of risk. In addition, laws stipulate that at least one-half of the company's income from contributions must come from members of the mutual insurance company and that the annual turnover of mutual insurance companies may not exceed BAM 2,000,000.00.[150]

98. The complex organization of B&H and the existence of two insurance markets with separate legislative and institutional frameworks require that the opening of company branches in another Entity must be separately regulated. To open an insurance company branch in the Entity other than the Entity where the company seat is located, it is necessary that the competent Entity Agency of the seat office submits to the competent Agency of the Entity where the branch is to be established a request with the extensive documentation: a business plan that determines the type of foreseen tasks and the structural organization of the branch; the address of the branch in the Entity where documents can be obtained and submitted and to which all notifications are sent; power of attorney for the authorized representative that must have sufficient powers to create liabilities on behalf of the insurance company and to represent the insurance company in relation with third parties, before courts, other bodies and organizations in that Entity and with the competent Agency; the authorized representative must reside in the Entity of the branch, represent the insurance company before courts and in company relations with public authorities and competent Entity agencies. Additionally, the competent Insurance Agency in RS, before the branches of the company start working in FB&H, forwards to the competent Agency in FB&H a request with the necessary documentation and the following attachments: decision on issuance of authorization to an insurance company from the RS for the establishment of a branch in the FB&H; decision on registration of branch establishment in the court register in FB&H; certificate of solvency of the insurance company, which establishes a branch in the FB&H, evidence of membership in the Green Card Bureau of B&H and evidence of membership in the Protection Fund of the FB&H, if it is an insurance company authorized to perform motor vehicle liability insurance business operations.[151] In opposite case of establishment of a branch of an insurance company from the FB&H in the RS, LI FB&H requires that such company must submit a request to the competent Agency in FB&H containing the statement that it intends to open a branch in the RS with the

148. Which after insurance legislation changes in FB&H, exclusively exist and operate in RS.
149. *See* the LIC RS, Art. 51(5).
150. *See ibid.*, Art. 50.
151. *See* the LI FB&H, Art. 47(2).

following documents: (a) decision on the establishment of a branch in the RS; (b) document on the internal organization and systematization of workplaces in the branch in the RS; (c) evidence of secured office space for the seat of the branch in the RS, as well as the internal organizational parts of the branch; (d) the decision on appointment of a natural person authorized to represent the branch in the RS, with specification of scope and the limits of authorization for representation in legal transactions; (e) evidence that the previously mentioned natural person (referred to in point d) has a temporary or permanent residence in the territory of B&H; (f) business plan and financial plan of the branch in the RS; (g) insurance conditions and premium rates for the types of insurance that the branch in the RS will perform; (h) single certified copy of all types of insurance policies (insurance contracts) that the branch in the RS will use in legal transactions in the RS; (i) a statement about the chosen business method within the insurance of the costs of legal protection, if it performs this type of insurance; (j) evidence on the Green Card Bureau of B&H's membership, if it is an insurance company authorized to perform motor vehicle liability insurance.[152]

99. The procedure to establish a branch includes verification of the business. If the administrative structure and financial standing of the insurance company, as well as the general and professional qualifications and experience of the directors and authorized representatives, are adequate, the Agency of the Entity where the company seat is located shall submit to the Agency of the Entity in which the branch is being established the above request together with documents and the certificate of solvency, within sixty days as of the completion of the request. The insurance company submitting the request will be notified thereon.[153]

100. Regarding the opening of branches in B&H's Entities, the laws stipulate the possibility that the Entity in which the branch is performing its insurance activity may ask the insurance company with its seat in the other Entity for periodical information about the general and special insurance contract terms and documents they intend to use for their clients.[154] This possibility is introduced for the purpose of protecting public interest and controlling the application of legal provisions pertaining to insurance contracts; however, the insurance company from which the documents have been requested must meet this request only if there is a legal obligation for insurance companies with their seats in that Entity to do so.[155]

101. The laws stipulate that access of foreign insurance companies to insurance markets in B&H is subject to authorization from foreign competent agencies. Additionally, foreign companies perform insurance activity on the territory of the B&H only as a branch after they obtain authorization from the competent agency in the Entity and are entered into the court registry.[156] A branch can perform either life or

152. *See ibid.*, Art. 48(1).
153. *See ibid.*, Art. 48(2) and the LIC RS, Art. 39(1).
154. *See* the LI FB&H, Art. 50(1) and the LIC RS, Art. 40(1).
155. *See* the LI FB&H, Art. 50(3) and the LIC RS, Art. 40(3).
156. *See* the LI FB&H, Art. 56. and the LIC RS, Art. 45.

non-life insurance in the overall territory of B&H. Conditions under which authorization for a branch can be given are stipulated in Article 55 of the LI FB&H and Article 46 of the LIC RS. *Inter alia*, the following conditions are laid down for foreign companies: they must be established as joint-stock insurance companies, mutual insurance companies or be established in any other insurance company form existent in the EU Member States; must be authorized in their country of origin to perform the types of insurance for which the authorization is requested in B&H; appoint an authorized representative of the branch in the Entity or Entities. In cases when the authorized representative is a legal person, it must have its seat in B&H and must appoint a natural person as a representative. Professional qualification requirements for persons managing insurance companies also apply to natural persons; the insurance company must be registered in the country that allows B&H companies to establish there according to the reciprocity principle, etc.

102. With the request for authorization of a branch, the Law stipulates in Article 56(2) of the LI FB&H and Article 46(2) of the LIC RS that the following documents must be submitted: document on establishment of the branch; an extract from the court or other suitable register of the home state of the parent insurance company and if information about the owners of the parent insurance company is not visible from the court extract, corresponding document in which the owners and their shares in the management of the parent insurance company are credibly stated must be submitted; the statute and proof of registration of the parent company issued by the competent body of the home country where the company seat is located; audited financial statements of the parent insurance company for the last three years; an extract from the court register or other suitable register of the state of the registered office for legal entities that have more than 10% share in the management of the parent insurance company; verified power of attorney for the appointment of an authorized representative with the statement that withdrawal of the appointment of power of attorney enters into force when the document is also submitted to the competent Agency; business plan which includes elements referred to in Article 22 of the LI FB&H and Article 34 of the LIC RS and the opinion of the branch's authorized actuary about it; evidence of the adequacy of the guarantee fund and guarantee deposit with the opinion of the branch's authorized actuary about it; documentation on the basis of which it can be determined whether the branch is in personnel, technical and organizational sense capable of providing the services to which the request for authorization refers.[157] Furthermore, the LIC RS requires: certificate of the supervisory authority of the insurance company's home country no older than three months from the day of submission of the request which confirms that the insurance company is operating and has an authorization to perform the types of insurance it intends to perform in the Entity; documents confirming that the branch meets the requirement of having the share capital in the Entity no less than the lowest capital threshold regulated by Article 49 of the LIC RS; a list of names and addresses of directors and executive directors; the business plan of the branch, which includes the elements provided for in Article 34 of the LIC RS; balance sheet

157. *See* the LI FB&H, Art. 56(2).

and income statement for the last three financial years, or for completed financial years if the applicant has been in business for less than three financial years.[158]

103. The LIC RS imposes an appointment of the authorized representative with residence in B&H who will represent the insurance company before the courts and in relations with state and public bodies and the competent insurance agency.[159] The authorized representative signs all insurance policies issued by the branch of a foreign company and assumes responsibility for the insurance company's steering board members.[160] Furthermore, the law requires that a foreign company operating in the territory of B&H must keep its ledgers in one of the official languages of B&H, and must prepare, publish and submit financial statements to the competent Agency.[161] Branches of foreign insurance companies operating RS fall under the competence of the courts of that Entity and are obliged to respect Entity accounting regulations and standards relating to joint-stock companies.[162]

158. *See* the LIC RS, Art. 46(1).
159. *See ibid.*, Art. 47(1).
160. *See ibid.*, Art. 47(2) and (3).
161. *See ibid.*, Art. 48(1).
162. *See ibid.*, Art. 48(2).

Chapter 3. Supervision

104. Entity-level insurance agencies have been authorized to conduct supervision over-insurance activities in B&H (the Insurance Supervisory Agency of FB&H and the RS Insurance Agency). Entity-level supervisory bodies were established by laws on insurance companies (LIC FB&H and LIC RS) in 2005, which regulated their activities and competence.

105. The insurance agencies were established as independent and non-profit institutions of the Entities that report to the Government (in the FB&H) and Parliament (in the RS). These agencies were assigned roles of supervisory and regulatory institutions on insurance markets in B&H that aim to protect persons entitled to insurance coverage and insurance benefit and work for the benefit of the insurance industry.[163] The agencies supervise the insurance operations of insurance companies and of branches that conduct insurance operations in the Entity (FB&H or RS), reinsurance companies, and insurance intermediaries and affiliated persons in the insurance industry.

106. As a rule, the main objectives of supervision over-insurance companies in the existing solvency regime in B&H are: providing an adequate level of protection to insured persons from unexpected losses and, at the same time, ensuring profitability and competitiveness of insurance companies, insurance market stability; early detection of potential financial and other business problems in insurers' operations and taking or requesting necessary measures to be taken in order to prevent potential problems or resolve them, if they exist already.

107. Supervisory powers assigned to the Entities' agencies include the following: control of the fulfilment of requirements for the establishment of insurance or reinsurance companies, of insurance intermediary companies and, in the RS, of companies for the management of voluntary pension funds and of voluntary pension funds themselves; performance of legal, technical and financial-accounting supervision over participants and products on Entity-level insurance markets; collection and processing of data on insurance companies and their activities and products,[164] as well as the analysis of the state of affairs and monitoring of insurance market tendencies; continuous reviews of: ledgers and other documents, methods of maintaining ledgers and reporting, business and internal control processes and procedures and other documents, with or without sending notification to the company;[165] information exchange in the field of supervision with other supervisory and regulatory bodies in B&H's financial sector and abroad;[166] imposition and implementation of different measures in order to ensure that activities of insurance market participants are compatible with the law and other regulations and to protect the

163. *See* the LI FB&H, Art. 126 and the LIC RS, Art. 6.
164. *See* the LIC FB&H, Art. 14 and the LIC RS, Art. 13.
165. *See* the LI FB&H, Art. 128(2) and the LIC RS, Art. 7(2).
166. *See* the LI FB&H, Art. 133 and LIC RS, Art. 18(3) and (4).

interests and gain confidence of insured persons and third parties – insurance beneficiaries, and to provide a stable and transparent functioning of the insurance market in B&H;[167] initiating court procedures when necessary (in insurance-related legal issues where the competent Agency has no powers to implement its supervisory functions and when an issue subject to court jurisdiction occurs in the supervision process);[168] supervision over reinsurance contracts concluded by insurance companies (identity control of other parties – reinsurers, control of conditions and provisions applied to reinsurance contracts and control of ceded risk proportion;[169] and supervision over Entity-level protection funds.[170]

108. There is a difference in supervisory powers between the Entity-level insurance agencies. Namely, as indicated above, the Insurance Agency of RS also has supervisory powers over companies for the management of voluntary pension funds and over voluntary pension funds defined in Article 85 of the Law on Voluntary Pension Funds and Pension Schemes (LVPFPS RS). When performing supervision in accordance with the LVPFPS RS provisions, the Agency is entitled to review ledgers and other documents, including electronic records, voluntary pension funds and companies that manage them, as well as legal entities that have property, management or business relations with management companies.[171] Supervision forms applied by the RS Agency are as follows: (a) indirect control, i.e., collecting, monitoring and checking reports and notifications submitted to it in accordance with the Law; (b) direct control, i.e., review of ledgers and other documents in the management company's premises or in premises of a third party in charge of administrative and marketing work of the management company.[172] On the basis of performed supervision, the Agency imposes supervisory measures and submits reports to the competent authorities in the event of the existence of grounded suspicion that the found illegitimate actions and irregularities include elements of a criminal or minor offence.[173] In the process of direct supervision of business operations, an authorized person from the Agency may review general acts, ledgers, bank statements, information systems, databases and other documents, not only of the management company but of a custodian bank too.[174] In a situation when illegitimate actions, irregularities or non-abidance by risk control rules are found in the process of supervision over a management company and the custodian bank, depending on the gravity of the found irregularity and the level of threat to the interests of voluntary pension fund members, the Law stipulates that the Agency may take one or several measures foreseen in Article 89 of the LVPFPS RS.

109. The supervisory body uses adequate instruments in the implementation of preventive and corrective measures if an insurance company fails to abide by the

167. *See* the LIC FB&H, Arts 8, 11, 12, 13, 15, etc. and the LIC RS, Arts 7, 11, 12, 13, 15, etc.
168. *See* the LIC FB&H, Art. 128(2) and LIC RS, Art. 7(2).
169. *See* the LI FB&H, Art. 135 and LIC RS, Art. 17.
170. *See* the Law on *See* the Law on Compulsory Insurances in Traffic, Art. 59(5).
171. *See* the LVPFPS RS, Art. 86.
172. *See ibid.*, Art. 88(1).
173. *See ibid.*, Art. 88(2).
174. *See ibid.*, Art. 88(5).

relevant regulations. There must be measures in case the insurance company management ignores requests of the supervisory body. Some of the measures prescribed by laws and by-laws are as follows: restriction on the volume of insurance operations (entire operations or a part thereof); withdrawal of operating authorization; prevention of the conclusion of new deals; prevention of the issuance of approvals for new activities or acquisitions; prevention of the disposal of, encumbrance or other specific ways of use of the company assets; entrusting (entirely or a portion thereof) company assets to a custodian; dismissal of management members; reorganization measures (introducing a temporary administrator, suspension of payments, suspension of an enforcement procedure and reduction of claim amounts), etc.

110. The supervisory body may impose the following measures: agree on a mandatory transfer of liabilities from the unsuccessful insurer's policy to an insurer willing to accept the portfolio; require a capital increase; prohibit certain financial transactions; prevent the transfer of assets; take over control over the insurer (introducing temporary administration).

§1. Solvency Control

111. One of the key supervision objectives is to ensure the insurance company's ability to orderly fulfil its obligations from the insurance contract. Insurance companies are therefore required to have financial guarantees: a solvency margin, a guarantee fund and technical reserves.

112. All insurance companies in B&H are obliged to determine a solvency margin for their entire operations, which should match the total assets reduced by intangible investments, prepayments and deferred expenses, losses, liabilities (including the mathematical reserve of life insurance) and for unearned positions (unearned premiums and reserved claims).[175] Elements and control of the solvency margin are defined by by-laws that were adopted by competent agencies. According to these documents, the solvency margin is calculated separately for life insurance lines, non-life insurance lines and reinsurance deals. The Agencies' by-laws accept calculation of the solvency margin in accordance with the first generation of European directives on life and non-life insurance. The solvency margin for non-life insurance deals and reinsurance deals is calculated by applying a premium index or damage index and equals to the higher result of the two. The solvency margin for life insurance deals is calculated as a sum of results calculated in the way prescribed by Articles 9 and 8 of the rulebooks on elements and control of solvency margin of insurance companies (FB&H and RS).[176]

175. *See* the LIC RS, Art. 52.
176. OJ FB&H, 82/2017, 95/2019; OJ RS, 103/12.

113. Insurance companies must also establish a guarantee fund that must constitute one-third of the solvency margin. Different, minimum amounts of the guarantee fund are defined in Article 73(3) of the LI FB&H and Article 53(2) of the LIC RS, depending on the type of insurance offered by the company.

114. Adequate technical reserves are intended for the fulfilment of obligations arising from the insurance contract, and they ensure sound operations of an insurance company. The Laws, therefore, stipulate that every insurance company must establish technical reserves for all insurance contracts concluded in the B&H's Entities or through branches, in accordance with regulations on technical reserves adopted by the agencies.[177]

115. Financial supervision by the agencies includes control of financial guarantees of insurance companies, aimed at ensuring abidance by relevant legal provisions. Competent agencies perform supervision of fulfilment of solvency requirements prescribed by Entity-level legislation by an insurance company: at the time of establishment – issuance of operating authorization; and while the company is active – periodical reporting and submission of year-end accounts. The competent Agency shall request the insurance companies seated in the Entity to occasionally declare their income, along with all the statistical documents required for supervision purposes. Within four months from the end of the financial year, the insurer must submit its balance sheet and income statement to the Agency, as well as all audit reports and financial reports with the format, content, data, details and confirmations defined by the Agency's decision.[178] Insurance companies are obliged to submit reports to the competent Insurance Agency for supervision purposes. The insurance company submits the following reports: monthly (on premium, claims and liquidity), quarterly (statistical data on premium and claims, investments, financial reports, calculation of solvency margin and of the guarantee fund, relations with affiliated persons, etc.), semi-annual and annual (aforementioned, actuary's opinion, the external audit report, etc.).[179]

116. In the event that an insurance company's solvency margin is lower than the amounts stipulated in Articles 71–72 of the LI FB&H and Articles 52–54 of the LIC RS, a company is obliged to submit a financial recovery plan to the supervisory body (insurance agencies),[180] i.e., a short-term financial programme to eliminate an observed shortfall.

---

177. *See* the LI FB&H, Art. 80 and the LIC RS, Art. 55.

178. *See* the LI FB&H, Art. 120(3) and the LIC RS, Art. 59(1) and (2).

179. *See* the FB&H Rulebook on reports of insurance and reinsurance companies, (OJ FB&H, 106/2018, 88/2020, 89/2022) and Rulebook on statistical standards and forms of financial reporting in insurance, (OJ FB&H, 95/2019, 88/2020, 89/2022) and the RS Rulebook on Content, Manner and Deadlines for Submission of Reports, Notifications and Other information of Insurance Companies (OJ RS, 91/14), as well as the RS Rulebook on Form and Content of Insurance and Reinsurance Companies' Supervision and Statistical Reports (OJ RS, 91/14).

180. *See* the LI FB&H, Art. 78(1) and the LIC RS, Art. 54(7).

117. In exceptional situations, when the Agency believes that the financial situation of an insurance company will further deteriorate or for the purpose of eliminating the shortfall completely, it may restrict or prohibit free disposal of all or a portion of the assets and take any other adequate measures to protect the interests of insured persons.[181] And if a company fails to harmonize its operations with measures contained in the recovery plan or short-term financial programme, agencies may withdraw the insurance company's authorization for all lines of insurance.[182]

118. In addition to the aforementioned measures, the agencies may impose sanctions prescribed in Article 216 of the LI FB&H and Article 77 of the LIC RS on the insurance company and its branches operating in the territory of the Entity within the Agency's jurisdiction, in cases when financial guarantees are not adequate.

119. Withdrawal of the operating authorization of an insurance company is one of the cases when the competent Agency initiates a liquidation procedure.[183] In FB&H procedures of liquidation and bankruptcy of insurance companies have been regulated by LI FB&H[184] while in RS they are regulated by provisions of legislation on bankruptcy and liquidation procedures on companies, except in cases when LIC FB&H stipulates otherwise.[185] In RS during and until completion of a liquidation procedure, the insurance company may not file for bankruptcy.[186] The liquidation and bankruptcy receiver determines the claims. Claims are categorized in LIC RS as follows: (i) life insurance policy beneficiaries; (ii) non-life insurance policy beneficiaries who reported the occurrence of the insured event and whose reports were recorded; and (iii) other persons who reported their claims in the time period specified herein.[187] While LI FB&H distinguishes between regular[188] and compulsory liquidation[189] of the insurance company, LIC RS distinguishes between special liquidation[190] and general liquidation.

120. The Law provides special regulation for privileged claims on insurance companies' investments from insurance beneficiaries and their heirs against all general or specially privileged claims, except for costs of the special liquidation process and costs of the bankruptcy procedure.[191] In case when an insurance company reaches a special or compulsory liquidation stage, the insurance beneficiary has privileged claims on all assets, whether they belong to the insurance company's investments or not, and this privilege puts them in a more favourable position than

181. *See* the LIC RS, Art. 54(8) and (10).
182. *See ibid.*, Art. 54(11).
183. *See* the LI FB&H, Art. 21(10) and (11) and the LIC RS, Art. 68(1).
184. *See* the LI FB&H, Arts 180–196.
185. *See* the LIC FB&H, Art. 69(2) and the LIC RS, Art. 68 (2).
186. *See* the LIC RS, Art. 68(4).
187. *See* LIC RS, Art. 69(3).
188. *See* the LI FB&H, Arts 173–179.
189. *See ibid.*, Arts 180–191.
190. *See* LIC RS, Arts 68–70.
191. *See* the LI FB&H, Art. 178(2) and the LIC RS, Art. 70(1).

all other creditors, except in the case of the claims for costs (enforced/special liquidation process costs foreseen in Articles 173–179 of the LI FB&H and Articles 68–70 of the LIC RS, as well as bankruptcy costs).[192] The privilege entails the settlement of claims of the insured and their heirs, including third parties having direct claims from the insurer arising from the insurance contract. Claims of other creditors can be settled from the insurance company's investments only if the claims of the insured have been fully paid out.[193]

121. The LI FB&H encompasses provisions on compulsory liquidation of a branch of a foreign insurance company.[194] Before issuing a decision on the initiation of compulsory liquidation and withdrawal of approval of a branch of a foreign insurance company, the Agency is obliged to inform (about the legal consequences and factual effects of such a procedure) all the competent authorities of the Member States in which the insurance company (whose branch is being liquidated) has branches.[195] Exceptionally, if it is not possible to postpone the start of the compulsory liquidation procedure due to protection of the insured, the Agency will notify the competent supervisory authorities immediately after the decision is made. During the compulsory liquidation procedure, the supervisory Agency is obliged to cooperate with the competent supervisory bodies of other Member States.[196] The liquidators are obliged to cooperate with each other in the compulsory liquidation procedure and to give each other all legally permitted notifications that may be of importance for the implementation of the procedure.[197]

§2. Supervision of Tariffs, Insurance Conditions and Market Behaviour

122. Basically, legal systems of insurance that were established at the Entity level do not foresee preliminary supervision of tariffs or insurance policy conditions where a competent body would provide explicit approval for their implementation. The positive opinion of an authorized actuary of the company concerned regarding the proposed business policy acts (and their potential amendments) that also include insurance conditions and tariffs, is a precondition for their adoption by the company management after which they are submitted to the competent Agency (in accordance with Article 54(13) of the LIC RS). Agencies do not provide prior approval to submitted conditions and tariffs but rely on positive opinions of authorized actuaries. The Agency tracks the implementation of submitted conditions and tariffs in the process of continuous supervision and exceptional or regular control of companies. Submitted conditions and tariffs come into force on the date of adoption by a competent body.

192. *See* the LI FB&H, Art. 178(3) and the LIC RS, Art. 70(2).
193. *See* the LI FB&H, Art. 178(4) and the LIC RS, Art. 70(3).
194. *See* the LI FB&H, Art. 189.
195. *See ibid.*, Art. 189(1).
196. *See ibid.*, Art. 189(4).
197. *See ibid.*, Art. 189(5).

123. Conditions and tariffs are subject to subsequent controls by the competent Entity-level agencies, both in terms of their compatibility with laws and by-laws and in terms of the adequacy of tariffs in view of assumed risk. There are certain differences in the control of tariff application and related non-life and life insurance conditions. Namely, control of life insurance tariffs is far stricter due to their long-term character and significance, and due to methods of calculation of reserve premiums in life insurance.

124. In non-life insurance, competent agencies adopted joint conditions and tariffs for compulsory liability insurance of motor vehicles for damage inflicted on third parties, and their implementation is mandatory. Conditions and tariffs for other insurance lines are independently created and adopted by companies.

125. After 2010 amendments to the LIC RS, the RS Agency may order a company to suspend the implementation or amendment to insurance conditions and tariffs, if it finds in the supervision process that the company has been violating risk management rules (liquidity and solvency rules, capital adequacy requirements, rules for establishing funds to support technical and mathematical reserves, reinsurance rules, restrictions in dividend payment, etc.) and rules for the protection of insured persons.

126. Pursuant to relevant legislation, the FB&H Agency provides opinions on insurance companies' documents that must be adopted in accordance with the Law (insurance terms, premium tariffs, rulebook on determination of unearned premiums and outstanding losses reserve, rulebook on the determination of the mathematical reserve and its change in life insurance, etc.).

127. Nevertheless, with regard to liability insurance for motor vehicles, the agencies adopted by-laws regulating joint conditions that define: insured risks and extent of coverage; uninsured (excluded) risks; loss of insurance rights; obligations of insured persons; insurers' rights and obligations; territorial validity of insurance; beginning and cessation of insurance coverage, definition, determination and payment of premiums, etc. The agencies also regulate the joint premium tariff and pricelist for liability insurance for motor vehicles through by-laws and control their implementation.

128. Of note, the agencies supervise reinsurance contracts concluded by insurance companies and also perform identity control of other parties-reinsurers and control of reinsurance terms and provisions and the proportion of ceded risk.[198]

---

198. *See ibid.*, Art. 135 and the LIC RS, Art. 17.

Chapter 4. Technical Reserves and Investments

129. Insurance companies are obliged to establish technical reserves to cover future liabilities arising from insurance and possible losses due to risks arising from insurance operations. As indicated above, Entity-level laws on insurance companies stipulate that any insurance company seated in one of the Entities must establish technical reserves for all insurance contracts concluded in the Entities (by the company or its branches). These technical reserves must be established in accordance with by-laws[199] adopted by the competent agencies[200] that determine methods and ways of calculating insurance technical reserves, contents of reports and manner of reporting to the competent agency on technical reserves of insurance companies.

130. An insurance company shall, in accordance with its insurance operations, form the following types of insurance technical reserves: unearned premium reserves; reserves for claims; reserves for bonuses and discounts; the mathematical reserve; and other technical insurance reserves.

131. A company may also form technical reserves for loss fluctuation in insurance lines for which statistics illustrate that significant deviations from the annual claim amount can be expected. Irrespective of the above, an insurance company must establish technical reserves for loss fluctuation if it performs operations of credit insurance.

132. An insurance company that offers life insurance and insurance to persons with cumulative savings or funds to cover risk in later years of insurance, such as insurance against accidents or multiannual health insurance that likelihood tables and calculations are applied to in the same way as to life insurance, mathematical reserves must be established.

133. An insurance company underwriting the insurance policies where the policyholder bears the investment risk is required to set up special reserves with respect to such insurance.

134. The reserve for unearned premiums with respect to individual lines of insurance needs to be established at the level of the portion of premiums written, which relates to insurance coverage for the insurance period after the accounting period for which the reserve is calculated.

135. The reserves for claims need to be established at the level of estimated liabilities of an insurance company under those insurance contracts where the insured event occurred before the end of the accounting period, including any expenses payable by the insurance company under those insurance contracts. In

---

199. The FB&H Rulebook on Technical Reserves (OJ FB&H, 80/2006) and the RS Rulebook on Technical Reserves (OJ RS, 116/2006).
200. *See* the LIC FB&H, Art. 56(1) and the LIC RS, Art. 55(1).

addition to the aforementioned estimated liabilities, the claims' reserves also need to include estimated liabilities with respect to incurred but unreported losses.

136. Provisions for bonuses and discounts shall be established in the amount of the payments to which the policyholders are entitled, based on: (1) The right to participation in the profits made under their insurance policies or other rights under insurance contracts (bonuses), unless the mathematical reserve is established in respect to such assets; (2) Future partial decrease of the premium (discounts); (3) The right to reimbursement of a portion of insurance premium on account of early termination (cancellation).

137. An insurance company is required to set aside another technical reserve with regard to the expected future liabilities and the risks of large claims arising from insurance against manufacturer's liability for pharmaceutical products, earthquake insurance, flood insurance, and other liabilities and risks in respect to which it has not set up certain forms of reserves.

138. By-laws adopted by competent Entity-level institutions regulate in detail calculation methods for each type of technical reserve.

139. Calculation of the aforementioned technical reserves is done by a certified actuary. The certified actuary confirms in his/her opinion the accuracy of the technical reserve calculation in financial reports, separately for each type of technical reserve. A company must obtain a positive opinion of a certified actuary prior to compiling financial reports, and such opinion is an integral part of the financial reports.

140. Regarding the investment of insurance companies' assets, both laws stipulate that insurance companies seated in one of the Entities may invest insurance assets in B&H or in a foreign country.[201,202] Investments outside of B&H require approval of the competent Agency (the FB&H Insurance Supervisory Agency or the RS Insurance Agency)· Agencies prescribe the amount and method of investing insurance companies' assets.

141. According to the LI F&H, the insurance company is obligated, depending on the type of insurance, to invest assets from the technical reserves of life and non-life insurance in a manner which guarantees safety, maturity compliance, profitability, marketability and diversity and dispersion of investments.[203] The insurance company is obliged to ensure that the amount of investment in assets determined by Law is at least equal to the calculated technical reserves.[204] Moreover, the Law prescribes obligation of insurance companies to invest the assets of technical reserves in different types of properties and up to the amount of individual investment, in

201. Such as Member States of EU.
202. *See* the LI FB&H, Art. 89(3) the LIC RS, Art. 56(1).
203. *See* the LI FB&H, Art. 88(1).
204. *See ibid.*, Art. 88(2).

order to preserve their real value and limit the risk of loss from investment.[205] According to one of the key investment principles, insurance company is obliged to manage the investments of assets in a way that ensures that all due obligations can be settled at any time, i.e., that the investment of assets does not call into question the promptness in the payment of obligations from the insurance contract in accordance with the law and by-laws.[206]

142. According to regulations adopted by Entity-level agencies on investing insurance companies' assets,[207] assets for covering the technical reserve in life and non-life insurance may be invested in: securities issued or guaranteed by B&H, FB&H, RS and BD B&H;[208] bonds and other debt securities issued or guaranteed by unit of local government in Entity/B&H; bonds and other debt securities traded in an organized securities market in the Entity/B&H; bonds and other debt securities that are not traded in an organized securities market, if they were issued by a legal person seated in B&H; shares traded in an organized securities market in the Entity/B&H; shares that are not traded in an organized securities market, if they were issued by a legal person seated in B&H;[209] loans to legal persons secured by lien on real estate (mortgage), if the lien was registered in land books and other real estate records in B&H and if the value does not exceed 40% (FB&H) or 60% (RS) of market value of the real estate;[210] loans secured by aforementioned securities; loans secured by a guarantee of a bank seated in B&H;[211] loans in the amount of insurance purchase value based on a life insurance contract from mathematical reserves; real estate and other rights over real estate if it cumulatively meets the following requirements: it was registered in land books in B&H and other real estate records in the Entities/B&H, it is free of any encumbrance, its value was appraised by a court expert or certified appraiser and it generates or is expected to generate yield; term deposits in banks seated in the Entities/B&H;[212] non-purpose deposit in

205. *See ibid.*, Art. 88(7).
206. *See ibid.*, Art. 88(10).
207. *See* the FB&H Rulebook on the Amount and Method of Investing Assets (OJ FB&H, 95/2019, 1/2023), and the RS Rulebook on Investing Insurance Companies' Assets (OJ RS, 117/2020, 23/2021, 118/2022, 1/23).
208. The RS Rulebook on investing assets of insurance companies additionally specifies securities issued by or guaranteed by the B&H Central Bank and funds specified in Art. 8 of the Law on the RS Investment-Development Bank (OJ RS, 56/2006, 28/13).
209. The FB&H Rulebook on the Amount and Method of Investing Assets foresees an additional requirement specifying that it must be a 'legal person that stated profit in its two most recent financial statements', *see* Art. 9(1)(e) also Art. 89 (1) e) of the LI FB&H.
210. Appraised by an authorized court expert or certified appraiser registered in B&H.
211. The FB&H Rulebook on the Amount and Method of Investing Assets foresees an additional requirement specifying that it must be a bank 'that stated profit in its two most recent annual financial statements', *see* Art. 9(1)(h).
212. The RS Rulebook on Investing Assets of Insurance Companies stipulates that these must be term deposits that the bank has no right to retain or other rights encumbering the insurance company, provided that the bank has positive opinion of certified auditor opinions regarding the financial statements.

banks seated in B&H;[213] and shares and stocks of investment funds with public offering, seated in the Entities/B&H. Also, according to the RS Rulebook on investing insurance companies' assets, insurance companies can invest in assets on insurance of the company's accounts.[214]

143. Technical reserve assets in life and non-life insurance may also be invested outside of B&H with prior approval of competent Agency in: securities issued by an EU, OECD or CEFTA Member State or their central banks,[215] or in securities guaranteed by some of the aforementioned subjects; bonds and other debt securities traded in an organized securities markets in Member States;[216] shares traded in an organized securities market of a Member State.[217] Additionally, the RS Rulebook on Investing Assets of Insurance Companies stipulates that assets may be invested in real estate, located in an EU, OECD or CEFTA Member States if it cumulatively meets the following requirements: it was registered in the land registers and other real estate records in the Member State, it is free of all encumbrances, its value was appraised by a certified court appraiser and it generates or is expected to generate yield.[218] Total investments outside of B&H may not exceed the total of 20% of assets, or 15% of assets per investment. As indicated above, investing assets outside of B&H is conditioned on the issuance of approval by the competent Agency.

144. Every individual submitting a claim for damages from insurance also has a privileged claim against assets comprising investments of the company for respective insurance lines (life or non-life) that the claim applies to. In this context, a privileged claim is the priority of a claimant over other creditors during the process of settling insurance claims.

145. An insurance company invests assets according to its type of activities, in order to guarantee life insurance, income and cash flow of the insurance company that is responsible for allocation and adequate schedule of the investments.[219] Similar to the above, the LI F&H prescribes that the insurance company is obliged to invest assets in a manner which will always ensure compliance with the types of insurance business it performs, timely compliance of deposited and invested funds

213. On which the bank has no rights of retention or other rights at the expense of the insurance company, provided that the bank has a positive opinion of the authorized auditor on the financial statements. *See* the RS Rulebook on Investing Assets of Insurance Companies, Art. 9(14).
214. *See* the RS Rulebook on Investing Insurance Companies' Assets Art. 9(16).
215. The RS Rulebook on Investing Assets of Insurance Companies also foresees that the aforementioned assets may be invested in securities of an international financial organization, *see* Arts 21 and 22(1).
216. The RS Rulebook on Investing Assets of Insurance Companies also foresees an additional requirement: that the assessment agencies established credit rating that at least matches Standard & Poor's rating A or appropriate rating of Fitch – IBCA or Moody's, *see* Art. 22(2).
217. The RS Rulebook on Investing Assets of Insurance Companies also foresees an additional requirement: that the stated shares were, at least in the past two years, included in the official stock exchange registration and that their minimum market capitalization at the time of investment amounts to EUR 500 million.
218. The RS Rulebook on Investing Assets of Insurance Companies also foresees that the aforementioned assets may be invested in securities of an international financial organization, *see* Art. 22(4).
219. *See* the LIC RS, Art. 56(6).

and the company's obligations based on calculated technical reserves, currency compliance of deposits and investments and liabilities from technical reserves, diversity of deposits and investments and their dispersion.[220]

146. As far as control by competent agencies is concerned, the Law in RS prescribes that the insurance company is obliged to inform the competent Agency about any investment of assets that the bank deposit secrecy is not applicable.[221] The insurance company must notify the competent Agency of any changes in the balance of investments within ten days from the date of change. For changes pertaining to real estate and loans secured by a mortgage, notification must be submitted fifteen days before the change.[222]

147. Further restrictions prescribed by the law in RS apply to the possibility of purchasing shares, other participations, bonds and other debt securities of the parent company or a company that controls the insurance company, at the time of their issuance or when making a payment for a public call for subscription and payment of securities.[223]

148. Control exercised by the competent Agency in RS includes: (a) on-the-spot control and requesting of all data about the financial situation: of the insurance company's subsidiary when insurance assets constitute the company's investments; of the insurance company's subsidiaries that manage the insurance company's investments; (b) requesting any data about the financial situation of bonds or debt securities of credit institutions that the insurance company possesses and disposes of in the investment of insurance assets; (c) requesting any data or performing control on the insurance company's premises for the purposes of implementing Articles 55–58 of the LIC RS.[224]

149. In case an insurance company fails to abide by legal provisions pertaining to technical reserves and the investment of the insurance company's funds and carrying out of supervision, competent institutions may decide to: prohibit investments of insurance assets and prohibit disposal with a part or with all free assets; withdraw or revoke the authorization for some or all lines of insurance, and take any appropriate measure in order to protect the interests of the insured persons, as well as any other person asserting their rights from the insurance contract.[225] The prohibition to freely dispose of the total or a part of the insurance company's assets, upon request of the competent Agency is entered in the public registers or in the ledgers of the bank in which the relevant deposit exists. This prohibition may be

220. *See* the LIC FB&H, Art. 86(3).
221. *See* the LIC RS, Art. 57(1).
222. *See ibid.*, Art. 57(2) and (3).
223. *See ibid.*, Art. 57(4).
224. *See ibid.*, Art. 55(5).
225. *See* the LI FB&H, Art. 98(1) and the LIC RS, Art. 58(1).

withdrawn entirely or in part by a decision of the Agency, and it must contain withdrawal conditions and deadlines; the competent Agency in the other entity must be notified thereof.[226]

150. In exceptional situations, when there is a risk of violating the existing provisions and statute of the insurance company, the competent Agency may decide to appoint certified auditors to perform an extraordinary audit, in accordance with international standards. The auditors' task is to conduct both financial and administrative audits of an insurance company as a part of the supervision performed by the competent Insurance agency, in order to determine whether the insurance company applies the existing legislation in the Entity.

151. Laws on insurance and insurance companies in FB&H and RS also include provisions regulating supervision over investments and assets of the insurance company. The Agency may issue an order to the insurance company about investing insurance assets of long-term life insurance, as follows: to refrain from investing insurance assets of a certain type for a certain period, and manner regulated by Articles 86 to 97 of the LI FB&H and Articles 56 and 81 of the LIC RS, if it is necessary to protect the interests of policyholders from immediate loss; to liquidate, within a set time frame, all or some items of a certain type of investment (regulated under Articles 86 to 97 of the LI FB&H and Articles 56 and 81 of the LIC RS or by a description provided by the company), if so required to immediately protect the interests of the insured persons from immediate loss.[227]

152. The Agency may prevent the disposal, encumbrance or certain ways of utilization of any form of the insurance company's assets. Such order may last no longer than six months but may be renewed as many times as necessary.[228]

153. The assets subject to orders referred to in Articles 131 of the LI FB&H and 11 of LIC RS may not be encumbered with a mortgage or any other form of encumbrance or restriction. In the event of insolvency, any mortgage or encumbrance on such assets shall be deemed void with respect to the rights of the liquidator or creditors.[229]

226. *See* the LI FB&H, Art. 98(2) and the LIC RS, Art. 58(2).
227. *See* the LI FB&H, Art. 131(1) and LIC RS, Art. 11(1).
228. *See* the LI FB&H, Art. 131(2) and LIC RS, Art. 11(2).
229. *See* the LIC FB&H/LIC RS, Art. 11(3).

Chapter 5. Accountancy

154. The legal framework in the field of accounting in B&H is extremely complex and comprised of four laws on accounting and auditing: the Law on Accounting and Auditing of B&H (LAA B&H),[230] the Law on Accounting and Auditing of FB&H (LAA FB&H),[231] the Accounting and Auditing Law of RS (LAA RS)[232] and the Law on Accounting and Auditing in BD B&H (LAA BD B&H).[233] The state-level Accounting and Auditing Law was adopted in 2004, and entity-level laws were originally adopted in 2005. The last, fourth law in this field was adopted in 2006 at the level of BD B&H.

155. Enactment of the state-level LAA B&H in 2004 was necessary, *inter alia*, for the following reasons: harmonization of accounting and auditing systems in B&H, harmonization of national legislation with *acquis communautaire*, development of the capital market and significant changes in applicable legislation, amendments to the existing and adoption of new regulations on banking, insurance, microlending, leasing, securities market, investment funds, etc.

156. The LAA B&H established a single framework that: introduced the obligation of applying the accounting and auditing standards, including the code of professional ethics for professional accountants and auditors for the entire territory of B&H; prescribed uniform requirements for obtaining qualifications and conducting training, testing, certification and licensing of professional accountants and auditors, as well as mutual recognition of qualifications of professional accountants and auditors; stipulated free performance of audits throughout B&H; and defined obligations pertaining to harmonization of implementations and other regulations of the Entities (FB&H and RS) and BD B&H with the provisions of the LAA B&H.[234] In addition, the LAA B&H also established an independent Accounting and Auditing Commission of B&H, which oversees the implementation of standards and performs other work in accordance with its powers defined in the LAA B&H in the territory of B&H.

157. The entity-level accounting and auditing laws (LAA FB&H and LAA RS) also prescribe the obligation to apply International Financial Reporting Standards (IFRS) and International Accounting Standards (IAS), and their provisions have also been largely harmonized with requirements from relevant EU directives and constitute the basis for the implementation of a corporate financial reporting reform and for enhancement and improvement of the accounting profession in the context of the EU integration process.

230. OJ B&H, 42/2004.
231. OJ FB&H, 15/2021.
232. OJ RS, 94/2015, 78/2020.
233. OJ BD B&H, 22/2016, 50/2018.
234. *See* the LAA B&H, Art. 1(1).

158. Entity-level laws include provisions that precisely regulate issues that are important for the establishment of a bookkeeping and accounting system, such as criteria for categorization of legal persons, titles and qualifications in accounting and auditing professions, organization and functioning of the accounting system, compiling, control and booking of bookkeeping of documents, rules pertaining to the obligations of making an inventory of assets and liabilities and other activities aimed at matching the bookkeeping and the actual balance, issues pertaining to standards and rules and the obligations to develop financial and consolidated reports in accordance with the rules from relevant IAS/IFRS, obligations and those obliged to develop periodical and annual financial reports, obligation and method of keeping business books, defining the issues of importance for the establishment of a public supervision system over the accounting and auditing professions.

159. In accordance with an adopted general internal act, legal persons regulate the organization of accounting in a way that ensures comprehensive recordkeeping, and also the detection and prevention of misrecorded business events, regulate internal accounting control procedures, determine accounting policies, determine persons responsible for legality and accuracy of occurrence of business events, and create and control accounting documents related to such events, determine the flow of accounting documents and define deadlines for their submission for further processing, determine procedures for preparation, compiling and presentation of financial reports, prescribe procedures for collecting, processing and presentation of data related to the preparation and creation of annual reports on performance, and financial data for statistical, taxation and other purposes, and regulate other issues of importance for establishing an efficient bookkeeping and accounting system in the legal person.[235]

160. Entity-level accounting and auditing laws have been harmonized to a great extent. However, there are certain deviations both between Entity-level laws and between Entity-level laws as opposed to the state-level law.

161. Pursuant to provisions of Articles 1, 2 and 3 of the LAA B&H and Articles 2, 33 and 73 of the LAA FB&H and Articles 6, 7 and 32 of the Statute of the Union of Accountants, Auditors and Financial Workers of FB&H, based on a Decision on authorizations for translation and publishing no. 2-11/06 of 10 March 2006,[236] the Management Board of the Union of Accountants, Auditors and Financial Workers of FB&H made a Decision in 2010 on publishing IFRS, including IAS and related interpretations of the International Accounting Standards Board.[237]

162. Operationalization and adjustment of provisions of the Entity-level accounting and auditing laws to the accounting needs of insurance and reinsurance companies were made through by-laws on the layout of chart of accounts, account

235. *See* the LAA FB&H, Art. 11(1) and the LAA RS, Art. 7(3).
236. OJ B&H, 81/2006.
237. Available at: http://www.srr-FB&H.org/msfi_mrs.asp.

content and application of the layout of chart of accounts[238] that define the function and content of accounts prescribed by the layout of chart of accounts. Namely, provisions of the 2010 Rulebook on the Layout of Chart of Accounts, Account Content and Application of the Layout of Chart of Accounts for Companies[239] apply to insurance companies in FB&H, and the 2009 Rulebook on the Layout of Chart of Accounts and Content of Accounts in the Layout of Chart of Accounts for Insurance Companies Applies to Insurance Companies in the RS.[240] Both of these rulebooks were adopted by Entity-level ministers of finance. Also, provisions of the by-laws on the contents and format of financial reports of insurance companies[241] prescribe contents and format of financial reports for insurance companies that are used to reporting on periodical and annual accounts.

163. Insurance companies must keep records in their business books (general ledger) by applying the layout of chart of accounts. Provisions of rulebooks on the layout of chart of accounts, its content and application define the function and content of accounts prescribed by the layout of chart of accounts.[242] Balance and changes in assets, capital and liabilities, revenues and expenditures and establishment of business results are recorded on basic three-digit accounts that comprise the layout of chart of accounts, in accordance with IAS and IFRS.[243] If needed, an insurance or reinsurance company may additionally break down the three-digit accounts within the prescribed layout of chart of accounts[244] to analytical accounts in a way compatible with rulebooks and a general act of the insurance company.[245] A company may not introduce or use three-digit accounts, except for accounts prescribed by the rulebooks.[246]

164. In subsidiary ledgers, a company records other data that arise from requests for publication of adequate IFRS or that is required for compiling other reports, in accordance with by-laws. Also, the rulebooks clarify the classification of individual accounting items, while requests for recognition and measurement are regulated by appropriate IFRS.

238. Layout of chart of accounts is an overview/list of all accounts comprised in the general ledger that may be opened in the bookkeeping of a company, which provides required clarity and organizational form to the bookkeeping, and guarantees order and clarity to the bookkeeping of the company.
239. OJ FB&H, 82/2010.
240. OJ RS, 90/2009, 93/2009.
241. The FB&H Decision on Reports of Insurance Companies (OJ FB&H, 64/2013, 31/2015) and the RS Rulebook on Content and Format of Financial Reporting Forms for Insurance Companies (OJ RS, 97/2009).
242. The FB&H Rulebook/RS Rulebook, Art. 1(1).
243. *Ibid.*, Art. 2(1).
244. Chart of accounts is an overview of all accounts actually opened in a company that are derived from the layout of chart of accounts. It is created by eliminating unnecessary accounts from the layout of chart of accounts and by proper breaking down of individual accounts in the general ledger. Chart of accounts does not introduce new balance or synthetic accounts against the layout of chart of accounts.
245. *See* the FB&H Rulebook/RS Rulebook, Art. 2(2).
246. *See ibid.*, Art. 2(3).

165. Provisions of the Entity-level accounting and auditing laws are applied to all companies, including insurance companies, microcredit companies, leasing companies, investment funds, companies for management of investment funds, broker companies-dealerships, stock exchanges and banks, and other financial organizations, cooperatives, profit and non-profit entities with a registered head office in the Entities.[247]

166. In light of the LAA FB&H and the LAA RS provisions, legal persons are categorized as small, medium-sized and large, depending on indicators established on the date of drafting financial reports in the business year, according to the following criteria: the revenue amount, value of assets, average headcount during the year.[248] Irrespective of the previously specified criteria, both laws categorize insurance companies as large legal persons, due to their specific nature.[249] Such classification implies, among other things, that financial reports of insurance companies are subject to a mandatory audit,[250] i.e., to a control and evaluation for the purpose of providing a professional and independent opinion on whether they objectively and truthfully, in all materially significant issues, present the balance of assets, capital and liabilities, business results, cash flows and changes in capital, in accordance with the IAS and IFRS and other regulations, in order to protect public interest in public presentation of financial reports.[251]

167. Therefore, according to the law in B&H, internal and external audits are obligatory for insurance companies. The LI FB&H regulates internal audits in insurance companies in FB&H. An insurance company shall organize work of the internal audit as independent and objective activity of providing a professional opinion, designed in such a way as to add value and improve the operations of the insurance company.[252] The internal audit must be conducted in accordance with the internationally recognized auditing standards, internal audit practice and internal auditors' code of ethics.[253]

168. The internal audit analyses and evaluates the activities of insurance companies and provides expert opinion, recommendations and advice on controls of forming in order to enable: performance of insurance business properly and in accordance with the Law and the regulations adopted on the basis of the Law and in accordance with the internal rules governing the operations of the insurance company; keeping financial records, recording business events on the basis of authentic accounting documents, evaluating accounting items and compiling financial and other reports in accordance with the Law and the regulations and in accordance with the internal rules governing the operations of the insurance company; systematic management of risks arising from the business activities of the insurance company

247. *See* the LAA FB&H/LAA RS, Art. 3(1).
248. *See* the LAA FB&H, Art. 4(1) and the LAA RS, Art. 5(1) and (2).
249. *See* the LAA FB&H, Art. 4(6) and the LAA RS, Art. 5(8).
250. *See* the LAA FB&H, Art. 49(3) and the LAA RS, Art. 28(2).
251. *See* the LAA FB&H, Art. 2(1) and the LAA RS, Art. 2(3).
252. *See* the LI FB&H, Art. 110.
253. *See ibid.*, Art. 111(2).

in accordance with the principles of stable business, including management of information technology resources and other associated technologies.[254]

169. The internal audit controls and evaluates the following: performance of insurance work in accordance with the FB&H Law on Insurance Companies and regulations adopted on the basis of this Law; adequacy and application of risk management policies and procedures in accordance with the going concern principle and stability principle; accounting procedures and organization of accounting work, including organization and management of the information system; and reliability, valuation and updating of financial data and information and other activities aiming to improve company operations.[255]

170. Organization and work of the internal audit are regulated by company acts. An insurance company must employ a minimum of one person to perform internal audit work, and if several people conduct internal audits, one of them manages the internal audit and is responsible for its work.[256] The minimum requirement for the performance of internal audit work is the title of a certified internal auditor.[257] An internal auditor may not perform other work in the company, may not have powers and responsibility for the preparation of acts and other documents that may be the subject of the internal audit, nor can it be a member of the management, supervisory board or audit board[258] The company management and employees are obliged to provide the internal audit with free and full access to all data, documentation and information on its operations. The internal audit submits reports to the audit board and to the company's board of directors.[259] Annual and semi-annual internal audit reports, along with the management report on measures taken to eliminate irregularities based on internal audit findings must be submitted to the supervisory board, and the annual report must be submitted to the company's assembly as well.[260] If during an audit the internal audit finds illegal operations or poor risk management that pose the risk of illiquidity, insolvency or jeopardize interests of policyholders, the auditor must immediately inform the board of directors, audit board and the supervisory board of the company.[261]

171. The LIC RS also contains two other provisions about the internal audit. Namely, the LIC RS foresees the obligation of an insurance company to organize the internal audit as an independent activity in a systematic and disciplined approach to the evaluation and improvement of efficiency of the management and

254. *See ibid.*, Art. 111(1).
255. *See* the FB&H Internal Audit Rulebook, Art. 3(2).
256. *See ibid.*, Art. 5(2) and (3).
257. *See* the LI FB&H, Art. 112(1).
258. *See ibid.*, Art. 112(4).
259. *See ibid.*, Art. 114(3).
260. *See ibid.*.
261. *See ibid.*, Art. 115.

control process[262] and prescribes that people who perform the internal audit work in an insurance company must be selected by the shareholder's assembly of the insurance company concerned.[263]

172. The Insurance Agency of the RS has adopted a by-law on the organization and procedures of an internal audit in insurance companies.[264]

173. The insurance company is obliged to organize an internal audit (proportional to the size of the organizational structure and the complexity of its activity), functionally and organizationally independent and independent from other organizational parts of the insurance company and the activities which audits.[265] Internal audit provides an independent and objective opinion on the issues subject to the audit, gives advice and recommendations for improvement of the existing internal controls system and business operations of the insurance company, and provides assistance to the audit board as well as to the assembly of shareholders in achieving their goals through applying a systematic, disciplined and documented approach to the evaluation and improvement of the existing methods of control, risk management and process management.[266] Establishment and work of internal audit in an insurance company must be regulated by the company's internal document drafted and adopted in accordance with the legal regulations governing the establishment and functioning of business companies, the International Framework for the Professional Practice of Internal Auditing and the RS Rulebook on Internal Audit in Insurance Company.

174. As in FB&H, the insurance company in RS is obliged to employ at least one person to perform internal audit.[267] The head of the internal audit (if that unit is organized in an insurance company) or at least one person who performs internal audit tasks (if that unit is not organized in an insurance company) are required to have the title of authorized internal auditor.[268] A person who performs internal audit duties is prohibited from performance of other duties in the insurance company and may not have the authority and responsibility for the preparation of documentation that may be subjected to internal audit, nor may she/he be a member of the company's body.[269] For internal audit of specific business areas, the insurance company may hire other experts for the relevant area.[270] The internal audit is directly answerable for its work to the audit board of the insurance company.[271] The internal auditor must have access to the necessary documentation and to all oral or written

262. *See* the LIC RS, Art. 59(9).
263. *See ibid.*, Art. 59(10).
264. OJ RS, 77/2019.
265. *See* the RS Rulebook on Internal Audit in insurance company, Art. 2(1).
266. *See ibid.*, Art. 2(2).
267. *See ibid.*, Art. 4(1).
268. *See ibid.*, Art. 4(2).
269. *See ibid.*, Art. 4(3).
270. *See ibid.*, Art. 4(4).
271. *See ibid.*, Art. 6(2).

information and data provided by the bodies of the insurance company and employees of the insurance company.[272] The authorities of the insurance company and the employees of the company must not, in any way, prevent, limit or hinder the functioning of the internal audit, or influence in any way the opinions and qualifications given by internal auditor in report.[273] According to the Article 8 of the RS Rulebook on Internal Audit in insurance company, internal auditor prepares a written report for every performed internal audit,[274] which must be based on the performed inspections and appropriate documentation.[275] The internal audit report is submitted to the executive board and responsible persons of the organizational part of the insurance company in whose authority are the business areas that were the subjected to the internal audit.[276] The internal audit of the insurance company prepares reports on the work of the internal audit in accordance with the deadlines set by the internal audit plans but no less than semi-annually and annually.[277] These reports are submitted to the audit board of the insurance company.[278] Shareholders' assembly of the insurance company reviews the annual report on the work of the internal audit, with the opinion of the audit committee, simultaneously with the financial statements of the insurance company.[279]

175. As indicated above, an external audit of insurance companies is mandatory and performed in accordance with the LAA FB&H, the LAA RS and the IAS. An external audit is performed by companies licensed in accordance with provisions of the LAA FB&H and the LAA RS by persons with a professional title of a certified auditor, licensed to work on the auditing of financial reports and who are employed or hired by the company to perform the audit.[280] In a report on auditing of financial statements, an opinion is given about whether the reports present truthfully and objectively, in all materially important issues, the financial situation and business results of the legal person, and changes in capital and cash flow in the accounting period that the revised financial statements apply to, and whether the reports were compiled in accordance with the IAS, i.e., IFRS.[281] Opinion of a certified auditor must be expressed in accordance with International Standards on Auditing (ISA) and it can be unqualified, qualified, adverse or a disclaimer opinion.[282] The audit of financial reports is performed for every business year individually[283] based on a contract signed between the legal person whose financial reports are to be audited

---

272. *See ibid.*, Art. 6(3).
273. *See ibid.*, Art. 6(4).
274. *See ibid.*, Art. 8(1).
275. *See ibid.*, Art. 8(2).
276. *See ibid.*, Art. 8(3).
277. *See ibid.*, Art. 9(1). The insurance company is obliged to submit these reports to the competent Agency within the following deadlines: (1) semi-annually, by 31 Jul. of the current year, (2) annually, by 30 Apr. of the following year, together with audited financial statements and an opinion audit committee. *See* the RS Rulebook on Internal Audit in insurance company, Art. 10(2).
278. *See* the RS Rulebook on Internal Audit in insurance company, Art. 9(3).
279. *See ibid.*, Art. 9(4).
280. *See* the LAA FB&H, Art. 50 and the LAA RS, Art. 31.
281. *See* the LAA FB&H, Art. 53(1) and the LAA RS, Art. 41(1).
282. *See* the LAA FB&H, Art. 53(2) and the LAA RS, Art. 41(2).
283. *See* the LAA RS, Art. 39(1).

and an auditing company no later than by the end of the business year for which the financial reports are prepared for audit.[284] The auditing company is entitled to remuneration for the performed audit, and the remuneration amount is determined in the audit contract.[285]

284. *See* the LAA FB&H, Art. 52(5).
285. *See ibid.*, Art. 52(7) and the LAA RS, Art. 39(5).

Chapter 6. Taxation of the Company

176. B&H has a complex tax system that is a reflection of its specific state organization. While the system of direct taxation is composed of three separate tax subsystems: FB&H, RS and Brcko District of B&H (BD B&H), the indirect taxation system is established at state level.

§1. Corporate Income Tax

177. Insurance companies and other legal entities performing an independent, permanent economic activity through the sales of products and provision of services on the market in order to generate an income are taxpayers when it concerns corporate income tax. As a direct tax, income tax is regulated at the Entities' level by the Law on Corporate Income Tax of the FB&H (LCIT FB&H)[286] and the Law on Corporate Income Tax of RS (LCIT RS)[287] and by the Law on Corporate Income Tax at the level of BD B&H (LCIT BD B&H).[288]

178. In the FB&H, the corporate income tax is determined and reported on the basis of data presented in the business books and records kept in accordance with the accounting regulations and IAS/IFRS, as well as data from the records and corrections which are prescribed by the LCIT FB&H and the Rulebook on the Implementation of the LCIT FB&H.[289]

179. Corporate income tax is paid at the rate of 10% on the determined tax basis on the tax balance.[290]

180. Taxpayers are insurance and reinsurance companies which generate income – on the market in FB&H, RS BD B&H or on the foreign market.[291] Taxpayers in the context of the company income tax are also non-resident insurance and reinsurance companies when they generate income from a resident of FB&H.[292] Resident companies, in terms of the LCIT FB&H, are those insurance and reinsurance companies whose head office (registration) is entered in the court register of business entities in the FB&H or companies whose actual management and supervision over the business operations are based in the FB&H.[293] A non-resident company is a company established outside the territory of B&H whose head office or actual management and supervision over business activities also lies outside the territory of B&H.[294]

286. OJ FB&H, 15/2016, 15/2020.
287. OJ RS, 94/2015, 1/2017, 58/2019.
288. OJ BD B&H, 17/2022, 38/2022.
289. OJ FB&H, 88/2016, 11/2017, 96/2017, 94/19, 87/2020.
290. *See* the LCIT FB&H, Art. 31.
291. *See ibid.*, Art. 3(1).
292. *See ibid.*, Art. 3(4).
293. *See ibid.*, Art. 5(1).
294. *See ibid.*, Art. 5(2).

181. The period in which the corporate income tax is determined is a calendar year, but this period may be even shorter in the case of cessation of business before the end of the calendar year; commencement of business operations during the year; status changes, etc. A taxpayer is obliged to submit a correctly and accurately filled out tax declaration with the tax balance, to the competent branch office of the Tax Administration: for the tax period ending with 31 December, that is, by the end of the year. A tax declaration with a tax balance and other supplements must be submitted to the competent tax office within a maximum of thirty days upon the end of the deadline prescribed for the submission of annual financial reports – that is, by 30 March of the current year for the previous year. As for the tax period ending in the course of the calendar year (cessation of business, status changes, etc.), the tax declaration with the tax balance and other supplements is submitted to the competent tax office within a maximum of ninety days from the last day of such tax period. In the second case, in accordance with the provisions of the LCIT FB&H, regulations on registration and all other regulations related to the business operations of a legal entity, the only valid date is the date of the status change from the court registry.

182. The tax basis of corporate income tax is determined in the tax balance by harmonizing expenditures and income and capital gains/losses declared in the financial statements in the manner as prescribed by the LCIT FB&H.[295] The tax basis is calculated as the profit declared in the financial statement increased by tax–unrecognized expenditures and other tax-unrecognized items and reduced by non-taxable items in accordance with the LCIT FB&H.[296] Every income and capital gain realized by a taxpayer is included in the tax basis, except for items that, in accordance with the LCIT FB&H, are not included.[297] The amount of corporate income tax is calculated by multiplying the tax basis with the income tax rate.[298] Pursuant to Article 8 of the LCIT FB&H, to determine the tax basis, all expenditures, income and capital gain/loss are recognized in the amounts declared in the business books, which are in accordance with the accounting regulations, unless otherwise prescribed by the LCIT FB&H.

183. According to the LCIT FB&H, expenditures for the formation of mathematical reserves, if they are formed in accordance with the regulations of the competent Agency, are recognized as tax–permissible to the insurance and reinsurance companies.[299] Furthermore, expenditures for the formation of technical insurance reserves are also recognized as tax–permissible (except for mathematical reserves), under the following conditions: (a) that they are formed in accordance with the regulations of the competent insurance Agency; (b) that the amount of increase in the reserve in the current balance sheet compared to the previous period does not

295. *See ibid.*, Art. 7(1).
296. *See ibid.*, Art. 7(2).
297. *See ibid.*, Art. 7(3).
298. *See ibid.*, Art. 7(4).
299. *See ibid.*, Art. 16(3).

exceed 20%.[300] Expenditures that exceed the amounts previously mentioned are not tax deductible expenditures and cannot be conveyed to a future tax period.[301]

184. According to the provisions of the LCIT FB&H (Articles 36–37), tax incentives are prescribed only in cases of relatively significant investments[302] and new employment. Regarding the latter, the taxpayer has the right to a tax-recognized expenditure in the amount of a twofold sum of the gross salary paid to newly hired employees if it meets the following conditions: (a) the duration of the employment contract must be at least twelve months full-time and (b) the newly hired employee was not employed by taxpayer or related person in the previous five years.[303]

185. When a taxpayer generates revenue or income through business activities performed outside the territory of B&H (directly or through its business unit) and pays corporate income tax on them, the tax paid abroad is incorporated into the paid tax, up to the amount of corporate income tax that would have been paid in the Federation on such income, with the obligation of the taxpayer to provide Tax Administration with evidence on payment of tax abroad for recognition of tax paid abroad.[304] Ratified treaties (agreements, conventions) on avoidance of double taxation, signed by B&H are implemented when taxing non-residents and prevail over the provisions of the LCITFB&H.[305]

186. Pursuant to the LCIT FB&H, the withholding or retention tax represents a type of tax that is calculated on revenue that has been realized by the non-resident in the territory of the Federation.[306] The withholding tax is calculated and paid by the payer at the payment of the income. The payer is obliged to file the report on calculated and paid withholding tax to the Tax Administration within ten days of the day of payment.[307] The basis for calculation of the withholding tax is the gross amount paid by the resident of the Federation to the non-resident on the basis, *inter alia*, insurance premiums for insurance or reinsurance of risk in the Federation.[308] The withholding tax is paid at the rate of 10%, (and on dividends at the rate of 5%).[309]

187. The LCIT FB&H and the Rulebook for the Implementation of the LCIT of FB&H prescribe: how to determine this type of tax, the filing of tax declarations, payment of tax obligations and their statute of limitations if they are not timely

300. *See ibid.*, Art. 16(4).
301. *See ibid.*, Art. 16(5).
302. *See ibid.*, Art. 36.
303. *See ibid.*, Art. 37(1).
304. *See ibid.*, Arts 32 and 33.
305. *See ibid.*, Art. 35.
306. *See ibid.*, Art. 38(1).
307. *See ibid.*, Art. 35(5).
308. *See ibid.*, Art. 38(1).
309. *See ibid.*, Art. 35(7).

determined and charged.[310] Pursuant to the Rulebook on the Implementation of the LCIT FB&H, the corporate income tax is determined after the end of the calendar year or other period for which it was necessary to calculate and state corporate income tax according to the tax basis precisely determined for that period.[311] Control, determination and collection of corporate income tax are performed in a manner and according to procedures prescribed by the FB&H Law on Tax Administration.[312]

188. The taxation of income generated by insurance and reinsurance companies as well as income of other legal entities on the territory of the RS is regulated by the LCIT RS which establishes the general legal framework for the taxation of the income of legal persons in the RS and foreign legal persons who generate revenues in the RS.[313] Pursuant to the LCIT RS, the taxpayers are: a legal person from RS for incomes obtained from any source whether in the RS, FB&H, BD B&H or abroad; a business unit of a legal person with seat in FB&H or BD B&H for income realized in the RS; a foreign legal person carrying out business activity and has a permanent place of business in the RS for the income that relates to that permanent place of business; a foreign legal person obtaining revenue from real estate located in the RS for the income that relates to that real estate and other legal persons specified in Article 3 of the LCIT RS. The business unit of a legal person from the FB&H or the BD B&H is a taxpayer of the corporate income tax in RS for income realized through performance of business activities in the RS.[314] The income of a foreign legal person is taxable if it is a result of activities performed in the territory of the RS through the permanent place of business of a foreign legal entity.

189. The tax basis of the legal person from the RS is the income generated in the RS and outside its territory, and the tax basis of a foreign legal person that has a permanent place of business in the RS is only the income generated in the RS.

190. The operating, financial, non-operating and extraordinary revenue and revaluation revenue calculated on the income balance in accordance with the law governing accounting, with the exception of revenue for which the LCIT RS prescribes another method of calculation, are recognized for the determination of tax basis in the tax declaration.

191. Corporate income tax is paid at the rate of 10% for the tax year in both the FB&H and the RS. The tax year for legal persons is the calendar year, unless the Ministry of Finance determines a different tax year to be used, which is not the calendar year.[315]

---

310. *See ibid.*, Arts 47–57.
311. *See ibid.*, Art. 47.
312. OJ FB&H, 33/2002, 28/2004, 57/2009, 40/2010, 27/2012, 7/2013, 71/2014, 91/2015, 44/2022.
313. *See* the LCIT RS, Art. 1.
314. *See ibid.*, Art. 3(2).
315. *See ibid.*, Art. 37.

192. The tax declaration for a tax year must be submitted no later than ninety days after the end of the tax year, and in the case of a calendar year, no later than 31 March of the current year for the previous year.

193. If a legal person from the RS obtains revenue in a foreign state and the revenue is taxed both in the RS and in that foreign state, whether paid directly or upon deduction by another person, then the tax paid in the foreign state is to be deducted from the RS corporate income tax, unless such legal person from the RS does not choose the foreign tax to be treated as expenditure that is deductible when determining the tax basis for the tax year.[316]

194. The reduction of corporate income tax for the tax paid abroad for the tax year may not exceed the amount of the corporate income tax calculated by applying the rate of tax of that legal person for that tax year in the RS. In case corporate income tax paid abroad exceeds the amount of tax on income realized in the RS, the excess amount is then transferred within a period of five tax years and is subject to the same limitations for those tax years.[317]

195. The third corporate income taxation subsystem in B&H is established on the territory of BD B&H. The Law on Corporate Income Tax of BD B&H (LCIT BD B&H) has established a general legal framework for the taxation of the income of legal persons based in the BD B&H, the business units of legal persons on the territory of the BD B&H based in the FB&H and the RS, and foreign legal persons that generate revenue in the BD B&H.[318]

196. Correspondingly to the solutions contained in the Entities laws on corporate income tax, the LCIT BD B&H prescribes that the taxpayers are defined as a legal person from the BD B&H for income obtained from any source whether in B&H or abroad; a business unit of a legal person with headquarters in the Entities for the income generated in the BD B&H; a foreign legal person carrying out economic activity from a permanent place of business in the BD B&H for the income that is attributable to the permanent place of business; a foreign legal person generating revenue from real estate located in the BD B&H for the income that is attributable to the real estate.[319]

197. Pursuant to the LCIT BD B&H, the tax basis for the tax year is taxable income determined in the tax balance.[320] Taxable income is determined by adjusting the revenue and expenditure of the taxpayer stated in the income statement, in accordance with the law, except for revenue and expenditures for which this Law prescribes a different method of calculation.[321]

316. *See ibid.*, Art. 50(1).
317. *See ibid.*, Art. 50(2).
318. *See* the LCIT BD B&H, Art. 1.
319. *Ibid.*
320. *See* the LCIT BD B&H, Art. 5(1).
321. *See ibid.*, Art. 5(2).

198. Taxable revenue with the aim of calculating the tax basis includes all revenue sources, whether in cash or in kind, and regardless of whether that revenue is linked to the operations of a legal person, other than revenue under Article 7 of the LCIT BD B&H.[322] The calculation of the tax basis, *inter alia*, does not include revenue in the form of interest from the securities that are issued or guaranteed by B&H, BD B&H, the Entities, the Central Bank, enterprises, insurance companies, investment funds and banks or other financial institutions.[323] When calculating the tax basis from revenue, the deductable expenditures are those directly attributable to the generated revenue.[324] Expenditures that are recognized and deductible from revenue, among others, are the insurance premiums paid by the employer for personal gain unless those premiums are included in employee salaries.[325]

199. Pursuant to the LCIT BD B&H, insurance legal persons, including banks and authorized credit institutions, are not allowed to have a deduction on the basis of written-off suspicious claims that arise in connection with the sale of goods or services, but only if the revenue from the sale was previously included in the tax basis of the legal person.[326] As for insurance and reinsurance companies, the deduction is allowed to increase reserves as registered in accounting documents in accordance with the law.[327] For insurance contracts, relating to reinsurance, reserves are reduced to cover only part of the risk borne by the insurance company and may not exceed 20% of the tax basis.

200. The income tax in the BD B&H is also paid at the rate of 10% on the tax basis for that tax year.

201. The general rule is that the tax year for legal persons is the calendar year – in the case when a legal person becomes a taxpayer during the tax year or ceases to be the taxpayer during the tax year, the tax year is the period in the calendar year when the legal entity was the taxpayer.[328] The tax declaration for a tax year must be submitted no later than ninety days upon the end of the tax year, and in case of a calendar year, no later than 31 March of the current year for the previous year.[329]

§2. Other Taxes

202. In addition to income tax, insurance and reinsurance companies can be taxpayers when it concerns real estate taxes and property taxes. Real estate tax is regulated in B&H at three levels: in the FB&H at the cantonal level, the level of the RS and the BD B&H. More specifically, in B&H there are currently twelve effective

322. *See ibid.*, Art. 6.
323. *See ibid.*, Art. 7.
324. *See ibid.*, Art. 8(1).
325. *See ibid.*, Art. 8(2).
326. *See ibid.*, Art. 10(2).
327. *See ibid.*, Art. 10(5).
328. *See ibid.*, Art. 21(1) and (2).
329. *See ibid.*, Art. 22(1).

laws on real estate tax: in FB&H, there are ten effective laws on real estate that have been adopted at the cantonal level, and one law in the RS and in the BD B&H. Also, special taxes on the property have been established by the relevant laws at the cantonal level in the FB&H.

Part II. The Insurance Contract: General

Chapter 1. Generalities

203. The insurance contract is primarily regulated by the Entities' laws on obligations (hereinafter referred to as the LO FB&H/LO RS) that have been transferred into the legal system of B&H[330] and partially adapted to the new circumstances.[331] The provisions relating to the insurance sector are contained in Chapter XXVII, more precisely in Articles 897–965. Although the LO FB&H/LO RS regulates in detail the insurance contract, they do not cover the whole sphere of insurance. The provisions of the aforementioned law do not apply to marine insurance, insurance of claims and reinsurance relations.[332]

204. The provisions relating to the contractual relationship in insurance are also contained in the Entities' legislation in the insurance sector: the Law on Insurance,[333] the Law on Compulsory Traffic Insurance,[334] the Law on Mediation in Private Insurance,[335] the Law on insurance Companies,[336] the Law on Compulsory Insurances in Traffic[337] and the Law on Representation and Mediation in Insurance and Reinsurance (LRMIR).[338]

205. The specific characteristic of the regulation of the insurance contract consists in the fact that although the LO FB&H/LO RS are regulations of dispositive nature, regulation of insurance has a largely imperative character. The insurance contract may depart only from those provisions of the LO FB&H/LO RS that explicitly allow such departure, and from provisions that leave to the contracting parties the option to proceed as they wish.[339] This approach has been influenced by multiple reasons: the need to preserve the equality of the parties in a contractual relationship in which one party (the insurer) is generally economically stronger and

330. Both Entities have taken over the Law on Obligations of the former Yugoslavia (OJ SFRJ, 29/78, 39/85, 45/89).
331. The Ordinance on Accepting of the Law on Obligations (OJ R B&H, 2/1992, 13/1994) and the Law on Obligations (OJ RS, 17/1993 and 3/1996).
332. *See* the LO FB&H/LO RS, Art. 899.
333. OJ FB&H, 23/2017, 103/2021.
334. *Ibid.*, 57/2020, 103/2021.
335. *Ibid.*, 22/2005, 8/2010, 30/2016.
336. OJ RS, 17/2005, 01/2006, 74/2010, 47/2017, 58/2019.
337. *Ibid.*, 82/2015, 78/2020.
338. *Ibid.*, 47/2017.
339. *See* the LO FB&H/LO RS, Art. 900(1).

therefore able through adhesion contracts whose content is predetermined by the general conditions, to impose on the other contracting party conditions that are not appropriate for them; insurance companies independently adopt insurance conditions, that are not subjected to external control, with their harmonization on a voluntary basis, which can result in different provisions; ensuring the application of principles underlying the insurance industry (that the risk that has already occurred cannot be covered by insurance, if that was known to the interested party; that the intentional causing of the insured event by the insured, policyholder or insurance beneficiary does not oblige the insurer to make any payments; the release of the insurer from obligation of payment of the insured sum to the insurance beneficiary when he/she intentionally caused the insured's death, etc.). Moreover, the LO FB&H/LO RS allows the departure from the other provisions with the fulfilment of two conditions: that it is not expressly prohibited by the LO FB&H/LO RS or another law, and if that departure is undoubtedly in the interest of the insured.[340]

206. The LO FB&H/LO RS defines the insurance contract as a contract where the policyholder is obliged to pool a certain amount in a community of insurance or community of risks (insurer), on the principles of mutuality and solidarity, and the community of risks is obliged, if an event takes place which represents the insured event, to pay to the insured, or to a third party, compensation or the agreed sum, or to do something else.[341] The LO RS also contains the above definition with modification and reads as follows: the insurance contract obliges the policyholder to pay a specific amount to the insurance organization (insurer), and the organization is obliged, if an event takes place which represents the insured event, to pay compensation, or the agreed sum to the insured, or to a third party, or to do something else.[342]

207. The general characteristics of the insurance contract are the following: it is a *nominate contract* – under the designation of the insurance contract, the LO FB&H/LO RS regulated the rights and obligations of contracting parties (thus for contract formation is sufficient consent of the contracting parties on its essential elements, and everything else what is not contracted, but is already prescribed by law, is considered to be arranged); the insurance contract is a *mutual (synallagmatic) contract* – at the moment of conclusion of the insurance contract obligations to perform actions prescribed by the LO FB&H/LO RS and the contract itself arise for each contracting party, and therefore each of them appears in a position of debtor and a creditor. The primary obligation of the policyholder is payment of contracted insurance premiums and of the insurer to pay the insured sum or annuity if the contracted insured event occurs; the insurance contract is an *aleatory contract* – at the moment of contract conclusion all the facts are not known, e.g., the amount and a mutual relationship of giving of the contracting parties (value ratio of the action and counteraction), because whether and in what amount one contracting party will gain or lose something, depends on the occurrence of an uncertain event; the insurance

340. *See ibid.*, Art. 900(2).
341. *See ibid.*, Art. 897.
342. *See* the LO RS, Art. 897.

contract is a *formal contract* – the insurance policy is a compulsory form of contract conclusion; the insurance contract is an *onerous contract* given that the policyholder is always burdened with the obligation of premium payment (there is no gratuitous insurance); the insurance contract is an adhesory contract (formulary contract or contract of adhesion) rights and obligations of the parties are determined by general and special conditions of life insurance issued by the insurer; the insurance contract is a contract of good faith and mutual trust *(uberrimae fidei)* – the principle of good faith or the principle of consciousness and honesty is one of the fundamental principles that the parties must follow when establishing the obligatory relationship and realization of the rights and obligations deriving from those relationships, which is also applicable to insurance contracts. The LO FB&H/LO RS regulates in detail the issue of the violation of the principle of good faith through the regulation of the violation of the obligation of the policyholder to report the circumstances relevant to the assessment of the risk and circumstances which relate to the change in risk.[343]

208. The insurance contract is regulated by general provisions applicable to all types of insurance (section 1) and special provisions relating to property insurance (section 2) and insurance of persons (section 3).

209. On the basis of the contract on property insurance, the insurer undertakes the obligation to compensate for the damage caused to the insured property due to the occurrence of the insured event. Compensation of the damage in whole or in part constitutes the purpose of property insurance, having in mind that the amount of compensation may never be greater than the damage suffered by the insured by the occurrence of the insured event,[344] since the purpose of insurance is not in making a profit but in returning to the state in which it was before the occurrence of the insured event (*restitutio in integrum*). General provisions contained in the segment dedicated to property insurance stipulate that property insurance may be concluded by any person who has an interest that the insured case does not happen because he/she would suffer some material loss.[345]

210. The insurance of persons, including life insurance and accident insurance, constitutes a contractual relationship in which the insurer is obliged to pay the insured sum upon the occurrence of the insured event, in the amount determined in the insurance policy by agreement of contracting parties,[346] and not dependant on the damage occurred. Thus, the principle of indemnity is not applicable to the insurance of persons.

211. Provisions in the LO FB&H/LO RS define the key characteristics of the insured event. Namely, according to Article 898 of the LO FB&H/LO RS, an

343. Articles 908, 909 and 914 of the LO FB&H/LO RS, although the consequences of the violation of the principle *uberrimae fidei* may be different, the most common consequence is the termination of the effects of the contract (by annulment or termination).
344. *See* the LO FB&H/LO RS, Art. 925(2).
345. *See ibid.*, Art. 924.
346. *See ibid.*, Art. 942.

insured event is an event serving as the basis for concluding insurance, which must be a future, uncertain event and independent of the exclusive will of contracting parties. The literature accepted a definition that the insured event is the event whose occurrence realizes a risk for which a contract of insurance is concluded.[347] The LO FB&H/LO RS regulates that the contract of insurance is considered null and void if, at the moment of its conclusion, the insurance event had already occurred, or was at the point of occurring or if it was certain that it was going to occur, or if, at that time the possibility of it occurring had ceased.[348] Therefore, a contract of insurance shall be null and void if, at the moment of its conclusion its two key elements are missing: the insured event and risk. The exception to the above rules is the provision contained in Article 898(3) of the LO FB&H/LO RS pursuant to which, if it was agreed that the insurance shall cover a certain period of time preceding the conclusion of the contract, the contract shall be null and void only if, at the moment of its conclusion, the interested party was aware that the insured event had already occurred, or that the possibility of its occurrence had ceased to exist. It stems from the above provision that the insurance contract does not necessarily have to be null and void in the case when it covers the period preceding its conclusion in which the insured event has already taken place, i.e., when the possibility of its occurrence ceased, but only if it was not known to the interested contracting party.

347. *See*: Bukljaš, Ivan & Vizner, Boris. *Komentar Zakona o obveznim (obligacionim) odnosima* (*Commentary to the Law on Obligatiry Relations*). Zagreb: Vlastita naklada, 2577 (1979).
348. *See* the LO FB&H/LO RS, Art. 898(2).

Chapter 2. Insurable Risk

212. When it comes to the risk in the insurance, 'at issue' is a term that is closely associated with the concept of an insured event. In fact, given that the insured event represents the realization of the insured risk, the risk itself represents danger of an adverse event or the possibility of the occurrence of the insured event. Although the LO FB&H/LO RS does not define an insurance risk, the content of the provision of Article 898(1) of the LO FB&H/LO RS may determine the basic elements of risk: that it is a future, uncertain event that is independent of the exclusive will of the policyholders.[349] However, the LO FB&H/LO RS envisages the possibility of insurance also in the case when the insured event has occurred, i.e., when the risk has already been realized. This is the so-called putative risk. Namely, the LO FB&H/LO RS provides that in the case where at the time of the conclusion of insurance contract, the insured event has already occurred, was occurring, or was likely to occur, or if the possibility for its occurrence had already ceased, such an insurance contract shall be null and void.[350] The exception of the above-mentioned rule is contained in Article 898(3) of the LO FB&H/LO RS according to which the insurance contract may cover a certain period preceding the conclusion of contract in which the insured event has already occurred, or in which the possibility of the occurrence of the insured event has stopped. Such a contract of insurance becomes null and void only if the interested party was aware of it.

213. In order for risk to be eligible for insurance, certain preconditions must be met:[351] the possibility of its realization; uncertainty of the occurrence of the event; it has to be recurrent; it must be independent of the will of the insured and other interested parties; and it must be allowed by law, public order and morality.

214. Apart from the fact that the LO FB&H/LO RS establishes certain restrictions of risk in terms of its characteristics, which it must have, they also provide the exclusions of certain insurable risks. In property insurance, the risk is limited to the degree of guilt assumed by the policyholder or the insured for damage caused (this does not apply to persons for whose actions he/she is liable), and in terms of damage caused by defects of the insured item, or with respect to damages caused by military operations, riots or unrest. In insurance of persons, the following risks are excluded from insurance: the conscious suicide of the insured; the intentional murder of the insured; and the intentional causing of an accident, death or the occurrence of an accident due to military operations.

215. Regarding the limitation with respect to the degree of guilt, the LO FB&H/LO RS has two different approaches: general and specific with respect to certain cases. The general approach is contained in the provision of Article 920 which is

349. *See ibid.*, Art. 898.
350. *See ibid.*, Art. 898(2).
351. Šulejić, Predrag. '*Pravo osiguranja*' (*Insurance Law*). Belgrade: Pravni fakultet u Beogradu, (2005), 95.

applicable to property insurance and insurance of persons and without the possibility of different contracting, which stipulates that the insurer has no obligation whatsoever if the policyholder, insured or the beneficiary caused the event covered by insurance intentionally or by fraud. The same position is assumed in property insurance where the insurer shall not be liable for damage caused intentionally by the policyholder, the insured or the insurance beneficiary, and the provision in the insurance policy which would specify such liability of the insurer is void.[352] Similar arrangements are contained in the insurance of persons under which the insurer is released from obligation to pay to the insurance beneficiary the insured sum if he/she deliberately caused the death of the insured,[353] as well as in the case where the insured deliberately caused the accident.[354]

216. The LO FB&H/LO RS excludes the so-called war and political risks by dispositive norms. In property insurance, in accordance with Article 931(1), an insurer is not obliged to indemnify any damages caused by war operations or rebellions, unless otherwise agreed by the contractual parties and the burden of proof that the damage was caused by some of these events is on the side of insurer.[355] Also, with regard to the insurance of persons when war operations are at issue, it is prescribed that if the death of the insured was caused by war operations, the insurer is not obliged to pay to the beneficiary the insured sum (but is obliged to pay him/her the mathematical reserve from the contract).[356] Furthermore, in accident insurance, the insurer is released from obligation from the insurance contract, if the accident was caused by war operations.[357] In addition to these exclusions, the LO FB&H/LO RS contains exclusion in property insurance, according to which when it concerns damage to insured items originating from their defects, the insurer is not obliged to indemnify such damage[358] and the exclusion of the risk of the insured's suicide in the case of life insurance.[359] In all mentioned cases of exclusions, except in the case of suicide of the insured, there is a possibility of different contracting.

217. In addition to the statutory exclusions or limitations, there exist contractual restrictions as a reflection of the autonomy of the will of the contracting parties. Namely, the LO FB&H/LO RS directly refers to this possibility in insurance of persons in a specific article,[360] according to which the insurance contract in the case of death or accident, may also exclude other risks from insurance. In property insurance, this possibility is indirectly included in Article 929(1) of the LO FB&H/LO RS, according to which, the insurer is bound to indemnify damages incurred

352. *See* the LO FB&H/LO RS, Art. 929(2).
353. *See ibid.*, Art. 950.
354. *See ibid.*, Art. 951.
355. *See ibid.*, Art. 931(2).
356. *See ibid.*, Art. 951(1).
357. *Ibid.*
358. *See* the LO FB&H/LO RS, Art. 930.
359. *See ibid.*, Art. 949.
360. *See ibid.*, Art. 953.

accidentally, or by fault of the policyholder, insured or the insurance beneficiary, unless regarding the specific damage, such obligation of the insurer is explicitly excluded from the insurance contract.

218. When it comes to the insurance practice, general insurance conditions of B&H's insurers provide the exclusion of a whole number of risks. In general conditions of property insurance, it is stipulated that the insurer is not obliged to indemnify damages caused by war operations or riots, civil war, revolution, rebellion, unrest resulting from such events, mines, torpedoes, bombs or other war weapons, imprisonment, seizures, constraints or detention and the consequences of these events or attempts to commit them by sabotage or terrorism performed for political reasons, detonations of explosives, if a person acts maliciously or because of a political motive, civil unrest, violence or other similar events, confiscation, requisition or other similar measures implemented or if they intend to implement some government or other similar organization that struggles for power or has power. Also, the indemnification of damages that occurred as a result of the intention of the policyholder, insured or beneficiary of insurance is excluded.

219. General conditions for the insurance of persons provide the exclusion in addition to the cases already foreseen by the LO FB&H/LO RS (suicide of the insured until the expiry of the first year of insurance, intentionally causing the death of the insured by the beneficiary, the death of the insured caused by war and similar events) and in the following cases: if the insured event occurred due to the attempt of suicide of the insured for any reason, if the insured event occurred during the preparation, attempt or execution of the commission of a criminal offence by the insured, if the death penalty was executed over the insured, if the death of the insured was caused by sabotage or terrorism committed for political reasons, violence or other similar event in which the insured participated. As for the general insurance conditions of accident insurance, they limit the risk if an accident occurs: during the performance of particularly hazardous jobs (e.g., mining, stunts), the races of motor vehicles, in sports participation in individual or organized training and public sports competitions, to persons who have recovered after some serious illness or are sick or have congenital or acquired physical handicap or defects causing reduction of their general work ability, and the risk is completely excluded in cases where the accident occurred due to: earthquakes, due to military operations or rebellion, management of aircraft, vessels and other motor vehicles without the required valid license, due to disorders of consciousness, seizure, heart attack or due to a diseased state of the insured, for participating in a physical confrontation, etc.

Chapter 3. Formation of the Insurance Contract

220. A contract of insurance constitutes the bases for the establishment of the rights and obligations between the contracting parties in relation to the insurance relationship. The contracting parties are the insurer and the policyholder. The insurer is obliged, if an event occurs that represents the insured event, to pay to the insured the insurance indemnity or the agreed sum for a certain amount.[361] Thus, the insurer is a contracting party in the concluded insurance contract, which for a certain price (the contracted premium) has assumed the obligation of protection against the risk of the insurance policyholder or the insured, i.e., the obligation to compensate damage or the insured amount, if the insured event occurs. In the context of the Entities' laws on insurance companies, the insurer is a specialized business company in the organizational-legal form of a joint-stock insurance company or mutual insurance company (as well as any other form of insurance company that is not from B&H), which is established and operating in accordance with the laws on insurance companies.[362]

221. The policyholder is a natural or legal person who meets the general requirements in terms of capacity to exercise rights, who concludes an insurance contract with the insurer and is obliged to pay the premium.[363] The policyholder does not necessarily conclude a contract of insurance on his/her own behalf, but may also do so on behalf of third parties. However, most often, the policyholder becomes the insured when concluding the contract in his/her own name and on his/her own behalf. The notion of the insured implies a person, who regardless of whether he/she is acting as the policyholder or as a beneficiary, is entitled to the rights from the insurance contract. In property insurance, the contract may be concluded by a person with the interest that an insured event does not occur, or he/she would otherwise suffer some material loss.[364] The rights from insurance may pertain only to the persons with a material interest that the insured event does not occur.[365]

222. The general rules of law on obligations on the formation of the contract also apply in the case of an insurance contract.[366] In order to conclude the insurance contract, there must be consented declarations of the will of the contracting parties. The contracting parties must agree on the essential elements of the contract. The LO FB&H/LO RS contains several provisions dedicated to the conclusion of insurance contracts.[367] The deviation from the above provisions is conditioned on the absence of an explicit prohibition (by the LO FB&H/LO RS or some other law) and if it is in the undoubted interest of the insured.[368]

361. *See ibid.*, Art. 897.
362. *See* the LI FB&H, Art. 2 and the LIC RS, Art. 2.
363. *See* the LO FB&H/LO RS, Art. 897.
364. *See ibid.*, Art. 924(1).
365. *See ibid.*, Art. 924(2).
366. *See ibid.*, Arts 26–45.
367. *See ibid.*, Arts 901–906.
368. *See ibid.*, Art. 900(2).

223. A contract is concluded at the moment when the offeror received the statement of the offeree that he/she is accepting the offer.[369] An offer in B&H's contract law is a proposal for conclusion of contract made to a specific person and containing all essential constitutive elements of the contract so that its acceptance would amount to the contract conclusion.[370] The most important elements of the insurance contract are the insured risk, the insured event, the subject of insurance, the premium and the insured sum. In addition to these elements, the contracting parties may agree on other elements that become, by the will of the contracting parties, the essential elements of the contract and must also be included in the offer. In insurance practice, the policyholder or the insured usually assumes the role of the offeror, who makes it (the offer) by completing the form – a form prepared in advance by the insurer, containing the most common questions about the risk and subject of insurance. The insurer may also have the role of the offeror, directly or through an agent. Sending price lists, lists of tariffs and premiums, and showing or handing over general business conditions is regarded only as an invitation to make an offer.[371] The insurer has the role of offeror in the following cases: when responding to a received offer, the insurer sends a modified or postponed response (acceptance of the offer) and when the insurer makes a general offer for contract conclusion to unspecified number of persons that contain essential elements of the insurance contract.[372] According to a general rule of the law on obligations, an offer of a contract for which conclusion Law demands special form, is binding on the offeror only if it is being made in such a form. The same rule applies with regard to the acceptance of the offer.[373]

224. As already specified, in insurance practice the offer is submitted on the form prepared in advance by the insurer. In B&H's law, an offer produces specific legal effects even before its acceptance. Specifically, an offeror is bound by his/her offer unless his/her obligation to honour the offer is excluded, or unless such exclusion stems from the circumstances of the business transaction involved.[374] With regard to the insurance contract, a written offer made to an insurer to enter into a contract of insurance is binding to the offeror, unless he has determined a shorter time limit, for eight days from the day the offer has reached the insurer, and if a medical examination is necessary, then in the course of thirty days.[375] In insurance general rules of contract law apply to the revocation of the offer, according to which, an offer may be revoked only if the offeree receives the revocation prior to receiving the offer, or simultaneously.[376] An offer is accepted when the offeror receives a

369. *See ibid.*, Art. 31(1).
370. *See ibid.*, Art. 32(1).
371. *See* Marjanski, Vladimir. *Ugovor o osiguranju* (*Insurance Contract*), Centar za izdavačku djelatnost Pravnog fakulteta u Novom Sadu, Novi Sad, (2007), 134.
372. *See* Šulejić, Predrag. '*Pravo osiguranja*' (*Insurance Law*). Belgrade: Pravni fakultet u Beogradu, (2005), 182.
373. *See* the LO FB&H/LO, RS, Art. 38.
374. *See ibid.*, RS, Art. 36(1).
375. *See ibid.*, RS, Art. 901(2).
376. *See ibid.*, RS, Art. 36(2).

statement from the offeree that he/she accepts the offer.[377] The silence of the offeree does not signify the acceptance of an offer.[378] The exception to this rule relating to insurance is contained in Article 901 of the LO FB&H/LO RS stipulating that should the insurer fail, within that time limit, to decline the offer in due time, which does not differ from the terms and conditions of his usual performance of the proposed insurance, it is then considered that the insurer has accepted the offer and that the contract has been concluded.[379] In such case, the contract is considered concluded at the moment when the offer has reached the insurer.[380]

225. The explicit provision of the LO FB&H/LO RS on the time of the insurance contract conclusion is contained in Article 901(1) of the LO FB&H/LO RS which stipulates that a contract of insurance is concluded after the contracting parties have signed the insurance policy or the list of coverage. There are two exceptions to this rule. The first exemption is when the insurer fails to decline the offer of the policyholder (offeror), which does not deviate from the conditions under which the insurer performs the proposed insurance within eight or thirty days from when it was received by the insurer.[381] The interpretation that the offer for the conclusion of the contract of insurance made to the authorized agent of the insurer is considered to have been made to the insurer was adopted in case law. Another exception is foreseen under Article 903 of the LO FB&H/LO RS stipulating that the contractual relationship of insurance can also arise by premium payment if this possibility is provided by insurance conditions.

226. In B&H's insurance law, the specificity of the insurance contract is reflected in the fact that the moment of its formal conclusion and the moment of commencement differ.[382] The commencement of the insurance coverage effect is conditioned by the payment of the premium. The time of the commencement of the insurance coverage is determined in general insurance conditions.

227. Generally speaking, an insurance contract is a contract in which there has been a deviation from the principles of informality and its validity is conditioned by a certain form. Pursuant to the LO FB&H/LO RS, a contract of insurance is concluded after the contracting parties have signed the insurance policy or the list of coverage.[383] There are some deviations from this rule, for instance when the offer made to the insurer is not in accordance with the terms under which the insurer performs the proposed insurance, and the insurer has not declined it within eight or thirty days period. In this case, it is deemed that insurer has accepted the offer. The insurance conditions may also provide that the insurance contract is created by the

377. *See ibid.*, RS, Art. 39(1).
378. *See ibid.*, RS, Art. 42.
379. *See ibid.*, RS, Art. 901(3).
380. *See ibid.*, RS, Art. 901(4).
381. *See ibid.*, RS, Art. 901(3) and (4).
382. *See ibid.*, RS, Art. 922.
383. *See ibid.*, RS, Art. 901(1).

premium payment itself.[384] Despite the aforementioned exceptions, the insurance contract in B&H's insurance practice is generally concluded in writing.

228. However, although the insurance policy is generally seen as a key document of the concluded insurance contract that contains all the relevant elements of the insurance contract pursuant to the provisions of the LO FB&H/LO RS, it is also the form of the concluded insurance contract, in which case, it is subject to the application of general rules of obligation law on formal contracts.[385] The following must be specified in the insurance policy: the contracting parties, the insured object, or insured person, risk covered by insurance, duration of insurance and period of cover, the insured sum or an indication that the insurance is unlimited, the insurance premium or contribution, the date of issuing the policy, and signatures of contracting parties.[386] In addition to elements which are fundamental for every insurance policy, a life insurance policy must include indication of the first name and last name of the person whose life is insured, his/her date of birth and the event or deadline which determines emergence of the right to request payment of the insured sum.[387] General and special conditions of insurance can be printed on the insurance policy.[388] In the case of a discrepancy between the provision of general or special conditions, and an insurance policy provision, the provision of the policy applies, while in the case of a discrepancy between a printed provision of insurance policy and a provision which is handwritten, the latter shall apply.[389] The insurance policy is a security, which, in accordance with the agreement of the contracting parties can be made out either to a specific person or by order, or to the bearer.[390] The life insurance policy may be made out either to a specific person or by order, but not to the bearer. The insurance policy may be temporarily substituted by a list of coverage, which includes the essential elements of a contract.[391] A list of coverage has the character of an insurance document that has the same elements as the policy but is of a temporary character.

229. The insurance contract may be: a contract in its own name and its own account, when there is no difference between the policyholder and the insured; a contract on its own behalf and for the account of a third party and a contract for the benefit of a third party in life insurance. The insurance contract may also be concluded through an agent acting on behalf of the insurer or the policyholder, who concludes the contract in the name and for the account of someone else, i.e., the insurer or the policyholder. Agents in the above case are not the contracting parties. The contracting parties are the persons in whose name and for whose account the insurance has been contracted. The LO FB&H/LO RS directly regulates the situation when an agent acts on behalf of the insurer with regard to the scope of their

384. *See ibid.*, RS, Art. 903.
385. *See ibid.*, RS, Arts 68–72.
386. *See ibid.*, RS, Art. 902(1).
387. *See* the LO FB&H/LO RS, Art. 943(1).
388. *See ibid.*, Art. 902(3).
389. *See ibid.*, Art. 902(5).
390. *See ibid.*, Art. 902(6).
391. *See ibid.*, Art. 902(2).

authority. Namely, if an insurer authorizes someone to represent him/her, failing to specify the scope of their authority, the agent is in that case entitled to conclude the contract of insurance on behalf of the insurer, and also to negotiate and conclude alterations of contracts or extend their validity, to issue the insurance policy, to collect premium payments, and to accept statements addressed to the insurer.[392] Should the insurer limit his agent's authority and this fact is unknown to the policyholder, such limitations are considered as if they had not existed.[393]

230. In case of insurance on another person's account or for the account of whom it may concern, the obligations of payment of insurance premium and other contractual obligations must be fulfilled by the policyholder, but he/she is not entitled to exercise the rights on the grounds of insurance, even after being in possession of the policy, without the consent of the person whose interest is insured and who is the holder of these rights.[394] When this kind of insurance contract conclusion is at issue, the policyholder is not obliged to hand over the policy to the interested party, unless the insurance premiums paid to the insurer are reimbursed to him/her, together with the expenses of the contract.[395] The policyholder has the right of priority in collecting these claims out of the owed indemnity, and the right to demand their payment directly from the insurer.[396] An insurer may raise all objections towards the beneficiary of insurance for another person's account which pertain to him on the grounds of the contract against the policyholder.[397]

231. In life insurance, there may be a difference between a person concluding the contract (the policyholder) and the person whose life is insured and the same applies to accident insurance.[398] In that case, the validity of the contract depends on the written consent of that person, which is specified on the insurance policy or in a separate letter at the time of signing the insurance policy, with an indication of the insured amount.[399] The same approach is applied in the conclusion of insurance in case of death of a person older than 14 years for whose validity is necessary to have written consent by his/her legal representative, and the written consent of the insured.[400]

392. *See ibid.*, Art. 906(1).
393. *See ibid.*, Art. 906(2).
394. *See ibid.*, Art. 905(1).
395. *See ibid.*, Art. 905(2).
396. *See ibid.*, Art. 905(3).
397. *See ibid.*, Art. 905(4).
398. *See ibid.*, Art. 946(1) and (2).
399. *See ibid.*, Art. 946(3).
400. *See ibid.*, Art. 947(2).

Chapter 4. Obligations of the Insured

232. The literature classifies the obligations of the policyholder or the insured according to the time when they should be fulfilled:[401] at the moment of contract conclusion (reporting of the circumstances of importance for the assessment of risk, the first payment of insurance premium); during the insurance period (payment of insurance premiums, informing the insurer on any changes in risk, prevention of the occurrence of the insured event); when the insured event occurs (notification of the insurer in connection with the occurred insured event, elimination and reduction of damages).

§1. Description of Risk

233. A policyholder is obliged to report to the insurer, at the moment of conclusion of the contract, all circumstances which are material in assessing the risk, and which are known, or could not have been unknown, to him/her.[402] Therefore, two key characteristics of the facts derive from the legal provision with respect to which the obligation to report has been set: that these circumstances are relevant for forming an opinion of the insurer about the risk and that they are known to the policyholder or that they could not have remained unknown.[403] Given the time when this obligation must be fulfilled, it does not strictly constitute a contractual obligation. Reporting of all circumstances of risk is significant in order for the insurer to be capable of assessing the extent of risk coverage, or to decline coverage in accordance with the principle of autonomy of the will of the contracting parties.

234. When implementing the obligation of reporting circumstances relevant to risk assessment, the policyholder is guided by a form prepared in advance by the insurer for certain types of insurance. Furthermore, the policyholder is liable for the accuracy of this data regardless of whether he/she himself filled the application (or offer) for the conclusion of the contract, or he/she just signed it. The obligation to report the circumstances of importance for the assessment of the risk is based on the general principles of law on obligations – the principle of conscientiousness and honesty. That principle is particularly evident in the insurance contract so the contract itself is called contract *uberrimae fidei* (utmost good faith).

235. The legal consequences of failure to comply with these obligations are different and depend on the conscientiousness of the policyholder or other subjects. Namely, in insurance on another's behalf, the knowledge and attitude of the beneficiary are of equal legal significance as the knowledge of the policyholder (in the case of insurance concluded in the name and on behalf of another, or for the benefit

401. *See* Marjanski, Vladimir. *Ugovor o osiguranju* (*Insurance Contract*), Centar za izdavačku djelatnost Pravnog fakulteta u Novom Sadu, Novi Sad, (2007), 203-223; Curak, Marijana & Jakovčević, Drago. *Osiguranje i rizici* (*Insurance and Risks*), Zagreb: RRIF Plus, 2007, 176–180; etc.
402. *See* the LO FB&H/LO RS, Art. 907.
403. *See ibid.*, Art. 907.

of a third party, or on behalf of others or on behalf of whom it may concern, if these persons knew of the inaccuracy of the report or the failure to disclose the circumstances of importance for the assessment of risk).[404] If the policyholder acts unconscientiously or if he/she deliberately makes a false report or deliberately withholds a circumstance of such nature that the insurer would not have concluded the contract had he known the true state of affairs, the insurer may request annulment of the contract.[405] The legal consequence, namely the sanction prescribed by the LO FB&H/LO RS in this situation is that the insurer retains the collected premiums and has the right to demand payment of the premium for the insurance period in which it requested the annulment of the contract.[406] The insurer's right to request annulment of the contract of insurance is terminated if, within a three-month period from the day of his becoming aware of the incorrectness of the report or of the suppressing of the facts, he fails to notify the policyholder about his intention to exercise that right.[407]

236. However, if the policyholder acts conscientiously, or he/she unintentionally makes a false report or fails to give due notice, the insurer has two options at his disposal. The first option is to declare contract termination within one month from the day of learning about the inaccuracy or incompleteness of the report. The insurance contract in this case ceases to exist after the expiration of fourteen days from the time when the insurer notified the policyholder about the termination of contract.[408] In case of termination, the insurer is obliged to return the part of insurance premium relating to the period until the end of the insurance period.[409] The other possibility of the insurer is to propose an increase in the insurance premium, proportional to the increased risk.[410] If the policyholder rejects the proposal that the premium is set to increase within a period of fourteen days from when it is received, the termination occurs by force of law.[411] Should the insured event occur prior to finding the incorrectness or incompleteness of the report, or after that but prior to the termination, or prior to reaching an agreement on the premium increase, the compensation is reduced proportionally between the rate of the paid insurance premiums and the rate of insurance premiums which would have to be paid according to the real risk.[412] An insurer who, at the moment of contract conclusion was aware, or could not have been unaware of circumstances relevant to assessing the risk, may not invoke incorrectness of the report or fact suppression.[413] Thus, the policyholder has no obligation to report the so-called notorious facts known to the insurer. The

404. *See ibid.*, Art. 910.
405. *See ibid.*, Art. 908(2).
406. *See ibid.*, Art. 908(2).
407. *See ibid.*, Art. 908(3).
408. *See ibid.*, Art. 909(2).
409. *See ibid.*, Art. 909(3).
410. *See ibid.*, Art. 909(1).
411. *See ibid.*, Art. 909(2).
412. *See ibid.*, Art. 909(4).
413. *See ibid.*, Art. 911(1).

same rule also applies if the insurer had learned of these circumstances during the insurance period, and failed to use legal powers.[414]

237. In life insurance, the LO FB&H/LO RS provides special rules for exceptions to the above-presented general rules concerning consequences of incorrect reporting and suppressing the circumstances relevant to the assessment of risk, which apply to the incorrect reporting of the insured's age:[415]

- a life insurance contract becomes null and void if the real age of the insured exceeds the limit up to which the insurer performs life insurance if the age was incorrectly stated at the moment of its conclusion. In this case, the insurer is obliged to return all received premiums;
- should it be incorrectly reported that the insured is of lower age, but his/her real age does not exceed the limit up to which the insurer performs the insurance, the contract is legally valid, but the insured sum is reduced in proportion to the stipulated insurance premium and the insurance premium provided for the life insurance for a person of the age of the insured;
- should the insured person be of a lower age than reported during the contract conclusion, the insurance premium is reduced to the corresponding amount, and the insurer is obliged to return the difference between the insurance premiums received and the premiums to which he/she is entitled.

So, for life insurance, there is no differentiation between conscientious and negligent actions of the insured, and the consequence of contract annulment signifies complete restitution for both contracting parties.

238. A specific kind of continuation of the obligation of reporting the circumstances relevant to the risk assessment when concluding the insurance contract[416] is the obligation to notify the insurer of any changes in the risk undertaken during the contract period. There is a correlation between the premium determined at the conclusion of the insurance contract and the risk. If in relation to the moment of conclusion of the contract, there is a change of risk (its reduction or increase), the previously determined premium is no longer adequate. The LO FB&H/LO RS contains specific rules relating to the change in risk depending on the type of insurance (property insurance or insurance of persons). Thus, a policyholder is obliged, in the case of property insurance, to notify the insurer of every change in circumstances which may be relevant for assessing the risk, and in case of insurance of persons, this obligation exists only if the risk has been increased because the insured person has changed profession.[417] A policyholder is obliged to notify the insurer without delay of the increase in risk if the risk is increased due to some act on his/her part, and if the increase in risk took place without his/her participation, he/she is obliged to notify the insurer accordingly within fourteen days after becoming aware of the

414. *See ibid.*, Art. 911(2).
415. *See ibid.*, Art. 944.
416. *See ibid.*, Art. 907.
417. *See ibid.*, Art. 914(1).

fact.[418] If the policyholder or the insured fulfils his/her obligation in terms of informing the insurer of the changes in the above-mentioned circumstances, the legal consequences then depend on the kind of increased risk in question. Should the increase in risk be of such scope that the insurer would not have concluded the contract if such situation had existed at the time of its conclusion, the insurer is then entitled to terminate the contract.[419] The termination of contract takes effect only *pro futuro*. But if the increase in risk is of such scope that the insurer would have concluded the contract but only with an increased premium, if such situation existed at the time of entering into contract, he is entitled to propose a new rate of insurance premium to the policyholder. If the policyholder declines the new rate of premium within a fourteen-day period after being notified about the new proposed rate, the contract is terminated by force of law.[420] But the contract remains in force and the insurer may not use the right to propose a new rate of insurance premium to the policyholder or to terminate the insurance contract, if such rights fail to materialize within a one-month period from the day of his becoming aware, by whatever means, of the increase in risk or if, even prior to the expiration of the one-month period, the insurer shows in some way his/her consent to the continuation of the contract (by accepting payment of the premium, by paying the indemnity for an event covered by insurance, which occurred after the increase of risk, etc.). In case when the insured event occurs before the insurer is informed of the increased risk, or after he was informed about the increased risk, but before he terminated the contract or achieved agreement with the policyholder on the increase of insurance premiums, the indemnity is reduced in proportion to the difference between the premiums paid and the premium that should have been paid in accordance with the increased risk.

239. However, in the case when due to a change in circumstances the risk reduction occurs after contract conclusion, the policyholder is entitled to demand a corresponding reduction of insurance premium, calculated from the day when he/she notified the insurer of such reduction of risk.[421] The reduction takes effect in the future. However, the insurer is not obliged to accept the reduction of insurance premium and may deny his consent. In that case, the policyholder may terminate the contract.[422]

240. Because the insurance contract is often concluded through insurance brokers, regulation governing the mediation in insurance often stipulates the obligation of brokers to notify the insurer of all the risks known to them or that had to be known to them in the context of fulfilment of the obligation to protect the interest of the insurer to the extent and scope of their obligation towards the policyholder.[423] Given the above, the legal consequences of failure to meet these obligations are the same as in the case of the failure of the policyholder to fulfil an obligation to report on the circumstances that are known or should be known to him/her.

418. *See ibid.*, Art. 914(2).
419. *See ibid.*, Art. 914(3).
420. *See ibid.*, Art. 914(5).
421. *See ibid.*, Art. 916(1).
422. *See ibid.*, Art. 916(2).
423. *See* the Law on Representation and Mediation in Insurance and Reinsurance, Art. 21(1).

§2. Payment of Premium

241. The payment of the insurance premium is the basic obligation of the policyholder whose fulfilment occurs when signing the insurance contract as well as during the period of duration of the insurance contract. The premium amount is determined by the average intensity of risk and expressed in tariffs of premium, which are adopted by the insurer for certain types of insurance. The premium is an element of the contract on which the parties reach an agreement when signing the contract. When concluding the insurance contract, there is an obligation to pay the first premium (if the current premium has been agreed) or a single premium. As a rule, the insurance premium is paid at the commencement of the period to which it relates, and the LO FB&H/LO RS stipulates that the premium should be paid by agreed deadlines, and if it is paid as a lump amount, it is paid during contract conclusion.[424] So, B&H's law assumes that the premium is paid when entering into the contract, or shortly after the conclusion of the contract. As a rule, the payment of the first premium is associated with the beginning of obligations of the insurer. Consequently, the payment of the premium may represent an element linked with the beginning of insurance effects, but it is also considered as the real form of the contract, i.e., the element linked with the moment of contract conclusion.

242. In practice, the first premium is paid upon delivery of the insurance policy or another document of insurance. The policyholder is primarily obligated to pay premiums, but the insurer is obliged to receive the payment of the premium from any person who has a legal interest that it is paid.[425] A policyholder on behalf of a third party, and in particular, for the account of another (and for the account of whom it may concern), by the contract he/she undertakes obligation to pay the premiums – he/she is the sole payer of premiums regardless of the fact that he/she may put on the account of the beneficiary payment of the premium. Only towards him/her, the insurer has to meet the requirement of the fulfilment of the obligation of paying a premium. The policyholder may also appear as a representative of the beneficiary of insurance; in this case, he/she acts in the name and on behalf of its principal, which is, legally speaking, the legal premium debtor. Also, the policyholder may conclude a contract in the capacity of agent without a mandate (*negotiorum gestor*) – even in this case, the policyholder is liable for the premium to the insurer as long as the transaction is not approved by the one in whose name it has been concluded. If the authorization is declined, the policyholder owes a premium for the insurance period in which the insurer is informed of the rejection of the order.[426] But an agent without a mandate is not liable for obligations from the insurance contract only if he/she has notified the insurer that he/she is acting without authorization on behalf of and for the account of another.[427] However, each of these persons

424. *See* the LO FB&H/LO RS, Art. 912(2).
425. *See ibid.*, Art. 912(1).
426. *See ibid.*, Art. 904(3).
427. *See ibid.*, Art. 904(4).

may be interested in payment of a premium and may appear as payers despite the fact that they are not burdened with the obligation to pay premiums.[428]

243. The place of the premium payment is the place in which the policyholder has its seat or permanent residence unless something else is agreed upon.

244. Should it be stipulated that the insurance premium is paid at the moment of contract conclusion, the obligation of the insurer to pay compensation or the sum specified by the contract, begins on the day following the day of payment of the insurance premium.[429] Should it be stipulated that the insurance premium is paid after contract conclusion, the obligation of the insurer to pay the compensation or the sum specified by the contract begins from the day determined in the contract as the day of commencement of insurance.[430]

245. Concerning the consequences of non-payment of the premium, the LO FB&H/LO RS provides in the case when the policyholder's premium, which is due after the contract conclusion is not paid until its maturity, or when this is not done by another interested party, the contract of insurance is terminated by force of law after the expiration of thirty days from the day the policyholder receives a registered letter of the insurer, notifying him/her of the maturity of the premium. However, such deadline cannot be terminated prior to the expiration of a thirty-day period from the day of maturity of the insurance premium.[431] In any event, the insurance contract is terminated by force law if the premium is not paid within one year from the date of maturity.[432] These rules do not apply to life insurance[433] where the payment of premium is optional. Should a policyholder of life insurance fail to pay some of the insurance premiums when they are due, the insurer is not entitled to demand payment through court proceedings.[434] The insurer must submit invitation to the policyholder by means of registered mail to pay the due premium within a certain period, which may be no shorter than ten days from the day of letter delivery. If the policyholder fails to pay the due insurance premium within the time limit indicated in the insurer's letter or should such payment not be made by another interested party, the insurer is entitled, if at least three annual insurance premiums have been paid by then, only to state to the policyholder that the insurance sum will be reduced to the level of the surrender value of insurance, or otherwise, state that he is terminating the contract.[435]

428. *See ibid.*, Art. 912(3).
429. *See ibid.*, Art. 913(1).
430. *See ibid.*, Art. 913(2).
431. *See ibid.*, Art. 913(3).
432. *See ibid.*, Art. 913(4).
433. *See ibid.*, Art. 913(5).
434. *See ibid.*, Art. 945(1).
435. *See ibid.*, Art. 945(2).

§3. Obligations in the Case of the Insured Event

246. Except in the case of life insurance, the insured person is obliged to notify the insurer about occurrence of the insurance, within three days at the latest, from the day of his/her learning about it.[436] This commitment in the practice of insurance does not mean just reporting the facts of the occurrence of the insured event, but also a series of circumstances related to the insured event, such as the submission of documents, evidence, etc., in accordance with the conditions of insurance, which are an integral part of the insurance contract. The sanction accepted in B&H's insurance law for failing to report the insured event is the obligation to compensate for damage which the insurer suffered due to that.[437] In practice, insurance conditions govern the detailed requirements related to the reporting of the insured event including the deadline for submission of report, content of report, etc.

247. In property insurance, an insured person is obliged to take prescribed, contracted and all other necessary measures to prevent the occurrence of the insured event, and if such event does take place, he/she shall be obliged to take every possible measure to limit its adverse consequences.[438] The insurer is obliged to compensate expenses, losses, and other losses caused by reasonable attempts to eliminate the direct danger of occurrence of the insured event, including the danger caused by the attempt to limit its damaging consequences, even if such attempts are not successful.[439] The insurer is obliged to pay such compensation even if, together with compensation of damage from the insured event, it exceeds the amount of insurance.[440] Should the insured person fail to fulfil his obligation to prevent the occurrence of the insured event, or the obligation of salvage, while having no justified reason, the obligation of the insurer is reduced by an amount equal to the increase of damage due to such omission.[441]

436. *See ibid.*, Art. 917(1).
437. *See ibid.*, Art. 917(2).
438. *See ibid.*, Art. 926(1).
439. *See ibid.*, Art. 926(2).
440. *See ibid.*, Art. 926(3).
441. *See ibid.*, Art. 926(4).

Chapter 5. Obligations of the Insurer

248. As in the case of the insured, obligations of the insurer are typically divided with respect to the time at which they should be performed:[442] the time prior to the contract conclusion (obligation of pre-contractual information of the insured); the time of the insurance contract conclusion (obligation of receipt of the insurance offer; obligation to inform the insured about the conditions of insurance and obligation to hand over the insurance conditions); during the insurance period (obligation to provide the insured with general and special conditions of the insurance contract as well as other information about the insurer and the contract; obligation of regular and proper performance of insurance business transactions; obligation to perform operations in relation to the insurance policy); when the insured event occurs (obligation of payment of indemnity from insurance or the insured sum; obligation of defrayment; obligation of reimbursement of the costs of rescue).

249. Prior to the conclusion of the insurance contract, an insurance company as the insurer is obliged to submit to the insured a range of data that relates to the insurer such as the name of the company and its organizational form and the name of the Entity in which the headquarters of the insurance company are based, or the branch that concluded the insurance contract. The insurer is also obliged to provide the elements of the insurance contract (pecuniary indemnity and other rights; the duration of insurance; the manner of contract termination; the amount, method and deadline of the premium payment; the calculation and distribution of shares in the profit of the insurance company or the mathematical reserve; the method of calculation of the surrender value or paid amounts and scope of their guarantee; information on the premiums for each compensation, for the main compensation and if necessary for additional compensation; if compensation from the insurance contract is related to investment units, information is required about the nature of the units to which compensation is related; information on the funds related to the investment units; conditions for withdrawal and termination of contract; information on the taxes applicable to this type of insurance contract; methods of processing of the indemnity request; and laws applicable when the parties do not have freedom of choice, or the law proposed by the insurer in cases when the parties have freedom of choice), and in accordance with Article 200(1) of the LI FB&H and Article 24(1) of the LIC RS.

250. A special significance in current insurance legislation is given to the obligation of pre-contractual information of the insured about the conditions for contract termination. Namely, the fulfilment of this obligation is a prerequisite to exercise the right to terminate the insurance contract that is provided by the

442. For example, *see*: Curak, Marijana & Jakovčević, Drago. *Osiguranje i rizici* (*Insurance and Risks*), Zagreb: RRIF Plus, 2007; Jankovec, Ivica & Miladinović, Zoran. *Pravo osiguranja* (*Insurance Law*), Niš: Centar za publikacije Pravnog fakulteta u Nišu, 2006, etc.

Consumer Law of B&H.[443] The aforementioned Law prescribes the right of the consumer to terminate the insurance contract, without stating specific reasons of any kind, if he/she informs the insurer in writing within fifteen days from the contract conclusion.[444]

251. The obligation of receipt of the offer for the conclusion of the insurance contract is not incorporated in the LO FB&H/LO RS due to its incompatibility with the system of party autonomy with regard to the conclusion of the insurance contract. This is evident from the LO FB&H/LO RS provision which stipulates that it is regarded that the insurer has accepted the offer and that the contract is concluded if he/she does not reject the offer within a certain period of time (eight or thirty days depending on whether a medical examination is necessary), which does not deviate from the conditions under which the insurer provided the proposed insurance.[445] However, the compulsory insurance situation is somewhat different because of the statutory obligation of the insured to conclude the insurance contract. Thus, the insured's obligation is the basis for the insurer's obligation to accept the offer in compulsory insurance under the condition that he performs this type of insurance.[446]

252. The general conditions of insurance are contractual in nature, and therefore in order to oblige the insured, they must be known to him/her at the moment of contract conclusion. This is a general rule of the law on obligations which is contained in the LO FB&H/LO RS in Article 142(3) 'general conditions oblige the contracting party if they were known to him/her, or should have been known at the moment of the contract conclusion'. Furthermore, the LO FB&H/LO RS provides that the general terms of the contract must be disclosed in the usual manner.[447] With regard to insurance contracts, the LO FB&H/LO RS contains an additional rule that the insurer is obliged to warn the policyholder that the general and special conditions of insurance are an integral part of the insurance contract and to hand him/her their copy if those conditions are not printed on the insurance policy.[448] The aim of this provision is to eliminate potential disputes between the insurers and the insured, which may invoke a lack of knowledge of provisions on general conditions. Both general and special terms must be handed to the policyholder during the contract conclusion, according to general insurance conditions practised in the Entities (FB&H and RS).

253. According to the Entities' laws on insurance companies, the obligation of the insurer to provide general and special insurance conditions during the insurance period is an additional measure introduced for consumer protection (LI FB&H and LIC RS). The insurer is also required to provide other information such as: any

443. OJ B&H, 25/2006.
444. *See* the Consumer Law of B&H, Art. 69.
445. *See* the LO FB&H/LO RS, Art. 901(3).
446. *See* the Law on Compulsory Insurances in Traffic FB&H, Art. 9(3) and the Law on Compulsory Insurances in Traffic RS, Art. 10.
447. *See* the LO FB&H/LO RS, Art. 142(2).
448. *See ibid.*, Art. 902(3).

changes (of the name of the insurance company, its legal form or address of seat and branch on the concluded contract); information relating to the elements of the insurance contract (pecuniary indemnity and other rights; the duration of the insurance contract; the manner of contract termination; the amount, method and deadline of premium payment; the amount of calculation and distribution of shares in the profit of the insurance company or the mathematical reserve; the method of calculation of the surrender value or paid amounts and scope of their guarantee; information on the premiums for each compensation, for the main compensation and if necessary for additional compensation; if compensation from the insurance contract is related to investment units, information about the nature of these units is required; information on the funds related to the investment units; conditions for withdrawal and termination of the contract; information on taxes applicable to this type of insurance contract; methods of processing of the indemnity request) in the case of modification of the insurance contract conditions or amendments of law applicable to the contract; and information on the level of participation in the insurance company's profit or in the mathematical reserve, which are given on an annual basis.[449] Additionally, LI FB&H stipulates: that the insurance company is obligated to notify the insured in writing once a year about the status of profit participation during the life insurance contract;[450] and that the insurance company must inform the policyholder during the insurance contract about the intention to conclude a contract with the co-insurer.[451] As in the case of pre-contractual informing, the information provided to the insured during the insurance period must be clear, accurate and in writing, and in one or more official languages of B&H.[452] The LIC RS provides that they may be in another language, if the insured, in accordance with the provisions of the LIC RS and the insurance contract, is entitled to choose the applicable law.[453]

254. Furthermore, the insurer is obliged to properly operate and conduct insurance business operations. General conditions provide the obligation of the insurer to operate in accordance with economic principles and to ensure that the collected financial means are safely and lawfully placed or invested thus creating the conditions for unconditional liquidity in the execution of contracts. The insurer also has the obligation for the formation and maintenance of the reserves. Insurance companies are required to form technical reserves for the coverage of future obligations from insurance and possible losses due to risks arising from the nature of the insurance business. Performance of this obligation is an integral part of regular performance of insurance companies and the proper way of conducting insurance business. The LIC RS stipulate that every insurance company that has its seat in one of the Entities is required to form technical reserves for all insurance contracts concluded in the Entities (by the company or subsidiary) in accordance with secondary

449. *See* the LIC FB&H/LIC RS, Art. 24(2).
450. *See* the LI FB&H, Art. 201(2).
451. *See ibid.*, Art. 201(3).
452. *See ibid.*, Art. 202 and LIC RS, Art. 23(1).
453. *See* the LIC RS, Art. 23(2).

legislation adopted by the competent insurance agencies (the Agency for Supervision of Insurance in FB&H or the Insurance Agency of RS),[454] which determine methods and means of reporting to the competent Agency on technical reserves. Depending on the insurance activities it performs, an insurance company is obliged to form the following types of technical reserves: reserves for unearned premiums; loss reserves; reserves for bonuses and losses; the mathematical reserve; and other technical reserves in insurance.

255. Finally, during the insurance period, the insurer has the obligation to take actions relating to the insurance policy. The general conditions of B&H's insurers provide that insurers must replace the missing insurance policy following a valid court decision, which declared the missing insurance policy invalid. The insurer may decide to replace the missing policy up to a certain amount of the insured sum without a decision on amortization. Given this, in addition to the rights of the insured to request the issuance of the insurance policy (or other insurance documents) the insured person has the right to require the issuance of the insurance policy's duplicate in the case of loss of the original.

256. The insurer is obliged to pay the contracted insured sum and/or the contracted indemnity in the case of realization of the insured event. The insurer is obliged to determine the extent of the harmful consequences caused by the insured event immediately after receiving a report on the occurrence of the insured event. With regard to the method of determination and assessment of damage, the rule is that the insurer and the insured work together. If a dispute arises, the assessment of these facts may be entrusted to experts. In practice, the contracting parties – the insurer and the insured often conclude an extrajudicial settlement and thereby resolve the issues related to the determination and assessment of the damage.

257. The law or insurance conditions determine the deadline within which the insurer is obliged to fulfil this obligation. The LO FB&H/LO RS provides the insurer's obligation to pay an indemnity or sum determined by the insurance contract when the insured event occurs. The payment must be made by an agreed deadline, which may be no longer than fourteen days, from the day the insurer was notified that the insured event had occurred.[455] The aforementioned provision is interpreted in general insurance conditions in a way that stipulates that the insurer must execute their contractual obligation within fourteen days when he has undoubtedly established the existence and amount of obligation. The LO FB&H/LO RS provides that this deadline may not be extended, but it may be shortened because that represents the undisputed interest of the insured.[456]

258. In practice, general insurance conditions stipulate that in the case when the beneficiary, policyholder or the insured does not provide the requested data, information or documentation on the occurrence of the insured event, or when criminal

454. *See* the LI FB&H, Art. 80(1) and the LIC RS, 55(1).
455. *See* the LO FB&H/LO RS, Art. 919(1).
456. *See ibid.*, Art. 900(2).

or administrative proceedings are initiated against them in relation to the insured event, the insurer has the right to postpone the resolution of the indemnity claim. These deadlines are determined by the general terms of the insurance. In the case when it takes longer to determine the obligation of the insurer or the sum, the LO FB&H/LO RS stipulates that the deadline starts from the date when the existence of the insurer's obligation and its sum are agreed.[457]

259. Also, the LO FB&H/LO RS contains provisions that regulate the insurer's obligation of reimbursement of the costs incurred as a result of undertaking measures in order to eliminate and reduce damage (salvage/rescue obligation) by the insured. These costs must have been incurred as a result of reasonable attempts to remove the immediate risk of occurrence of the insured event and to limit its harmful effects, even if these attempts were unsuccessful.[458] The insurer is obliged to compensate all expenses, losses and other damages caused in this manner, even if they exceed the insured sum.[459]

§1. Non-Life Insurance

260. Non-life insurance represents the second basic category of insurance in contemporary insurance law of B&H. It includes all types of insurance that do not fall into life insurance in accordance with decisions on the type of insurance adopted by the relevant Entity agencies for insurance.[460] In recent years, classification of insurance into life and non-life categories has been given a key position in relation to the earlier, traditional insurance classifications such as: classification into property insurance, insurance of persons and marine insurance; and classification of insurance into compulsory and voluntary insurance. This change is a result of harmonization of national legislation with EU legislation in the field of insurance.

261. The main obligation of the insurer when it concerns non-life insurance is indemnity of damage, which ensues due to the occurrence of the insured event.[461] However, indemnity of damage within this type of insurance should be considered outside the framework of the general rules of the law on obligations regarding the indemnification of damages.[462] The fundamental principle is the principle of indemnity according to which the amount of indemnity cannot be higher than the actual

457. *See ibid.*, Art. 919.
458. *See ibid.*, Art. 926.
459. *See ibid.*.
460. *See* Decision on distribution of types of risks by groups and types of insurance of the Agency for Supervision of Insurance in FB&H (OJ FB&H, 82/2017); and Decision on the Type of Insurance of Insurance Agency of RS, (OJ RS, 57/2006).
461. *See* the LO FB&H/LO RS, Art. 925(1).
462. For more information on the general concept of indemnification of damage developed in contractual law in B&H, *see*: Bikić, Abedin, *Obligaciono pravo – opći dio* (*Law of Obligations: General Part*). Sarajevo: Pravni fakultet Univerziteta u Sarajevu, 2004.

loss caused by the insured event and suffered by the insured.[463] The purpose of this principle is to prevent profit on the basis of damage.

262. The principle of insurable interest is also an important principle in property insurance, according to which the insurance contract is only valid if the insured is in a position of financial loss when the insured event occurs. This principle is regulated by the provisions of the LO FB&H/LO RS on insurance interest contained in Article 924. According to the LO FB&H/LO RS, the insurance contract may be concluded by any person who has an interest that the insured event does not occur because otherwise he/she would suffer a material loss.[464] The rights from the insurance may only apply to persons who at the time of the damage had a material interest in the insured event not occurring.[465] Through these provisions, the LO FB&H/LO RS prevents the misuse of insurance by persons who have an interest in the insured event to occur so that they may cause or influence its occurrence in order to get indemnity from the insurance.

263. Both of these principles constitute the specific characteristics of property insurance. However, the primary position within property insurance belongs to the principle of indemnity, which is in the LO FB&H/LO RS closely connected with concepts of over-insurance, under-insurance, and multiple and double insurance, which are not applicable to the insurance of persons (life insurance and accident insurance).

I. Over- and Under-Insurance

264. The notion of over-insurance indicates a contractual relationship in insurance in which the insured sum agreed upon is higher than the actual value of the insured item. Over-insurance can happen at the moment of contract conclusion or throughout the contractual relationship. In the first case, the LO FB&H/LO RS provides different implications depending on whether the contracting parties were unconscientious or conscientious. If during the insurance contract conclusion, the agreed insured sum is higher than the actual value of the insured item due to fraud committed by one contracting party, the LO FB&H/LO RS stipulates that the conscientious contracting party may request annulment of that insurance contract.[466] The conscientious insurer keeps the received premiums and is entitled to the non-reduced premium for the current period.[467] Therefore, the rule on restitution does not apply to the insurer. However, if neither contracting party acted unconscientiously, the contract remains in force, the insured sum is reduced to the actual value of the insured item and the premiums are proportionally reduced.[468] Analogous to the aforementioned case, the conscientious insurer keeps the received premiums and

463. *See* the LO FB&H/LO RS, Art. 925(2).
464. *See ibid.*, Art. 924(1).
465. *See ibid.*, Art. 924(2).
466. *See ibid.*, Art. 932(1).
467. *See ibid.*, Art. 932(3).
468. *See ibid.*, Art. 932(2).

is entitled to the non-reduced premium for the current period.[469] As previously indicated, over-insurance may occur during the contractual relationship. In the case when the insured value is reduced in the insurance period, each contracting party is entitled to the corresponding reduction of the insured sum and premium starting from the day on which he/she communicated his/her request for reduction to the other contracting party.[470]

265. Under-insurance exists when the value of the insured item is higher than the insured sum. Under-insurance may occur during or after the conclusion of the insurance contract. The LO FB&H/LO RS regulates situations when under-insurance existed at the beginning of the insurance period: 'when it is established that in the beginning of the respective insurance period the value of the insured item was higher than the insured sum, the amount of indemnity owed by the insurer is reduced proportionally, unless otherwise agreed'.[471] Unlike over-insurance, in under-insurance, there is no possibility of violation of the principle of indemnity. In under-insurance, the rule of proportionality is applied according to which, in cases when the insured sum is smaller than the value of the insured item, the insurer is obliged to compensate the damage in the ratio that exists between the insured sum and the value of the insured item.[472] Derogation from the rule of proportionality is provided in Article 936(2) of the LO FB&H/LO RS according to which the insurer is obliged to give full indemnity up to the amount of the insured sum if it is agreed that the relations between the value of item and sum of insurance are irrelevant for determining the amount of indemnity.

II. Subrogation

266. The segment of the LO FB&H/LO RS dedicated to property insurance contains special rules that regulate the transfer of the insured's rights towards the responsible person to the insurer, this is known as the principle of subrogation (section 6 of the LO FB&H/LO RS). Certain adverse events result in two claims from the insured regarding the indemnification of damage. The insured may have a claim towards the insurer if he/she has concluded the insurance contract so that the adverse event represents the insured event, and towards the person who committed the tort, which caused damage to the so-called injurer. Therefore, claims have different foundations and exist independently from each other. But, if simultaneous realization of both claims (their cumulation) were to happen, it would violate the principle of indemnity. Thus in property insurance, a rule is applied that allows the insured to exercise rights from both legal bases only to the extent of the damage he/she suffered or after settlement on the one legal basis that he/she may contact another debtor only if the settlement from the first debtor was partial and related to the unrealized portion of indemnity. However, these rules create the possibility that

469. *See ibid.*, Art. 932(3).
470. *See ibid.*, Art. 933.
471. *See ibid.*, Art. 936(1).
472. HCC Rev-1253/85 from 04.09.1985. PSP 30/11986, p. 68, para. 52.

the injurer is not liable for indemnification of damage caused to the insured if the insured first exercises his/her right with respect to indemnification of damages. In order to prevent the previously presented situation and preserve the principle of indemnity in property insurance, the principle of the recourse right of the insurer was introduced in contractual law: 'according to the law, payment of the insurance indemnity transfers, up to the amount of paid indemnity, all rights of the insured toward the person who is responsible for damages on any basis'.[473] From the aforementioned legal definition of subrogation, it follows that it is conditioned with the payment of insurance indemnity to the insured and with the existence of the insured's right to indemnity towards the person who is responsible for the damage, while the basis of liability is irrelevant. All rights towards the person liable for the damage are transferred to the insurer after the payment of indemnity. The rights transferred to the insurer are in entirety equal to the rights of the insured. However, all objections to which the insured was exposed may be raised with the insurer. For example, an injurer who did not participate in litigation where a court settlement was concluded between the victim and the insurance company as insurer is entitled to point out all objections that might be raised in the proceedings in which the settlement was reached in the recourse lawsuit that the insurer leads against him; this means that the injurer may raise to the insurer the objection of exclusive or shared liability of the victim, the objection to the amount of the damages or objection on the grounds of their own material circumstances.[474]

267. If the insurer has indemnified only part of the resulting damage to the insured (e.g., due to under-insurance), both the insured and the insurer have claims against a third party. This situation raises the question of who has the advantage during settlement. According to the LO FB&H/LO RS 'Transfer of rights from the insured to the insurer cannot be to the detriment of the insured and if indemnity that the insured received from the insurer is lower than the damages suffered, the insured is entitled to the payment of the remaining part of the indemnity from the funds of the liable person before the payment of the insurer's claims on the basis of the rights transferred to him/her'.[475] The justification behind the implementation of the aforementioned rule, which favours the interests of the insured, is based on the purpose of insurance itself – the indemnification of the insured.

268. Exceptionally, from the principle of the insurer's subrogation according to the LO FB&H/LO RS, it is allowed to derogate when it concerns certain persons who are in a particular relationship with the insured.[476] Namely, the rights of the insured do not transfer to the insurer if damage is caused by a person directly related to the insured, a person for whom the insured is responsible, or anyone living with the insured or employed by them. The LO FB&H/LO RS provides two exceptions from the aforementioned rule on derogation. The first exception exists in the case

473. *See* the LO FB&H/LO RS, Art. 939(1).
474. HC FB&H, 45 0 P 001341 08 Rev from 22 Dec. 2009, DSP 41/2010, p. 33 and Report of the HC FB&H, 1/2010, para. 38.
475. *See* the LO FB&H/LO RS, Art. 939(3).
476. *See ibid.*, Art. 939(4).

when those persons caused the damage deliberately,[477] and the second when one of the aforementioned individuals is insured from the liability and the insurer has recourse rights towards the insurer of that individual.[478]

269. Given that the insured can reduce or take away the insurer's rights with their actions, which they can exercise after the payment of the indemnification to the third liable party (e.g., the release of debt, settlement, by waiving the right to indemnification, etc.), the LO FB&H/LO RS sanctions such conduct of the insured and releases the insurer from the obligation of indemnification in appropriate measure: 'If the fault of the insured disabled this transition of rights to the insurer, wholly or partly, the insurer is relieved from his/her obligation toward the insured to an appropriate extent.'[479]

III. Multiple Insurance

270. Multiple insurance exists when a certain object is insured by two or more insurers from the same risk, for the same interest and for the same time so that the total of the insurance sum does not exceed the value of that object.[480] Under the previously mentioned conditions, multiple insurance is valid and every insurer is responsible for the implementation of obligations arising from the contract he/she concluded in their entirety. When the insured event occurs, the policyholder is obliged to notify each insurer of the same risk and inform him/her about the names and addresses of other insurers and about the insured sums from individual contracts that are concluded with them.[481]

271. If the total of the insured sum exceeds the value of the insured item, it is considered double insurance.[482] The situation of double insurance may exist also in the case when some of the contracts are concluded without any indication of the insured sum or with unlimited coverage; therefore, the LO FB&H/LO RS takes a stand that in this situation the contract is concluded with the highest sum insured.[483]

272. Insurance contract law differentiates between consciously and unconscionably concluded double insurance. If the insurer acts consciously, the LO FB&H/LO RS provides that all of these insurances are legally valid and each insurer is entitled to an agreed premium for the current period of insurance, and the insured is entitled to request indemnity from each insurer in accordance with the contract concluded with him/her, but no more than the amount of the damage.[484] However, when the insured acts unconscionably upon the occurrence of double insurance,

477. *See ibid.*, Art. 939(4).
478. *See ibid.*, Art. 939(5).
479. *See ibid.*, Art. 939(2).
480. *See ibid.*, Art. 934(1).
481. *See ibid.*, Art. 934(3).
482. *See ibid.*, Art. 934(2).
483. *See ibid.*, Art. 934(5).
484. *See ibid.*, Art. 934(2).

each insurer may request annulment of the contract, retain the premium and request the unreduced premium for the current period.[485]

273. The LO FB&H/LO RS provides that in cases where the policyholder concludes an insurance contract which creates double insurance without knowing about the previously concluded insurance, he/she may within one month from the day of learning about that insurance, request corresponding reduction of the insured sum and premiums of the later insurance where no importance is given to the circumstance of whether the previous insurance is concluded by the policyholder or by someone else.[486] The position taken in insurance law of B&H is that in the previously mentioned case, the insurer keeps the received premiums and is entitled to the premium for the current period. According to the position developed in case law, the insured may request a reduction of the insured sum and premium by the mentioned deadline only from the latter insurer.[487]

274. If double insurance occurs due to the reduction of the value of the insured item during the insurance period, the policyholder is entitled to appropriate reductions of the insured sum and premiums, starting from the day when he/she informed the insurer about the request.[488]

275. The insurer is obliged to pay indemnification in accordance with the concluded contract when the insured event occurs; however, the insured does not have the right to collect more than the amount of the damage.[489] If some of the contracts are concluded because of the possibility of uneven burden of individual insurers, since the insured can collect different amounts of contractual obligations from each insurer, the LO FB&H/LO RS provides that after payment of the indemnity to the insured, each insurer bears the part of the indemnity in proportion of the insured sum to which he/she committed in relation to the total of insured sums, and the insurer who paid more has the right to demand compensation for the overpaid amount from other insurers.[490] In the case when one of the insurers cannot fulfil his/her obligation, i.e., to pay his/her share, other insures are liable for him/her in proportion to their parts.[491]

§2. Life Insurance

276. In contracts to insurance of persons (life insurance, accident and causality insurance) the amount of the insured sum that the insurer is obliged to pay when the

485. *See ibid.*, Art. 934(9).
486. *See ibid.*, Art. 934(7).
487. HC B&H, Pž-154/86, 30 Jun. 1986, Report of the HC B&H, 3/1986, para. 48.
488. *See* the LO FB&H/LO RS, Art. 934(8).
489. *See ibid.*, Art. 934(2).
490. *See ibid.*, Art. 934(4).
491. *See ibid.*, Art. 934(6).

insured event occurs is determined in the insurance policy in accordance with the agreement of the contracting parties.[492]

277. In insurance of persons, the insurer who paid the insured sum cannot be entitled on any basis to indemnity from a third party responsible for the occurrence of the insured event.[493] The right to indemnity from a third party, responsible for the occurrence of the insured event belongs to the insured or the beneficiary regardless of his/her right to the insured sum.[494] These provisions do not apply in cases when accident and causality insurance is contracted as liability insurance.[495]

278. The contract of insurance in the event of death does not include the risk of suicide if suicide occurred in the first year of insurance.[496] In the event that suicide occurs within three years from the conclusion of the contract, the insurer is not obliged to pay the insured sum to the insured, but only the mathematical reserve of the contract.[497]

279. The insurer is freed from the obligation to pay the insured sum to the beneficiary if she/he intentionally caused the death of the insured, but the insurer is obliged to pay the mathematical reserve to the policyholder if at least three annual premiums were paid until that moment, and if he/she is insured, then to pay his/her heirs.[498]

280. The insurer is released from the obligation from the contract of accident and causality insurance if the insured intentionally caused the accident.[499]

281. If the death of the insured is caused by war operations unless something else is agreed upon, the insurer is not obliged to pay the insured sum to the beneficiary but he/she is obliged to pay him/her the mathematical reserve from the contract.[500] Unless something else is agreed upon, the insurer is relieved from his/her obligation from the contract of accident and causality insurance if the accident was caused by war operations.[501]

282. The LO FB&H/LO RS provides special rights to the policyholder of life insurance before the occurrence of the insured event: the right to request the redemption of the insurance policy; the right to request the advance payment and the right to pledge the insurance policy.

---

492. *See ibid.*, Art. 942.
493. *See ibid.*, Art. 948(1).
494. *See ibid.*, Art. 948(2).
495. *See ibid.*, Art. 948(3).
496. *See ibid.*, Art. 949(1).
497. *See ibid.*, Art. 942(2).
498. *See ibid.*, Art. 950.
499. *See ibid.*, Art. 951.
500. *See ibid.*, Art. 952(1).
501. *See ibid.*, Art. 952(2).

283. At the request of the policyholder of life insurance concluded for the lifetime of the insured, the insurer is obliged to pay him/her the surrender value of the insurance policy if at least three annual premiums are previously paid.[502] The policy must state the conditions under which the policyholder may request the payment of its surrender value and the manner in which that value is calculated in accordance with insurance conditions.[503] Under case law in FB&H, the policyholder may not request the surrender value of the insurance policy without the knowledge and consent of the insured, if the determination of the beneficiary becomes irrevocable and it is irrelevant from whose funds premiums are paid.[504] According to the LO FB&H/LO RS, the right to request surrender cannot be exercised by the creditors of the policyholder or the insurance beneficiary, but the surrender value must be paid to the beneficiary at his request if determination of the beneficiary is irrevocable.[505] The exception to this rule exists in the case of creditors to whom the insurance policy is pledged, who may request the surrender of the insurance policy if the debt secured by the pledge is not settled on its maturity.[506]

284. At the request of the policyholder of life insurance concluded for the lifetime of the insured, the insurer may pay him/her in advance part of the insured sum up to the surrender value of the insurance policy, which the policyholder may return at a later date.[507] The policyholder is obliged to pay a certain interest rate on the received advance payment.[508] If the policyholder is late with payment of the due interest rate, the same procedure as in the case of the request for the surrender applies.[509] The insurance policy may stipulate conditions for, the possibility that the sum received in advance is returned to the insurer, the level of interest rate, and consequences of the non-payment of the due interest rate, as specified in the insurance conditions.[510]

285. Life insurance policies may be pledged.[511] Pledging the insurance policy has an effect towards the insurer only if he/she is informed in writing that the policy is pledged to a certain creditor.[512] When the policy states per order, pledging is performed by means of endorsement.[513]

---

502. *See ibid.*, Art. 954(1).
503. *See ibid.*, Art. 954(2).
504. HC FB&H, no: 070-0-Rev-07-001079, from 11 Sep. 2008. Report HC FB&H, 2/2008, para. 14 and DSP 33/2009, pp. 31–32.
505. *See* the LO FB&H/LO RS, Art. 954(3).
506. *See ibid.*, Art. 954(1).
507. *See ibid.*, Art. 955(1).
508. *See ibid.*, Art. 955(2).
509. *See ibid.*, Art. 955(3).
510. *See ibid.*, Art. 955(4).
511. *See ibid.*, Art. 956(1).
512. *See ibid.*, Art. 956(2).
513. *See ibid.*, Art. 956(3).

Chapter 6. Insurance and Third Parties

286. In the insurance law of B&H, the insurance contract is concluded between the insurer and the policyholder.[514] Typically, the insurance contract is concluded by the policyholder in his own name and for his/her own account, and therefore he/she is not merely the policyholder but also the insured and insurance beneficiary. When the policyholder concludes a contract on somebody else's behalf, a differentiation is made between the person who is the contracting party and the person who is the insurance beneficiary. In this situation, the insurance beneficiary does not participate in the conclusion of the insurance contract and he/she is entitled to indemnity. Obligations from the concluded insurance contract belong to the policyholder. Namely, the LO B&H/LO RS provides in Article 905(1) that 'the obligation to pay the premium and other obligations from the contract must be executed by the policyholder'. However, the insurance beneficiary is entitled to the rights arising from the contract. The policyholder may exercise the rights from the insurance contract only with the consent of the person whose interest is insured and to whom they belong under circumstances where the fact that the policyholder holds the insurance policy is without importance.[515] The policyholder is not obliged to submit the insurance policy to the insurance beneficiary until the paid premiums to the insurer are reimbursed to him/her as well as the costs of the contract.[516] Also, the policyholder is given priority when collecting the mentioned claims from the owed indemnity and has the right to request payment directly from the insurer.[517] According to insurance contract law of B&H, even though the rights of the insurance beneficiary arise from the insurance contract irrespective of the policyholder, they are in certain aspects comprehended from the position of the relation between the policyholder and the insurer. Thus, the insurer is entitled to file to each insurance beneficiary all objections that he has against the policyholder, on the basis of the insurance contract.[518]

287. Apart from the insurance beneficiary or the insured, there may be other persons with an interest in the concluded insurance contract, such as property rights holders on the insured item, the acquirer of the insured item, a third damaged party in liability insurance, creditors of the policyholder, creditors to whom the insurance policy is pledged, etc.

288. The LO FB&H/LO RS prescribes specific protective rules regarding the holders of proprietary rights on an insured item. Namely, if the rights of pledge and other rights (usufruct, easement) on the insured item existed before the occurrence of the insured event, the holders of these rights may, after the occurrence of the insured event, immediately request payment of their claims from the insurer, within the limits of the insured sum and in accordance with the statutory order for payment

514. *See* the LO B&H/LO RS, Art. 897.
515. *See ibid.*, Art. 905(1).
516. *See ibid.*, Art. 905(2).
517. *See ibid.*, Art. 905(3).
518. *See ibid.*, Art. 905(4).

of their claims.[519] The insurer cannot pay indemnity to the insured without the consent of the holders of those rights. However, if the insurer did not know or could not have known about these rights at the moment of payment, the performed payment to the insured remains valid.[520] The insurer can only file objections against the claims of these persons before the occurrence of the insured event.[521]

289. The acquirer of the insured items and items whose use is covered by liability insurance also belongs to the group of people who have a specific interest regarding the insurance relationship. The LO FB&H/LO RS stipulates that when such items are alienated, the rights and obligations of the policyholder transfer to the acquirer unless otherwise agreed.[522] Therefore, there is a transfer of the insurance contract to the acquirer who is taking over the role of the contracting party in relation to the insurer. However, if the policyholder fails to notify the insurer that the insured item is alienated the transfer of the obligation to pay the premiums will not occur and the policyholder remains obliged to pay the premiums, which are due even after the date of alienation.[523] The circumstances of alienation may have an effect on the possibility of occurrence of the insured event in a way that it reduces or increases the probability of its occurrence. Thus the general provisions of the LO FB&H/LO RS on the increase or decrease in risk are applied accordingly.[524] The insurer and the acquirer of the insured item can withdraw from the insurance contract with a notice period of fifteen days, provided that the notice on withdrawal is submitted no later than thirty days from the day they learned about the alienation.[525] In addition, the LO FB&H/LO RS stipulates that an insurance contract terminates on the basis of law in relation to the alienated items when only one part of the insured items is alienated, which in terms of insurance does not make a separate unity.[526] However, an insurance contract cannot be terminated if the insurance policy is issued to the bearer or by order.[527]

290. In the case of liability insurance, there is a third injured party/victim that may have a direct relationship with the insurer, which is realized through indemnity on the basis of direct action.[528]

291. Creditors of the policyholder in certain situations may appear as third parties who have a specific interest in the insurance contract. Their interest in the context of the LO FB&H's/LO RS' provisions is that they may request the handover of the part of the premiums that exceeds the possibilities of policyholder, which were

519. *See ibid.*, Art. 938(1)(2).
520. *See ibid.*, Art. 938(3).
521. *See ibid.*, Art. 921 (2).
522. *See ibid.*, Art. 937(1).
523. *See ibid.*, Art. 937(4).
524. *See ibid.*, Art. 937(3).
525. *See ibid.*, Art. 937(5).
526. *See ibid.*, Art. 937(2).
527. *See ibid.*, Art. 937(6).
528. *See ibid.*, Art. 941.

unreasonably high in comparison to his/her possibilities at the time when they were paid, and they may refute the actions of the policyholder that have been taken to their detriment.[529]

292. The creditor to whom the insurance policy is pledged may also act as a third party with interest in the insurance relationship, given the right of the policyholder to pledge the insurance policy prior to the occurrence of the insured event. In order that the pledge of the insurance policy takes effect on the insurer, he/she must be notified in writing that the insurance policy is pledged to a certain creditor.[530] The LO FB&H/LO RS provides in Article 954(4) the exception where the repurchase of the insurance policy may be requested by the creditor to whom the policy was pledged, if the claim for purpose of which the settlement of the pledge is given, is not settled at maturity.

529. *See ibid.*, Art. 961(2).
530. *See ibid.*, Art. 956(2).

Chapter 7. Termination of the Insurance Contract

293. In B&H's insurance law, the moment of formal termination of an insurance contract differs from the moment of cessation of the insurance effects. The following text will concisely outline the different reasons and conditions for the termination of insurance contracts.

294. Termination of a contract by expiry of the period for which it was concluded represents one of the most frequent modes of termination of insurance contracts. A contract concluded for a certain period of time terminates when that period expires and the insurance produces effects until the last moment of the given period in accordance with the provision of the LO FB&H/LO RS contained in Article 922(1). The said provision prescribes that, unless otherwise agreed, the insurance contract produces its effects starting from the twenty-four hours of the day that is indicated in the insurance policy as the day of commencement of insurance until the end of the last day of the period for which the contract is concluded. However, there are insurance contracts in which the end of the contractual relationship, i.e., insurance is not determined by a certain date, but it is related to certain actions, for example, the delivery of goods in a warehouse or in a port in transport insurance.[531]

295. An insurance contract may also be terminated by cancellation. Namely, insurance contracts with indefinite duration usually contain the right to cancel the contract, which belongs to both parties. The LO FB&H/LO RS contains specific rules regarding property insurance contracts when the duration of a contract is not determined. The first rule is that each contracting party may terminate the contract within a day of maturity of the premium by notifying in writing the other party no later than three months before maturity of the premium.[532] The second rule is that when the insurance contract is concluded for a period longer than five years, each party may notify the other party in writing that he/she is terminating the contract after the expiration of this period, with a cancellation period of six months.[533] Finally, the LO FB&H/LO RS expressly proscribes that the right of each contracting party to terminate the contract in the aforementioned ways cannot be excluded by the contract.[534]

296. An insurance contract is terminated when the subject of insurance ceases to exist. The reasons why the subject of insurance ceased to exist may be covered by insurance (occurrence of the insured event) or lie outside of insurance. If cessation of the insurance subject is a result of the occurrence of the insured event, the insurance contract is terminated. In insurance of persons, this occurs when the person specified in the contract lives to a certain age or dies. Regarding property

531. *See* Jankovec, Ivica & Miladinović, Zoran. *Pravo osiguranja* (*Insurance Law*), Niš: Centar za publikacije Pravnog fakulteta u Nišu, 2006, 297.
532. *See* the LO FB&H/LO RS, Art. 922(2).
533. *See ibid.*, Art. 922 (3).
534. *See ibid.*, Art. 922 (4).

insurance, a distinction is made between total and partial destruction of the insurance object.[535] The insurance contract is terminated only in case of total loss.

297. In the event that the reasons for the cessation of the insurance subject have extra-contractual nature, i.e., they are not covered by insurance, the LO FB&H/LO RS provides identical consequences: 'If the insured item or item whose usage is related to the conclusion of liability insurance, perishes during the insurance period due to an event not provided for in the policy, the insurance contract will cease to exist in the future and the insurer is obligated to return part of the premium to the policyholder in proportion to the remaining time.'[536]

298. The LO FB&H/LO RS provides numerous reasons for an insurance contract annulment due to the circumstances that existed at the moment of its conclusion. If these reasons were known, the contract would have never been concluded.

299. An insurance contract may be annulled, if at the time of its conclusion an insured event had already occurred, was in the process of occurring, was likely to occur, or if the possibility of the event occurring had ceased.

300. Besides, in property insurance, the LO FB&H/LO RS stipulates that if one party committed fraud during the contract conclusion and the contracted insured sum was higher than the actual value of the insured item, the other contracting party has the right to request annulment of the contract.[537] In this case, the conscientious insurer retains the received premiums.

301. Furthermore, the insurance contract can be annulled if the contract provides that the obligation of the insurer exists even if the insured person were to deliberately cause the insured event.[538]

302. Third-party insurance against accident or death may be annulled if, in the course of the contract conclusion, there was a failure to obtain consent from the third party.[539]

303. A life insurance contract may be annulled: if an insurance contract is concluded in the case of the death of a third person under the age of 14, or a person who is completely deprived of his/her civil capacity,[540] or if during the conclusion of a life insurance contract, the age of the insured person is incorrectly reported and his/her real age exceeds the limits under which the insurer provides life insurance

535. *Ibid.*
536. *See* the LO FB&H/LO RS, Art. 928(2).
537. *See ibid.*, Art. 932(1).
538. *See ibid.*, Art. 929(2).
539. *See ibid.*, Art. 946.
540. *See ibid.*, Art. 947(1).

in accordance with their conditions and rates.[541] The consequences of a life insurance contract annulment in these cases are that the insurer is obliged to return all the premiums received on the basis of such a contract.[542]

304. The insurer may request a contract annulment during the conclusion of the insurance contract, if the policyholder intentionally made a false report, or deliberately withheld a circumstance of such nature that the insurer would not have concluded the contract had he/she known the true state of the matter.[543] The insurer may lose the right to demand annulment of a contract if they fail to notify the policyholder of their decision to exercise that right within three months of finding out any inaccuracies in the report submitted by the policyholder.[544]

305. The consequences of the annulment of a contract are reflected in the fact that both parties have the obligation to return what they have received. This means that the insurer is obliged to return the received premiums, and the insured is obliged to return the amount of compensation paid out for the possible damage or the insured sum. If the policyholder had intentionally made a false report or withheld circumstances of such nature that the insurer would not have entered the contract had he/she known, as stated in Article 908(1) of the LO FB&H/LO RS, the insurance contract specifies that the insurer has the right to retain the collected premiums and to demand payment of the premium for the insurance period in which he/she requested annulment of the contract.[545] This solution is essentially a particular form of damage compensation.

306. However, when the policyholder unintentionally submits an incorrect report or fails to give due notice, the LO FB&H/LO RS provides that the insurer has two options, which must be used within one month from the day the report was discovered to be inaccurate or incomplete.[546] The first option for the insurer is to enunciate the termination of the insurance contract to the policyholder. In this case, the contract expires following a fourteen-day period from the day the insurer notified the policyholder of their intention to terminate the contract. Another option for the insurer is to propose to the policyholder to increase the premium in proportion to the increased risk. In this case, termination occurs on the basis of law if the policyholder does not accept the proposition within fourteen days from the day he/she received it. In the case of termination, the insurer is obliged to return the premiums relating to the period of time until the end of insurance.[547] When circumstances relevant to the assessment of risk, incorrectly reported or withheld by the policyholder, are known or could not have been unknown to the insurer, the insurer may not invoke inaccuracy of the report.[548] This rule applies even if the insurer had

541. *See ibid.*, Art. 944.
542. *See ibid.*, Arts 947(1), 944.
543. *See ibid.*, Art. 908(1).
544. *See ibid.*, Art. 908(3).
545. *See ibid.*, Art. 908(2).
546. *See ibid.*, Art. 909.).
547. *See ibid.*, Art. 909(3).
548. *See ibid.*, Art. 911.

learned about the circumstances from the insurance period but failed to use his/her authorization prescribed by the LO FB&H/LO RS.

307. The insurance contract may be terminated due to reasons that arise after its conclusion. Termination may occur because of a change of circumstances or failure of one contracting party to fulfil its obligations. In the first case, there is a change in circumstances that existed at the time of contract conclusion that affect the increase or decrease in risk, which has already been discussed in the previous section. As already stated, if the increase in risk is so high that the insurer would not have entered into the contract had that condition existed at the moment of its conclusion, the insurer can terminate the contract.[549] If the increase in risk is so high that the insurer would have only concluded the contract with a higher premium, he/she can propose a new premium rate to the policyholder.[550] If the policyholder does not agree with the new premium rate, within fourteen days from the day of receipt of the proposal, the contract terminates on the basis of law.[551] With regard to risk reduction after contract conclusion, according to the LO FB&H/LO RS, the policyholder has the right to terminate the contract if the insurer does not agree with the corresponding reduction of the premium.[552]

308. The second most common reason for the termination of an insurance contract is non-payment of the insurance premium. The LO FB&H/LO RS provides different possibilities for the termination of a contract depending on the type of insurance. Regarding property insurance, if the premium is not paid when it is due, the insurer is obliged to inform the policyholder and extend the deadline for thirty days to pay the premium. If the premium is not paid within that period, the contract is terminated by law.[553] The insurance contract is terminated by law in any case if the premium is not paid within one year from maturity.[554] In the case of life insurance, if the policyholder does not pay the due premium within a certain period of time no shorter than one month at the request of the insurer, the insurer can only if the policyholder had previously paid at least three annual premiums, notify them that he/she will be reducing the insured sum to the amount of the surrender value of insurance. Otherwise, the insurer may inform the policyholder of the termination of the insurance contract.[555] In the insurance of persons against accidents, the procedure is similar to that of property insurance. If the premium is not paid within one month from the date of its maturity, the insurance contact is terminated and the insurer has the right to the premium until contract termination.

309. Termination of an insurance contract may occur as a result of cessation of the contracting parties. Due to the specificity of the insurer as a legal entity, the LO FB&H/LO RS contains specific rules on termination of the insurance contract in

549. *See ibid.*, Art. 914(3).
550. *See ibid.*, Art. 914(4).
551. *See ibid.*, Art. 914(5).
552. *See ibid.*, Art. 916.
553. *See ibid.*, Art. 913(3).
554. *See ibid.*, Art. 913(4).
555. *See ibid.*, Art. 945(2).

case of bankruptcy of the insurer. Namely, in the case of bankruptcy of the insurer, the insurance contract is terminated upon expiration of thirty days from the opening of bankruptcy.[556] However, in the case of bankruptcy of the policyholder, insurance continues and each party has the right to terminate the contract within three months from the opening of bankruptcy. In this instance, part of the paid premium that corresponds to the remaining insurance period belongs to the bankruptcy estate of the policyholder.[557]

310. In the case of alienation of the insured item, or the item in relation to which usage liability insurance was concluded, the insurance contract does not end, only the insurable interest of the initial policyholder.[558] The rights and obligations of the policyholder are transferred on a legal basis to the acquirer unless otherwise agreed.[559] The policyholder who fails to notify the insurer that the insured item is alienated remains obliged to pay premiums which fall due after the day of alienation.[560] The insurer and the acquirer of the insured item may opt out of the insurance with a notice period of fifteen days, provided that they submit the cancellation no later than thirty days from the day of learning about the alienation of the item.[561] If only one part of the insured item is alienated, which in terms of insurance does not class as a separate whole, the insurance contract will be terminated by force of law with regard to alienated items.[562] The insurance contract cannot be terminated if the insurance policy was issued to bearer or order.[563]

311. Previously presented methods of terminating an insurance contract can be categorized into two major groups: termination of contract by force of law and termination of contract by unilateral termination. An insurance contract is terminated by force of law: if at the time of conclusion of the contract the insured event had already occurred, was in the process of occurring, was likely to occur, or if there was no longer a possibility of it ever occurring;[564] if the insured item perishes due to an unforeseen event in the policy;[565] if an insurance contract has a determined duration, the contract terminates on the last day of the deadline;[566] due to bankruptcy of the insurer after expiration of thirty days from the opening of the bankruptcy proceedings;[567] if the insured has passed the age limit up to which the insurer provides life insurance;[568] if the premium is not paid for thirty days from maturity, or a notice is not given in the form of the recommended letter from the insurer, or if the premium is not paid within one year from the day of maturity, the insurance

556. *See ibid.*, Art. 932(2).
557. *See ibid.*, Art. 923(1).
558. *See ibid.*, Art. 937.
559. *See ibid.*, Art. 937(1).
560. *See ibid.*, Art. 937(4).
561. *See ibid.*, Art. 937(5).
562. *See ibid.*, Art. 937(2).
563. *See ibid.*, Art. 937(6).
564. *See ibid.*, Art. 898(2).
565. *See ibid.*, Art. 928.
566. *See ibid.*, Art. 922.
567. *See ibid.*, Art. 932(2).
568. *See ibid.*, Art. 944.

contract terminates by force of law.[569] If within fourteen days, the insured does not accept the new higher rate of the premium proposed by the insurer because of the increase in risk (due to the unintentional incorrect or incomplete report or due to the changes in circumstances), the contract terminates on the basis of law.[570]

312. The second group of methods of terminating an insurance contract entail a unilateral termination in the following cases: if the policyholder intentionally makes an incorrect report, or withholds circumstances of such nature, that the insurer would not have concluded the contract if he/she had been previously informed;[571] if the policyholder unintentionally makes an incorrect report or fails to give due notice within one month from the day of learning about the inaccuracy or incompleteness of the report;[572] if the increase in risk is so high that the insurer would not have concluded the insurance contract if that condition existed at the moment of its conclusion;[573] if the insurer disagrees with the reduction of the premium due to a reduction in risk;[574] or with the maturity of the premium, or if the duration is not determined in the contract with written notification of the other contracting party no later than three months before maturity of the premium;[575] if the insurance contract is concluded for a period longer than five years after expiry of the cancellation period of six months;[576] within three months from the opening of bankruptcy of the insurer;[577] if during the conclusion of the insurance contract one contracting party commits fraud and contracts over-insurance;[578] if during the occurrence of double insurance the policyholder acted unconscientiously;[579] if the policyholder (or some other interested party) does not pay a due premium upon invitation of the insurer in a deadline defined in the recommended letter, which cannot be shorter than one month.[580]

569. *See ibid.*, Art. 913.
570. *See ibid.*, Arts 909(2), 914(5).
571. *See ibid.*, Art. 908(1).
572. *See ibid.*, Art. 909(1).
573. *See ibid.*, Art. 914(3).
574. *See ibid.*, Art. 916(2).
575. *See ibid.*, Art. 922(3).
576. *See ibid.*, Art. 922(4).
577. *See ibid.*, Art. 923(1).
578. *See ibid.*, Art. 932(1).
579. *See ibid.*, Art. 934(9).
580. *See ibid.*, Art. 945(2).

Part III. Property and Liability Insurance

Chapter 1. Fire Insurance

313. In insurance practice, fire insurance is offered not only as a type of civil insurance but also as a type of industrial insurance. This insurance may be individually contracted (e.g., building insurance), or as part of a comprehensive insurance policy (e.g., in the case of home insurance). Fire insurance can provide coverage for almost all types of real estate and all parts of buildings, including the foundations and basement walls, and all built-in installations and other built-in mechanical equipment (e.g., elevators, central heating with fuel tanks, radiators, etc.). Also, other types of real estate may be insured such as bridges, roads, tunnels, railways, etc. Besides real estate, fire insurance may insure movables outdoors or contained in buildings (personal items/belongings, equipment, supplies and products). The insured is a person whose property and/or proprietary interest is insured. Generally, the policyholder and the insured are the same person except in the case of insurance on behalf of others.

314. The scope of fire insurance determined by general insurance conditions usually covers destruction or damage of insured items caused by the following basic hazards: fire, lightning, explosion, storm, hail, impact of the insured's motor vehicle, aeroplane crash, manifestations and demonstrations.

315. Fire is in general conditions of insurance defined as fire that originates from a certain outside source or spreads from it and expands by its own force. However, if the insured item is destroyed or damaged because of exposure to useful fire or warmth in order to be processed or for other purposes (e.g., ironing, drying, roasting, baking, cooking, heating, etc.) or because it fell or someone put it in a fireplace (oven, stove), this is not covered by insurance. Moreover, insurance does not cover damage caused to the insured property by negligent use of cigarettes, embers/hot coals, lamps, etc., or damage to chimneys that occur during their use.

316. Lightning is defined as damage caused to the insured property by the thermal and destructive power of lighting or by the impact of the object destroyed or thrown by lightning. According to the general conditions of insurers in B&H, fire insurance does not cover damage to electrical machines, appliances and power lines caused by the activity of the flow of electric power, or overheating because of overload and atmospheric influences (static tension and induction due to atmospheric discharges or similar occurrences). Also, insurance does not cover damage caused by a lightning stroke with transmission of electricity through power lines, or damage to the fuse, protective contacts, arresters of voltage, the lightning arrester and similar devices.

317. An explosion is defined as a sudden release of force that occurs because of expansion of gases and steam. Fire insurance does not cover damages resulting from mining, explosions in the engine cylinder, regular explosions in the production process, explosions of biological character, the breaking of the sound barrier and explosions in pressurized containers.

318. A storm is a wind with a speed of at least 62 km per hour (8 degrees on the Beaufort scale). If the speed of wind is uncertain, the insured must provide data from the hydro meteorological institute as proof. Insurance covers only losses that occur due to the direct action of a storm, or direct impact of the object thrown at the insured item by the storm. Insurance also covers damage resulting from the penetration of precipitation through the openings made by the storm. But insurance does not cover damages caused by penetration of precipitation through open windows or other openings in buildings, damage to the objects placed in open space or under the eaves and in open buildings, damage to the building that is not constructed in a conventional manner, etc.

319. Hail is defined as damage caused when the solid form of precipitation (balls or lumps of ice) impacts the insured property in such a manner that the property is broken, ruptured, chipped or transformed due to the impact. Insurance also covers damage resulting from the penetration of precipitation through the openings made by hail. Usually, damages that occur on deteriorated and poorly maintained buildings are not covered.

320. Regarding the risk of damage caused by the impact of a motor vehicle, insurance usually covers only damages to insured buildings resulting from the impact of the insured's motor vehicle or mobile work machines. Moreover, damage that occurs when an aircraft falls on insured property or hits into it is also covered with this type of insurance.

321. Manifestations and demonstrations are defined as organized or spontaneous public expressions of the mood of a group of people. However, insurance covers only losses that result from the manifestations or demonstrations allowed by the competent state authority. The insured event occurs when a participant of the manifestation or demonstration destroys or damages the insured property (breaking, demolition, arson, etc.).

322. If an additional and specially arranged premium is paid, supplementary insurance may also cover destruction or damage of insured items caused by one or more additional hazards: floods, water spills, landslides, avalanches, impact of a motor vehicle not owned by the insured, leakage, auto-ignition (pyrolysis) and spillage of incandescent mass.

323. Insurance also covers the disappearance of the insured items if an insured event occurs. In addition to the indemnity, the insurer is obliged to reimburse the costs due to the cleaning, demolition and removal incurred by the insured when eliminating the adverse consequences of the insured event.

324. Insurance only covers damage caused to insured items due to the insured risks, but not other indirect damages resulting from the occurrence of the insured event (liability, loss of rent, business interruption, impairment and other similar losses caused by the occurrence of the insured event). Fire insurance does not cover damages caused by nuclear radiation or radioactive contamination, or by basic and additional hazards that are directly connected with earthquakes.

325. The value of the insured object in general insurance conditions is determined in the following manner: for buildings – it is the price of construction of a new building according to local prices and reduced to the amount of the estimated rebate. For supplies of goods and raw materials – it is the purchase price, and if market price is lower than the purchase price, market price is then increased for dependent costs. For supplies of finished products – it is the production price and if that price is lower than market price – it is the market price. For machinery, devices, installations, means of transport, inventory and household items – the purchase price of new items is reduced to the amount of estimated rebate (technical and economical). For forests – it is the cost of re-plantation or, the value of the wood mass, which should be determined in each particular case. For items made of precious metals, precious stones, plans, drawings, models, manuscripts, collectors' items, money, securities, archive materials, for museums and exhibitions of items, etc. – the amount agreed upon by the insurer and policyholder.

326. The amount of insurance indemnity in the case of the destruction or disappearance of the insured object is determined according to the value of the insured object reduced to the value of the remains. In the case of damage, the costs of repair and the price of materials and work at the time of occurrence of the insured event are reduced to the amount of estimated rebate and the value of the remains, unless otherwise agreed. Higher repair costs are borne by the insured if changes and improvements were made during the repair of the damaged items. It is considered that the object is destroyed if repair costs exceed the value of the remains. The remains of the destroyed or damaged items are left to the insured and their value is calculated at market price at the conclusion of liquidation of the insured event and according to the state they were found immediately after the insured event.

Chapter 2. Loss of Benefits Insurance

327. The legal regime established in B&H after the reform influenced by EU legislation includes insurance against miscellaneous financial losses as a type of non-life insurance.[581] This insurance gives coverage of the following risks: risk of loss of employment, insufficiency of income (general), bad weather, loss of benefits, permanent general expenses, unexpected trading expenses, loss of market value, loss of rent or revenue, indirect trading losses other than previously mentioned, other financial loss (non-trade) and other forms of financial loss. Furthermore, the types of risks in insurance against miscellaneous financial losses in insurance practice are divided into: insurance of financial losses because of business interruption caused by the risk of fire or risk of machinery breakdown, insurance of various events against precipitation, insurance against damage caused by the purchase of counterfeit currency, insurance against damages in relation to the funds on current accounts and debit and credit cards, insurance of financial risk against cancellations of tourist travel, other insurance against financial losses.[582]

328. The most important types of insurance against miscellaneous financial losses in insurance practice are insurance against business interruption caused by the risk of fire and insurance against risk of machinery breakdown. Both of these types of insurance are of special interest to companies and trade unions because they both ensure uninterrupted payment of personal income to the employees. The first type covers business interruption due to destruction or damages of insured property caused by basic hazards, such as fire, lightening, explosion, storm, flood, hail, impact of the motor vehicle of the insured, fall of an aircraft, demonstrations and protests. Business costs specified in the insurance policy are the subject of insurance for business interruption against fire. If specified, the subject of insurance may also be the profit from the business. Business costs are defined as all necessary costs incurred during the period of interruption, which are in proximate cause with production and trading performed by the insured. According to B&H's accounting standards, those are the costs of services, amortization, costs of labour and other costs.

329. Insurance does not cover costs for the purchase of goods, raw materials, auxiliary and operating materials not intended for maintenance. In terms of this type of insurance, profit is considered as profit for the entire business year, in accordance with B&H's accounting standards. Damage due to business interruption represents business costs and profit (if especially agreed) the insured could not cover or achieve. Insurance does not cover damages caused by business interruption if it is caused by: extraordinary events that occurred during the interruption; local and other restrictions in the reconstruction of damaged property or facility, the lack of funds for timely construction, repair or purchase of damaged and destroyed property, changes and improvements in the reconstruction of damaged facilities, delay

581. *See* the Decision on the types of insurance in RS, (OJ RS, no. 57/06), Art. 2.
582. *See* the Decision on the distribution of types of risks by groups and types of insurance in FB&H (OJ FB&H, 82/2017), Art. 4 and the Guidelines on the Application of Decision on the Types of Insurance in RS, (OJ RS, 57/06), Art. 2.

in the work of the insured facility, which affected the operation of another facility unless otherwise agreed, the consequences to others with whom the insured has business relationships or subcontracts, because of disappearance or destruction of money (in cash), securities, business books, documents, etc. The conclusion of insurance against business interruption caused by the risk of fire is preconditioned by the existence of fire insurance, and damage due to business interruption is covered only with pre-existing coverage of material loss under fire insurance. The insured sum is determined as a fixed amount or on the basis of actual annual business expenses and the profit from the business.

330. Insurance of business interruption because of machinery breakdown may be included in the coverage of business costs, and with an additional agreement, it may also cover lost profit due to the occurrence of the insured event, which is covered by the insurance against machinery breakdown.

Chapter 3. Transport Insurance

331. In insurance practice in B&H, transport insurance is an umbrella term for several types of insurance that cover specific risks: cargo insurance, insurance of carrier's liability, insurance of freight forwarder's liability and insurance of means of transportation (hull insurance). Given that aviation insurance and motor vehicle insurance are covered in other chapters, the following will focus on cargo insurance and carrier's liability.

332. According to insurance conditions in B&H, cargo insurance of goods in transportation covers physical damage, destruction or theft of goods in transport by one or more means of transport at the insured distance. Insurers offer coverage of basic and all hazards so that the insured can decide on the scope of insurance coverage based on: the kind of goods, destination and type of means of transport. Basic insurance coverage insures consignment against hazards, such as traffic accidents, force majeure, natural disasters, fire or explosion of means of transport, burglary and plundering raid.

333. With insurance coverage against all hazards, the insurer covers all risks of loss, damage or destruction of insured goods except for damages resulting from the defect or natural characteristics of goods, hidden defects of goods or damage due to usual shortage of goods during transport. Sensitive goods may also be additionally insured against the so-called special hazards.

334. Unless specifically agreed and an additional premium is paid, insurance does not cover damages and costs arising from war, coup d'état, revolution and similar risks, effects of strikes, excluded worker or a person participating in any work unrest, resistance, terrorism or a person acting with a political motive, natural qualities of things in transport, etc. Insurance coverage excludes damages and costs caused by: a nuclear reaction, radiation or radioactive contamination, chemical or biological weapons and cybernetic attacks, hidden errors on the cargo, intentional or gross negligence of the insured, policyholders or their representatives, improper or insufficient packaging, improper loading and insufficient protection of goods in transport, improper or incorrect declaration of goods, etc.

335. Besides the liability for damages caused by their means of transport, carriers are also liable for the goods they transport. Activities of carriers are regulated by national and international regulations (Convention on the contract for the international carriage of goods by road – CMR) that contain provisions on the liability of carriers for damage to transported goods. Registered carriers may insure their liability for damage, destruction or loss of goods that are received for transport with appropriate documentation. In insurance practice, an insurance contract containing such coverage protects against indemnity requests by victims/injured persons (owner of the goods) as well as against recourse requests of insurers on the basis of paid transport (cargo) damages. Insurance coverage relating to transport in certain areas (e.g., Eastern Europe) or for specific kinds of goods has certain limitations.

Generally, the insurer regardless of the geographic area does not cover some damages for which the carrier is usually liable (such as malicious or criminal intent, gross negligence, damage due to exceeding the specifically determined transportation deadline, etc.).

336. As previously stated, in insurance practice transport insurance also includes insurance of freight forwarders' liability. Liability and activities of freight forwarders are regulated by the provisions of the LO FB&H/LO RS and General business conditions of international freight forwarders. In such insurance, the insurer gives coverage up to a certain limit for damages on the basis of liability that arise during the performance of shipping activities. Insurance coverage excludes liabilities for damages due to intent or negligence of the insured, the choice of inadequate means of transport, etc.

337. In insurance practice, hull insurance of water vessels provides adequate insurance coverage for the insured's vessel. This insurance covers physical loss, destruction and damage to the hull of the ship, its machinery, appliances and equipment as well as the usual supplies of fuel and other items on the vessel. This insurance provides coverage of physical loss, destruction and damage to the hull of the ship, its machinery, appliances and equipment, as well as the usual supplies of fuel and other things on board. The owner can insure the vessel against marine hazards during navigation and during the slipway; danger of explosion, fire and lightning; damage to the vessel during boarding, reloading or unloading of cargo; risk of a falling aircraft or parts thereof; damage at departure, pulling or lifting on the shore; the risk of burglary, violent actions of third parties or any unauthorized use of the vessel. When the insured event occurs, the insurer covers the costs of salvage, general average and awards for the rescue.

Chapter 4. Liability Insurance

338. The essence of liability insurance is that the insurer provides indemnification of a third party and payment of the indemnity for an event caused by the insured, i.e., the insurer has a specific contractual obligation to give coverage of the consequences of the insured's civil liability. Furthermore, the insurer is obliged to provide to the insured protection against indemnity claims of third parties and defence against excessive or unfounded indemnity claims.

339. Liability insurance in B&H's insurance law is considered part of the property insurance system primarily because of its indemnifying character. However, several features of this type of insurance distinguish it from the common concept of property insurance, such as the subject of liability insurance is property in its entirety and not just one object, the insured value is generally not determined in advance and the only criteria are the damage caused and the insured sum, the insurer's obligation is limited by the insured sum, absence of rules related to the insured sum (under-insurance, over-insurance, double insurance), liability insurance provides double protection (protection of the insured and victim), existence of the insurer's interest in the procedure of establishment of the liability and damages, special position of the third party in liability insurance, coverage of the liability includes damages caused by gross negligence of the insured, the insurer does not obtain the right to recourse from the injurer after the payment of indemnity, etc.[583]

340. In addition to typical obligations of the insurer arising from the insurance contract, in liability insurance the insurer is obliged to give the insured legal protection that includes, *inter alia,* conducting legal proceedings for the insured if the victim exercises its right to indemnity in civil proceedings. However, this obligation is subordinate to the main obligation of the insurer to indemnify damage. In accordance with the relevant legislation, the insurer is liable for damages caused by an insured event only if a third injured party/victim requests its compensation, i.e., the fulfilment of the indemnity claim. Contractual and non-contractual liability of the insured may be covered by insurance.

341. The established legal framework on liability insurance is complex. Besides the detailed rules on the liability of owners or users of motor vehicles, aircraft and water vessels contained in the Law on the Compulsory Insurance in Traffic FB&H,[584] [585] and the Law on the Compulsory Insurance in Traffic RS,[586] the LO FB&H/RS contains several legal rules on liability insurance contracts contained in Articles 940–941.

583. *See* Šulejić, Predrag. '*Pravo osiguranja*' (*Insurance Law*). Belgrade: Pravni fakultet u Beogradu, 2005, 385–387.
584. OJ RS, 82/2015.
585. OJ FB&H, 57/2020, 103/2021.
586. OJ RS, 82/2015, 78/2020.

342. According to the provisions of law on obligations in case of insurance against liability, the insurer is responsible for damages caused by the insured event only if a third injured party/victim requests its compensation.[587] The insurer bears the cost of the dispute on liability of the insured within the limits of the insured sum.[588]

343. In case of liability insurance, the victim may request compensation for damage sustained in an event for which the insured is liable directly from the insurer, but only up to the amount of the insurer's obligation.[589] From the day of occurrence of the insured event, the victim must have, his/her own right to compensation from insurance and therefore any subsequent change in rights of the insured against the insurer has no effect on the victim's right to compensation.[590]

§1. Liability Insurance of Private Persons

344. In insurance practice, liability insurance of private persons is ordinarily part of a comprehensive household insurance policy. Although the precise extent of insurance coverage may vary, it usually includes liability of the insured for damages caused to the life, health or property of third persons as the owner, user and tenant of a living space or the user of common areas of construction of the building in which the living space is located. Insurance also covers liability of the insured in the capacity of employer towards persons employed in the household and in the capacity of holder of domestic animals (unless the animals are held for economic purposes). Insurance usually covers liability of the insured and members of their household as well as persons employed in the insured's household while conducting activities in that household. If part of a residential building is used for performing a profession, insurance does not cover the liability from the content of that part of the building.

345. However, insurance of liability of private persons does not cover: the liability of the insured for intentionally caused damage, unless the damage is caused by the person employed in the household; liability for damage caused by storage and use of motor vehicles, aircrafts and water vessels; liability for damage suffered by the insured and members of his/her household; liability for damage caused by cold weapons and firearms regardless of the existence of a permit; liability for damage caused by defective products, liability for damage caused by conscious behaviour contrary to regulations; liability for damage to other peoples' property caused by the performance of the insured's professional activity (processing, reparation, examination, etc.); liability for damage that is a consequence of the pollution of air, water and soil; liability for damage that is a consequence of the occupational disease of employees; liability for damage to other peoples' property that was taken into lease,

587. *See* the LO FB&H/LO RS, Art. 940(1).
588. *See ibid.*, Art. 940(2).
589. *See ibid.*, Art. 941(1).
590. *See ibid.*, Art. 941(2).

transport, reparation, etc. Furthermore, insurance policies do not usually cover damages caused to property due to the permanent influence of temperature, gas, steam, moisture, mould, etc. which can result in the gradual occurrence of damage or damage caused by landslides and depression of land.

§2. Liability Insurance of Legal Entities

346. Liability insurance policies usually provide a guarantee for damages because of third parties' civil claims for compensation for damage against the insured due to an unexpected event. The sudden event (accident) may arise from the activity, ownership or legal relationship specified in the insurance policy that results in bodily injuries, disease, death or destruction, damage or disappearance of property. In the context of general liability insurance, employees of the insured are also considered to be third parties unless otherwise stipulated.

347. Liability insurance, if specified, covers liability for damage from the source of danger for which the applicable premium system determines a special premium or an extra premium. Only if especially agreed, liability insurance includes liability for pure financial loss caused by unintentional actions, omissions or errors. If the registered activity falls within the scope of pure financial loss, liability is insured separately. Insurance coverage excludes indemnity claims made before foreign courts or claims due to violation of foreign law or activity abroad, overrun of pro forma invoice and credit, violations of a purchase deadline, mediation or recommendations in monetary, land and other business activities, claims for damages caused by deficits in managing the cash register, errors in payment and embezzlement of the insured's employees, claims for damage caused by conscious violation of the regulations or instructions or any other conscious violation of the obligation, and claims for damage as a result of calculation errors or in a survey of the draft.

348. Within the source of danger covered with insurance, insurance of the liability resulting from the activity includes liability of the insured for the use, possession or lease of land, buildings and areas that are used exclusively for the purposes of the insured, the use or lease of facilities intended exclusively for employees (canteen, bathing resorts, vacation homes and sports fields), the use of personal or cargo elevators, any liability of the insured for the damage, theft or disappearance of property of their employees except money, valuables, watches, technical objects (camera, laptop, etc.), under the condition that they are held in locked spaces. Furthermore, it includes liability of legal representatives of the insured or persons who manage insured facilities or their parts, as long as they have that role. It also includes liability of the other employees for any damages caused by performance of their work. However, the insurer does not guarantee or compensate for damage if it is caused deliberately by the insured. The notion of intent includes behaviour that does not cease regardless of its expected harmful consequences, acting contrary to present regulations and knowledge of corruption and faulty goods, products or services.

349. Unless otherwise agreed, the insurer does not give a guarantee for accidents caused by active partaking at equestrian, bicycle, motorcycle or car races, competitions or combat sports events, including test races and fights or preparations for test races and fights and claims because of damage to property that the insured takes care of (lease, storage, processing, etc.). Liability insurance coverage excludes claims due to: damages to objects or instruments of processing, damage to persons or things caused by products put into circulation by the insured, impairment of health and damage caused to persons because of treatment, medical and other interventions and procedures, impairment of health and damage caused to animals because of treatment, medical and other interventions and procedures, damage caused by environmental pollution (ecological damage), damage to property as a result of the gradual adverse effects of temperature, gas, humidity, precipitation, etc., claims made by the insured and his/her family members as well as the insured's business associates and their families, damage to persons a consequence of nuclear energy except liability for a radioisotope used for peacetime purposes (in medicine, biology, industry, agriculture, etc.), damage resulting from the use or possession of an aircraft, all types of water vessels, and land vehicles and trailers, claims because of damage from the liability of the insured based on his/her contractual extension to cases for which they are not otherwise liable for under the law, etc.

350. If the insured event in liability insurance occurs at the same time as the adverse event, an indemnity claim against the insured may be accepted. Upon occurrence of the insured event, the insured is obliged to inform the insurer about the accident without delay. Also, without delay, the insured must inform the insurer about punitive measures or criminal investigation or charges imposed upon him/her, or the person for which he/she is liable, or if a decision in criminal – administrative procedure has been issued. Correspondingly, the obligation to inform the insurer is stipulated in the case of damage claims or a damage lawsuit against the insured, where original documentation containing such claims must be submitted.

351. The insured must leave litigation to the insurer and give legal powers to the person determined by the insurer. Furthermore, the insured must leave the processing of the claims to the insurer, which is why the insured is not entitled to decline the claim or more importantly to accept it. In the case that the insured precludes the insurer from solving the claims with a settlement, the insurer is not obliged to pay the indemnity excess, interest rate and costs incurred because of it.

352. The insurer's obligation is to study the soundness of the indemnity claims in terms of their adequacy and amount and to comply with justified claims as well as to take care of the defence of the policyholder/insured against unfounded or excessive indemnity claims. The insurer guarantees for reasonable costs of the insured and damage resulting from the reasonable costs, which are awarded to the victim only if proceedings are directed by the insurer or person appointed by the insurer, in accordance with previously indicated rules. The insurer guarantees the costs of defence of the insured in criminal proceedings only if he/she explicitly agrees with the defence and commits to the payment of these costs. The insurer covers only part of the reasonable costs that match the ratio between the insured sum and part of the indemnity awarded to the victim. If that is not possible to determine, obligation of the insurer regarding reasonable costs is determined by the ratio between the insured sum and the height of the actionable claim.

353. The capitalized value of the annuity that should be paid to the victim and the extent of the insurer's participation in the payment of the annuity are determined using life tables for annuity insurance of the insurer. In the case of an underage user of annuity, who acquired the right to annuity because of the death of the person who was obliged to support him/her, it is calculated that he/she will receive the annuity until 20 years of age. The insurer may deposit the insured sum or its remaining part as a savings deposit in favour of the insured, in relation to the payment of the annuity; a possible excess of the deposit counts as the remainder of the insured sum. The insurer is also entitled to use the insured sum or part of it as a savings deposit to cover damage due to the payment of the annuity until the insured sum is exhausted.

354. The insured sum is the upper limit of the insurer's liability regardless of the number of injured parties/victims. Several time-related damages represent a single damage if they are incurred by the same cause.

355. Obligation of the insurer only exists if an accident occurs within the warranty period. According to the terms of the insurance policy, if the cause of an event derives from the time before the conclusion of insurance or from the time when the insurer's warranty was terminated, insurance covers damage only if the cause was unknown to the insured.

356. A general insurance policy may also include various specific clauses drafted in accordance with the particulars of the insured. Unless otherwise agreed, liability insurance covers only liability for accidents that occur in the state of B&H.

§3. Liability Insurance of Professionals

357. A special type of liability insurance in B&H covers the liability of insured persons that perform specific professional activities (notaries, attorneys, insurance brokers, auditors, expert witnesses, etc.) for the damage incurred by their clients. Such types of liability insurance in B&H often have a compulsory nature. Although liability insurance of professionals usually covers extra-contractual liability, if specified, it may also cover contractual liability.

358. In insurance practice, such insurance products may be designed as a separate policy but most commonly they are an integral part of the comprehensive insurance policy covering other risks as well. Furthermore, in the latter case liability insurance gives coverage not only to the insured but also to his/her permanent employees. Usually, such insurance guarantees pure financial loss for which the professional is liable. For example, in case of liability insurance of expert witnesses, insurance covers liability of the insured for actions, omissions or errors that he/she may commit in the process of expertise. And in this case, insurance covers pure financial loss that the expert may cause to third parties due to negligence, errors or omissions in the course of expertise in the judicial and administrative proceedings.

359. Generally, the insurance policy covers personal injury claims and/or damage to property on the territory of B&H.

Chapter 5. Legal Aid Insurance

360. Legal aid insurance includes coverage of the costs of judicial proceedings and the provision of other services from the insurance contract.[591] In insurance practice, legal aid insurance gives coverage of costs of representation of the insured in criminal and administrative proceedings. However, this insurance does not cover pecuniary fines resulting from those proceedings. The insurer covers attorney costs in accordance with the relevant attorney's tariff in the place of the attorney's seat, costs of judicial or administrative proceedings that the insured has to bear (such as judicial and administrative fees, costs of expert witnesses, interpreters and witnesses). However, it excludes the costs of execution in criminal and administrative proceedings, in civil procedures for payment of compensation of damage and the costs of the opposite party if they have to be paid by the insured. Under the same conditions, the insurer covers costs of the opposing participant in criminal or administrative proceedings if he/she acts as a subsidiary plaintiff or victim.

361. One of the main obligations of the insured in such insurance is to consult the insurer on the probability of success before judicial or administrative proceedings and especially before rebuttal of a court decision or conclusion of settlement. If the insured does not respect the opinion of the insurer and after the procedure it is established that the insurer was right, the insurer is entitled to refuse payment of the indemnity or to reduce it in accordance with the accuracy of their opinion and the outcome of the proceedings.

362. Usually, the insured is entitled to choose an attorney who will represent him/her in legal proceedings. However, this right of the insured is limited in the following manner: the insured can only choose an attorney who has a seat in the place of the competent court or administrative body, which is responsible for conducting first-instance proceedings. An attorney answers for its work to the insured, and the insurer does not take any responsibility for the work of the attorney.

363. The insured's demands for payment of costs that are paid by the insurer in accordance with the legal aid insurance policy are transferred to the insurer. The insured is obliged to help the insurer with the collection of costs from the other person and to surrender a statement of cession on the demand of the insurer.

591. *See* the Decision on the types of insurance in the RS, Art. 2.

Chapter 6. Aviation and Space Insurance

364. Aviation insurance in insurance practice represents a fragment of transport insurance that provides insurance of aeroplanes and other aircraft against any hazards and damages in the insurance period during the derailleur, on the grounds that is done with the aircraft's own engines or with haulage, take off or standstill. Furthermore, this insurance includes insurance of aircraft equipment, goods and other transported movables, insurance against liability of owners and users for damages caused to third parties.

365. The hull of an aircraft with engines, propellers, standard instruments and equipment and all parts necessary for flying are generally considered subjects of aviation hull insurance. Subject of insurance may also be equipment attached to the aircraft that is not needed for flying (e.g., equipment for aerial photography or for towing advertising signs) but only if specified and paid with an additional insurance premium.

366. Aviation hull insurance covers damage due to physical loss or damage of the aircraft and costs that arise due to an extraordinary event on the insured aircraft in the determined interval.

367. According to the insurance conditions of B&H's insurers, insurance does not cover damage due to loss, damage of aircraft and costs incurred if: the insured aircraft is used for illegal purposes or for purposes not specified in the insurance policy, during transportation (unless transport is a consequence of the insured event), during landing or take off or during attempts of these activities on the ground not permitted by the aircrafts' manufacturer or the competent authorities (except in the case of a forced landing), due to improper loading of the aircraft, due to war, invasion, activities of armed groups, revolutions, rebellions or attempts at these activities, strikes, riots and rebellion of workers, sabotage, etc. Usually, insurance conditions provide that the insured participates with a franchise that is specified in the policy with a certain percentage of the insured sum or the total amount at every insured event, except in the case of total loss of aircraft. The insurer also covers any damage to air vessels caused by acrobatics, training, competitions, test flights of prototypes, training of pilots and by treatment of agricultural and forest areas with aircraft.

368. Although aviation insurance is mostly voluntary, it also includes compulsory liability insurance of aircraft owners against damages caused to third parties on the ground and compulsory insurance for passengers within public air transport.

369. Space insurance is not regulated in the relevant insurance legislation, and it is not present in insurance practice in B&H.

Chapter 7. Theft and Embezzlement Insurance

370. Theft insurance is not explicitly regulated in insurance legislation of B&H, but being part of property insurance all rules of this type of insurance are fully applicable. Risk of embezzlement is excluded from the coverage. The insurance against risks of burglary and robbery can be taken out not only in the form of separate policy but also as part of a comprehensive policy (such as insurance of the house/apartment and residential movables). In the insurance conditions of insurers in B&H, this insurance is named burglary and robbery insurance. Such insurance gives coverage against risks of execution or attempt of burglary or robbery, as well as acts of vandalism against insured property during the burglary. Insurance does not cover damages incurred by burglary or robbery if they are executed by a family member who lives in the same household with the insured; and if it is performed with the participation of one of the family members who lives in the same household of the insured as an instigator or accomplice. Also, insurance does not cover damages incurred by fraud, 'normal' theft, indirect losses caused by the occurrence of the insured event (e.g., loss of profit), and shortages established by inventory.

371. Burglary is defined as theft, when a perpetrator breaks into the premises where the insured objects are located, by entering by force through the doors or windows, attic, walls, floors, or by opening the premises with false keys or any other device that is not intended for regular opening, and the perpetrator leaves a trace. Theft also occurs when the perpetrator opens the premises with actual keys or their duplicates acquired in an illegal manner or enters through an opening not intended for entry by overcoming the barriers that prevent effortless entering, or seamlessly prowls into the place of insurance where he/she hides and performs the theft while they are locked. Items are insured against the risk of burglary only while they are inside closed and locked premises listed in the insurance policy. Robbery is defined as taking away the insured objects by using force or by endangering the health and life of the *insured* or persons who are connected with the insured (e.g., as household members, workers, etc.). Also, it is considered that force is used when devices for disabling resistance are employed.

372. Objects of insurance against risks of burglary and robbery may be all movables except the items exhibited at fairs, land vehicles, self-propelled machinery, floating vessels and aircraft of all kinds. Insurance covers only items that are specified in the policy and only if they are property of the insured or persons living in the same household with the insured. Items that belong to workers and others, which are taken in for repair, on loan, pledged or secured are insured only if specifically agreed.

373. This insurance does not cover costs of elimination or reduction of risks or the costs for intervention of the fire department or other organizations that in case of the occurrence of the insured event by the nature of their work must provide their services free of charge.

374. The insurer guarantees indemnity only up to the contracted insured sum unless otherwise agreed. If the insured sum is equal to the value of the insured item or higher, the insurer at conclusion of liquidation must pay the calculated damage in full but only up to the value of the insured item. In the case of under-insurance, the insurer must pay calculated damages in proportion between the insured sum and the value of the insured item, but without exceeding the insured sum. In the case of insurance against the so-called first risk, the insurer pays calculated damages for the total amount, but only up to the amount of the agreed insured sum. In the case of the conclusion of double first risk, the insurer pays calculated damages per individual item from the collection of insured items in the full amount, but not more than the lower insured sum, provided that the total damage to the entire sum of items cannot exceed the higher insured sum. Provisions on under-insurance are not applied in such cases. The insurer must pay back in full the necessary costs for measures aimed at removing or reducing damages that are undertaken upon the occurrence of the insured event on the basis of the insurer's order, regardless of the insured sum.

Chapter 8. Agricultural Insurance, Hail Insurance, Livestock Insurance

375. Although agricultural insurance is an important segment of the insurance system in B&H, this type of property insurance is insufficiently developed. In insurance practice, agricultural insurance usually encompasses insurance of crops and fruit and insurance of animals.

376. The insurance of crops and fruit covers damages to insured crops and fruit if they are destroyed or damaged during the insurance period due to hail, fire or lightning. If specially contracted, insurance coverage can be extended for the following hazards: insured crops and fruit from risks of spring frost, storms and floods; and insured orchards and vineyards from risks of salty wind.

377. Insurance does not cover damages resulting from natural disasters not specified in the insurance conditions. Furthermore, insurance does not cover damages caused by plant diseases. Insurance does not cover damages due to nuclear reactions, nuclear radiation or radioactive contamination.

378. The subjects of insurance are crops, fruit, grass, herbs, and horticultural plants, planting material, orchards and vineyards, and willows for weaving. If specially arranged insurance can provide coverage of green orchards and vineyards as well as agricultural crops in greenhouses. The insured sum for the insurance of crops and fruit is equal to the amount of expected yield evaluated at the contractual price.

379. In insurance practice, the insurer is entitled to examine and determine the state of the insured crops and fruit, which is carried out by the insurer and the insured. On the basis of a detailed review of the state of crops and fruit, the insurer is entitled to request corrections of the insured sum at the moment when the insured event has not yet occurred. The insured value of crops and fruit is equal to the amount of achieved yield evaluated at wholesale prices at the time of storage of yield. According to the single provision of the LO FB&H/LO RS dedicated to the insurance of crops, fruit and other land products, the amount of damage in such insurance is based on the value of those products at the time of collection, unless otherwise agreed.[592]

380. The insurance of animals generally covers numerous hazards that are endangering the life, reproduction and economic effects of livestock at farms and production plants. Livestock insurance covers the following basic perils: death, emergency slaughter or killing, and slaughter or killing for economic reasons. Insurance provides coverage of damage resulting from death, emergency slaughter or killing of animals due to accident or disease or immediate danger from those perils and coverage of damage resulting from slaughter or killing for economic reasons if

592. *See* the LO FB&H/LO RS, Art. 925.

the animal due to accident or disease becomes incapable of any kind of economic activity and there is no hope for recovery. The insured may perform slaughter due to economic reasons only after the insurer's approval on the basis of written veterinary opinion. If especially agreed and if additional premium is calculated, insurance may also cover medical costs, disappearance or theft of animals and the liability of the owner of the animal.

381. Accident and disease are defined as any sudden, unforeseen event independent from the will of the insured that results in the death of animals, slaughter out of necessity or economic reasons, as well as the treatment of animals. Accidents are fire, lightning, explosions, storms, floods, snow and earth landslide, high or low air temperatures, trampling or collision with vehicles, injuries from weapons, the fall or slip of an animal, animal poisoning with chemicals and other events that result in death or injury of the insured animals. Disease as an insured risk is an organic change in the normal functions of the body in response to internal and external irritation. Disease is considered to be a difficult birth, stroke, hernia, colic and other similar cases. Insurance does not cover damages resulting from earthquakes, nuclear radiation or radioactive contamination, infectious diseases (except swine fever, inflammation of the udder, trichophytia), asthma or chronic disease of the joints, tendons and bones that is the result of long-term, excessive or unreasonable use of animals or untimely treatment, hereditary diseases, etc.

382. The insured loses rights from insurance due to: untimely treatment of the affected animal (if that is the insured's fault); slaughter or killing of animals without any real need or slaughter or killing of animals because of economic reasons without consent of the insurer, or failure to take protective measures specified in the insurance conditions.

383. Insurance subjects can be the following domestic animals: hoofed animals, stallions, cattle, pigs, small livestock, poultry, fish, bees, dogs and cats and exotic animals. The value of insured animals is their market value unless something else is agreed.

Chapter 9. Catastrophe Insurance

§1. General

384. Generally speaking, catastrophe insurance gives coverage against specific, low-probability, high-cost events such as natural disasters (flooding, storms, earthquakes, landslides, etc.), fire, explosions, war, terrorist attacks, nuclear risks, etc., which are in insurance practice usually excluded from insurance coverage. Therefore, special insurance policies against catastrophe risks must be contracted and this usually involves reinsurance pools.

§2. Nuclear Risks

385. Nuclear risks are excluded in B&H's insurance practice from insurance coverage, and there is no possibility to insure such risks even if an additional premium is paid. Special risk-sharing mechanisms, such as insurance and reinsurance pools for covering nuclear risks, are not established in B&H.

§3. Natural Catastrophes

386. B&H is characterized by high exposure to certain types of natural disasters such as floods and landslides but unfortunately, the insurance against those natural disasters is generally neglected in the portfolio of non-life insurance, and in insurance practice, insurers mostly offer earthquake insurance. A flood is defined as an event when permanent water (rivers, lakes, seas) accidentally floods the land on which the insured items are situated after water descends across hills, penetrates banks, causes dams to collapse, or where it spills because of exceptionally high tides, waves or due to the extraordinary influx of water from an artificial lake. A landslide represents a slide of the ground with clearly visible cracks and creases of soil if these movements cause dangerous static deformations or wide cracks in the buildings in a short period of time. An earthquake is defined as ground motion caused by natural processes in the earth's crust. The risk of earthquakes is usually covered in fire insurance, computer insurance and insurance against delays in operations specified as an additional hazard. In terms of insurance of companies, subjects of such insurance are all types of buildings and movables. Earthquake insurance covers destruction or damage of insured property that results directly from an earthquake or as a result of a causal connection with it.

Chapter 10. Credit and Caution Insurance

387. Credit insurance is a type of non-life insurance[593] in which the insurer covers the insured's loss suffered as a result of a default in obligations of one or more debtors towards the insured for the payment of a premium. Such insurance includes general insolvency, export credit, credit paid in instalments, mortgages, agricultural credit, etc. Credit insurance covers a wide range of risks of credit activities and particularly the risks of insolvency and inability to pay and failure to perform contractual obligations.

388. In insurance practice, several types of credit insurance are offered: consumer credit, insurance of home loans, credit insurance of small businesses, credit insurance of legal entities, etc.

389. Contracts on insurance of claims such as the contract of insurance of payment of credit are excluded from the application of provisions of the LO FB&H/LO RS.[594] Credit insurance is ordinarily divided in insurance practice and literature,[595] into three main types: *del credere* credit insurance, caution credit insurance and insurance of trust (credit insurance against abuse of trust).

390. *Del credere* credit insurance represents insurance against the risk of non-collection of financial claims against debtors that is concluded between the insurer and creditor, who pays the insurance premium, has status of the insured and is entitled to submit the indemnity claim to the insurer. However, the debtor is usually unaware that the creditor has insured his/her claim against him/her.

391. Caution credit insurance is such insurance wherein a borrower from a particular legal relation concludes a contract with the insurer. In other words, this insurance guarantees to the creditor that his claim will be paid, that is the insurer pays the creditor if the debtor does not.

392. In insurance practice, caution insurance is defined as an insurance contract whereby the insurer guarantees the fulfilment of obligations of the policyholder to the user, from the letter of guarantee or creditor legal relationship on the basis of regulation or a business relationship. The types of such insurance offered by insurers in B&H are insurance of customs debt, bid guarantee, guarantee of good performance of commitments, insurance of contractor's obligations or services for refund of advance, insurance against insolvency of travel organizers and insurance of guarantee.

---

593. *See* the Decision on the distribution of types of risks by groups and types of insurance in FB&H, Art. 3 and the Decision on the types of insurance in RS, Art. 2.
594. *See* the LO FB&H/LO RS, Art. 899.
595. *See* Marović, Boris & Avdalović, Veselin. Osiguranje i upravljanje rizikom (*Insurance and Risk Management*), Subotica: Biografika, (2005), 223–227.

393. Insurance in the case of insolvency of travel organizers is compulsory and a condition for obtaining a licence prescribed by legislation for tourism activities. By issuing a letter of guarantee for ensuring payment of costs of returning people from tourist travel to the place of their permanent residence, the insurer jointly guarantees with the organizer of tourist travel payment for those costs.

394. Insurance against the abuse of trust represents the employer's protection from the damage that he/she may suffer as a result of the actions of his/her employees.

395. After payment of the insured sum upon the occurrence of the insured event, the insured transfers to the insurer all rights towards the debtor on the basis of the concluded credit contract.

396. The basic coverage is in the form of non-payment of loans or credit annuities due to the bankruptcy of the debtor. The coverage may be broadened subject to payment of an additional premium, whereby it also covers the risks of insolvency or intentional non-payment of annuities.

Chapter 11. Technical Insurance

397. In insurance practice in B&H, technical insurance is an umbrella term covering specific risks relating to the construction of buildings, use of machinery and electronic equipment. The most relevant types of this insurance offered by insurers in B&H are construction insurance and machinery breakdown insurance.

398. General insurance conditions provide that construction insurance gives coverage of destruction or damage of insured items caused by basic hazards, such as fire, lightning, fall of an aircraft, explosions, storms, hail, manifestations and demonstrations, water spillage, frost, ice and snow, snow avalanches, rain, etc. It also covers construction accidents, clumsiness, negligence, malice and burglary. Upon special agreement and payment of a premium, a construction insurance policy includes insurance coverage of damage or destruction of insured items against one or more additional risks of flood, landslide, liability of the policyholder and contractual liability of the policyholder during the warranty period. Such insurance covers damage caused to mechanical and electrical equipment that is already installed or will be installed in an insured building under construction. The extent of damage to that equipment covered by insurance is determined in accordance with general conditions for montage insurance. Upon the occurrence of the insured event, the insurer also covers the disappearance of insured objects and costs of cleaning, demolition and removal. However, this insurance does not cover contractual penalties and indirect damages or losses due to the insured event (lost rent, business interruption, impairment, and similar losses). Furthermore, nuclear risks are excluded.

399. The subjects of construction insurance are objects under construction, construction and installation materials, and equipment and auxiliary facilities for construction. Upon the payment of an additional premium, construction insurance also covers existing objects which are under renovation, reconstruction and adaptation, existing objects close to the insured object, auxiliary building materials, property of employees, business and technical documentation, etc. The insured value of the object in construction or the value of its parts is the actual price of material and work without exceeding the price of material and price for this object in the construction contract.

400. Machinery breakdown insurance gives coverage against damages or destruction caused by mechanical breakage, defects in construction, materials or production, effects of electrical power, failure of protective or regulative devices as well as falling and overturning and clumsiness, negligence or intent of the worker or another person. This insurance excludes risks covered with other types of insurance: fire, lightning, explosions, storms, hail, the aircraft's fall, water spillage, landslides, avalanches, demonstrations and protests, obvious defects or errors that existed at the time of conclusion of insurance, violation of legal and technical regulations, insufficient investment maintenance, excessive moisture, calculus, rust, direct consequences of permanent influence of chemical, thermal or mechanical conditions, installation and trial operation of machinery, overload and overvoltage of machinery, mechanical and electrical equipment, etc. Machinery breakdown insurance also does not cover damages incurred during the warranty period for which the manufacturer or trader is liable, maintenance costs, indirect damages resulting from the insured event, damage caused by the disappearance of the insured item, damage due to nuclear risks, etc.

401. The subject of this insurance includes machinery, mechanical devices, electronic devices, appliances and installations. If specially agreed, the subjects of insurance are also power lines, gas lines, water and sewer networks, metal silos, antenna towers, electronic computer programs installed into machinery and devices, etc. The value of the insured item, unless otherwise agreed, is the value of a new item reduced to the amount of estimated rebate (technical and economic).

402. The insurance contract may cover all machines (in a group) or individual machines that belong to the insured. The amount of indemnity is determined in the case of destruction in accordance with the value of the insured item at the time of the insured event, reduced for the value of the remains, unless otherwise agreed. In the case of damage, the amount of indemnity is determined by the amount of costs of repair reduced for the amount of rebate and value of the remains, unless otherwise agreed. The insurer is obliged in addition to the payment of indemnity to reimburse costs of cleaning and clearing in relation to the occurrence of the insured event, as well as the necessary costs resulting from the reasonable attempt of the insured to undertake measures when the insured event occurs in order to eliminate and reduce detrimental consequences of the occurrence of the insured event. However, the insurer is not obliged to reimburse costs resulting from the removal of causes of damage. This insurance also covers, if agreed upon, other risks such as the loss of profit due to business interruption caused by damage to machinery.

403. In addition to the aforementioned types of technical insurance, insurers in B&H also offer computer insurance, montage insurance, insurance of guarantee and insurance of goods in freezers.

404. Given the voluntary nature of technical insurance, insurers may provide various products that cover various risks in accordance with specific needs of the insured.

Part IV. Motor Vehicle Insurance

405. Progress in motor insurance significantly influenced the development of contemporary insurance in B&H. Motor vehicle insurance is part of property insurance and entails different types of insurance against potential risks resulting from the use of a motor vehicle. The notion of motor vehicle insurance usually refers to compulsory motor vehicle liability insurance and motor hull insurance, as the two most common types of motor vehicle insurance in B&H. However, in practice, other types of insurance are also offered, such as insurance for drivers against accidents, roadside assistance insurance, insurance of persons against consequences of accidents in motor vehicles, legal aid insurance and insurance for treatment after injuries in traffic accidents. In insurance practice, all these types of motor vehicle insurance may be contracted in addition to compulsory and/or motor hull insurance.

§1. Motor Vehicle Liability Insurance

406. Motor vehicle liability insurance is the most common type of compulsory insurance in B&H,[596] which is prescribed in detail by the Entities' laws: the Law on Compulsory Insurance in Traffic (LCIT FB&H),[597] which in 2020 replaced the Law on Insurance against Motor Liability (LIML) and other Provisions on Compulsory Insurance against Liability in the FBiH (LIML FB&H)[598,599] and the Law on Compulsory Insurance in Traffic (LCIT RS),[600] which replaced the Law on Insurance against Motor Liability and other Provisions on Compulsory Insurance against Liability in the RS (LIML RS).[601] Both of these laws regulate the elements of motor vehicle liability insurance contracts.

407. According to the LICT FB&H, owner of the vehicle is obliged to conclude insurance contract against liability for damage caused to third parties, before the

596. *See* the Insurance Agency of B&H (2022), *2021 Annual Report of the Insurance Agency of B&H*, http://www.azobih.gov.ba/dokumenti/publikacija-en-21.pdf (accessed: 22 Dec. 2022), 45.
597. OJ FB&H, 57/2020, 103/2021.
598. *Ibid.*, 24/05.
599. As well as Arts 69–72 and 93–95 of the Law on Insurance of Property and Persons in FB&H (OJ FB&H, 2/95, 7/95, 6/98 i 41/98).
600. OJ RS, 82/2015, 78/2020.
601. *Ibid.*, 17/2005, 64/2006,12/2009.

vehicle starts to be used in traffic, and renew it as long as the vehicle is used in traffic.[602] Damage caused to third parties by the use of the motor vehicle due to death, bodily injury, impairment of health, destruction or damage to property.[603] The LCIT RS also prescribes that the owner of the vehicle is obliged to conclude a contract of motor vehicle liability insurance for any damage caused to third parties due to bodily injury, impairment of health, destruction or damage of possessions.[604] Therefore, possessors or owners of motor vehicles must conclude an insurance contract with the insurance company that offers coverage of the risk of civil liability resulting from the use of a vehicle on the territory of B&H. However, the LICT FB&H and LCIT RS explicitly stipulate that it is the obligation of the insurer to conclude a contract of compulsory insurance in accordance with the law, insurance conditions and tariffs of insurance premiums.[605] The insurer may not refuse the offer to conclude the contract of compulsory insurance if the insured accepts the conditions under which the insurer provides that type of insurance.[606]

408. Regarding the qualitative scope of coverage, compulsory motor vehicle liability insurance covers the liability of the owner and user of the vehicle, towards third parties who have a claim for compensation for damage caused to them, in accordance with the provisions of the LO FB&H/LO RS.[607] Furthermore, motor vehicle liability insurance covers damage to persons and damage to belongings of passengers in motor vehicles that caused the damage;[608] damage to persons and damage to property suffered by pedestrians, cyclists and other non-motorized participants in a traffic accident;[609] and damage caused to a third party as a result of items falling from the vehicle.[610]

409. Compulsory motor vehicle liability insurance does not cover the carrier's liability for the items he has received for transportation.[611] Additionally, the right to compensation for damages based on motor vehicle liability insurance doesn't belong to: the driver of the motor vehicle that caused the damage; the owner, co-owner, and every user of the vehicle that caused the damage, who was not the driver of the vehicle whose use caused the damage, for compensation for damage to property; relatives and other natural persons, for mental pain due to the death or physical injury of the driver who caused the damage; a passenger who voluntarily entered a vehicle that caused damage and was driven by an unauthorized driver or a driver under the influence of alcohol or narcotic drugs, if the responsible insurance company proves that the passenger should have been aware of this circumstance; damaged person to whom damage was caused due to: (i) the use of vehicles

602. *See* the LCIT FB&H, Art. 5(1).
603. *See ibid.*, Art. 22(1).
604. *See* the LCIT RS, Art. 21(1).
605. *See* the LCIT FB&H, Art. 9(1), and the LCIT RS, Art. 10(1).
606. *See* the LCIT FB&H, Art. 9(3), and the LCIT RS, Art. 10(2).
607. *See* the LCIT FB&H, Art. 22(2).
608. *See ibid.*, Art. 22(3).
609. *See ibid.*, Art. 22(5).
610. *See ibid.*, Art. 22(6).
611. *See ibid.*, Art. 24(1).

at sports events that are held on a road or part of the road closed to traffic for other drivers, and the goal of which is to achieve the highest or highest average speed, i.e., at practice sessions for those events; (ii) direct or indirect effects of nuclear energy or radiation generated during the transportation of nuclear or other radioactive materials; (iii) war, rebellion or terrorist activities; (iv) the use of the vehicle that was mobilized, from the moment of collection by the competent authorities until the moment of returning the vehicle to the owner.[612]

410. Correspondingly, the LCIT RS provides qualitative coverage in contracts of motor vehicle liability insurance which covers the liability of the vehicle owner or user towards third parties who have claims for indemnity from the person responsible for causing the damage, in accordance with the laws on the obligation relationship.[613]

411. The contract on insurance against automobile liability covers damages caused to passengers and their belongings in the vehicle that caused the damage[614] and damages suffered by pedestrians, cyclists and other non-motorized participants in the traffic accident.[615] The contract also covers damage caused to third parties due to objects falling off the vehicle.[616] When the vehicle and connection vehicle are owned by the insured whose liability is insured by different insurers they are jointly liable for any damages and the injured party may submit an indemnity claim to either insurer.[617]

412. With regard to the quantitative scope of compulsory insurance coverage, the LICT FB&H stipulates that the minimum amount of the insured sum cannot be lower than BAM 2,000,000.00 in the case of physical injury of the person and regardless of the number of victims included in the same accident; and BAM 400,000.00 per adverse event in the case of property damage, regardless of the number of victims.[618] If there is more than one insured person and if the total compensation exceeds the amount of BAM 2,000,000.00, the amount of the compensation will be proportionally reduced.[619] If an accountable insurance company pays the claimant an amount higher than he/she is entitled to, given the proportional reduction of the indemnity due to the fact that they did not know about the other people entitled to indemnity, the company will still be liable towards the other persons only up to BAM 2,000,000.00.[620] Currently in the RS, insured sums obligatory for a motor vehicle liability insurance contract cannot be less than BAM 1,000,000.00 per one adverse event, regardless of the number of injured parties in the same accident.

612. *See ibid.*, Art. 24(2).
613. *See* the LCIT RS, Art. 21(2).
614. *See ibid.*, Art. 21(3).
615. *See ibid.*, Art. 21(5).
616. *See ibid.*, Art. 21(6).
617. *See ibid.*, Art. 21(7).
618. *See* the LICT FB&H, Art. 27(1).
619. *See ibid.*, Art. 27(2).
620. *See ibid.*, Art. 27(3).

In the case of damage to property, the insured sum cannot be less than BAM 350,000.00 per adverse event, regardless of the number of claims arising from the same accident.[621]

413. The minimum territorial validity of the policy of motor vehicle liability insurance towards third parties issued in the Entities of B&H is the territory of the B&H.[622] The Law of RS similarly stipulates that a contract of compulsory insurance of the owner or user of a vehicle against liability for damage caused to third parties covers damage that occurs not only on the territory of B&H but also on the territories of Member States of the Green Card System and states that they are parties to the multilateral agreement when the multilateral agreement is signed with B&H.[623]

414. In the FB&H registration of motor vehicles, renewal of registration and issuance of test registration plates may be performed only after the submission of a valid insurance policy or certificate on insurance against automobile liability insurance of third parties to competent authorities responsible for the registration or issuing of trial registration plates.[624] Correspondingly, LCIT RS also provides that the owner of a vehicle is obliged to conclude a contact of compulsory insurance before the vehicle is used in traffic and to renew the insurance as long as the vehicle is in use.[625] The competent authority for registration of vehicles may not register or extend the registration without evidence that the contract of compulsory insurance is concluded.[626] Therefore, all registered vehicles must have motor vehicle liability insurance.

415. The LCIT FB&H/RS provide that insurance companies who perform different classes of compulsory insurance are obliged to adopt the conditions of motor vehicle liability insurance and to submit them to the competent Insurance Agency no later than eight days from the day of their adoption.[627] The Management Board of the Agency adopts a common premiums' tariff and a price list for motor vehicle liability insurance, which are valid for five years from the date the legislation entered into force.[628] On the date of expiry of the common premiums' tariff and price list aforementioned, the insurance company becomes entitled to use its own premiums' tariff and price list for the motor vehicle liability insurance for which it has obtained prior approval of the Agency.[629] The insurance company must submit its own premiums' tariff and price list for motor vehicle liability insurance to the Agency for approval no later than ninety days before the expiry of the five-year

621. *See* the LCIT RS, Art. 30.
622. *See* the LICT FB&H, Art. 10(2).
623. *See* the LCIT RS, Art. 11(2) and (3).
624. *See* the LICT FB&H, Art. 5(2).
625. *See* the LCIT RS, Art. 5(1).
626. *See ibid.*, Art. 5(3).
627. *See* the LICT FB&H, Art. 11(1) and the LCIT RS, Art. 12(1).
628. *See* the LICT FB&H, Art. 11(2) and the LCIT RS, Art. 12(2).
629. *See* the LICT FB&H, Art. 11(6) and the LCIT RS, Art. 12(6).

period.[630] The Agency's approval ceases to be valid upon the end of October 2025, and after that period the insurance company's obligation to obtain the Agency's prior approval to the premium tariff and price list for motor vehicle liability insurance ceases.[631]

416. The LCIT FB&H/RS provide that if during the insurance period the owner changes, the new owner is obliged to conclude the contract of insurance of his/her liability for the use of the vehicle which he/she acquired.[632] The contract concluded with the previous owner of the vehicle ceases to have effect at the moment when the new owner of the vehicle concludes a contract on automobile liability in his/her own name.[633] Following the termination of the aforementioned contract on compulsory insurance, the previous owner is entitled to reimbursement of part of the premiums for the unused period of coverage, provided that he/she informed his/her insurer about the change in ownership of the vehicle and in the event that there was no damage during the insurance period under the specified policy.[634]

417. The injured party/victim is entitled to submit a claim directly to the liable insurance company.[635] However, if the insurance company does not solve the victim's indemnity claim within sixty days from the day of its submission, or if the victim has other reasons, he/she may start court proceedings against the liable insurance company.[636] In FB&H, the responsible insurance company is obliged to determine the legal basis and the amount of the compensation claim within thirty days from the date of completion of the claim, along with submitting a reasoned offer, to pay the ascertained compensation within a further period of fourteen days.[637] The deadline for submitting a complaint to the insurance company cannot be shorter than fifteen days from the day when the injured party received a reasoned offer or a reasoned answer from the insurance company.[638] The deadline for resolving complaints is fifteen days from the date of submission of the complaint by the injured party.[639] The injured person has the right, in addition to the amount of compensation, to statutory default interest starting from the first day after the deadline for payment of damages.[640] In the procedure of peaceful resolution of the compensation claim in the insurance company, the responsible insurance company is not obliged to compensate the costs of legal and any other representation to the injured party.[641] The injured party has the right to submit a complaint to the Insurance

630. *See* the LICT FB&H, Art. 11(3) the LCIT RS, 12(3).
631. *See* the LICT FB&H, Art. 11(7).
632. *See ibid.*, Art. 45(1) the LCIT RS, Art. 32(1).
633. *See* the LICT FB&H, Art. 45(3) the LCIT RS, Art. 32(3).
634. *See* the LICT FB&H, Art. 45(4) and the LCIT RS, Art. 32(4).
635. *See* the LICT FB&H, Art. 12(1) and the LCIT RS, Art. 13(1).
636. *See* the LCIT RS, Art. 24(1).
637. *See* the LICT FB&H, Art. 13(1).
638. *See ibid.*, Art. 13(5).
639. *See ibid.*, Art. 13(6).
640. *See ibid.*, Art. 13(7).
641. *See ibid.*, Art. 13(8).

Ombudsmen on the insurance company's decision based on the submitted complaint, for the purpose of further out-of-court settlement of the dispute arising from the claim for compensation.[642]

418. The LICT FB&H/RS prescribe the right of subrogation to the insurer.[643] Namely, the insurer who paid indemnity to the injured party/victim is entitled to compensation of the paid amount of the indemnity and all the actual and reasonable expenditures from the insured or person who is liable for the damage in the following cases: if the driver used the vehicle for an unintended purpose; if the driver used the vehicle without obtaining a proper license, unless it was a candidate training for a driving test in compliance with all regulations governing learner drivers; if the driver used the vehicle during a safety measures order or violated protective measures in traffic (complete or partial ban on driving, etc.); if the driver operated the vehicle under the influence of alcohol above the prescribed limit, narcotics, psychoactive medicines or other psychoactive substances or refused to take a breathalyser test, and a test for the presence of drugs, psychoactive medicines or other psychoactive substances; if the driver caused the damage intentionally; if the driver fled the scene of an adverse event; if the driver committed an offence of violent driving in accordance with safety regulations of road traffic.[644] The aforementioned right of the insurance company does not affect the right of the victim to indemnity from the responsible insurance company.[645]

419. Regarding the persons who are not entitled to indemnity on the basis of motor vehicle liability insurance, the LCIT RS provides that the contract of insurance does not cover the liability of the carrier for any transported goods.[646] The right to indemnity on the basis of motor vehicle liability insurance excludes the driver of the vehicle that caused the damage; the owner, co-owner and every user of the vehicle that caused the damage, but who was not operating the vehicle at the time of the accident. The right to indemnity on the basis of motor vehicle liability insurance also excludes damaged possessions, or any emotional and mental pain caused by the death or bodily injury to the driver who caused damage to their relatives, the passenger who voluntarily entered the vehicle causing the damage while driven by an unauthorized driver or driven by a driver under the influence of alcohol or drugs, if the responsible insurance company proves that the circumstance should have been known to the passenger,[647] persons injured by the use of a motor vehicle during car racing shows or during the practice for those shows, the direct or indirect effect of nuclear energy or radiation occurring during the transport of nuclear or other radioactive materials; war, rebellion or terrorist activities; the use of a vehicle that has been mobilized from the moment of its expropriation until the return of the vehicle to the owner.[648]

642. *See ibid.*, Art. 13(9).
643. *See ibid.*, Art. 16 and the LCIT RS, Art. 28.
644. *See* the LICT FB&H, Art. 25(1) and the LCIT RS, Art. 28(1).
645. *See* the LICT FB&H, Art. 25(2) and the LCIT RS, Art. 28(2).
646. *See* the LCIT RS, Art. 27(1).
647. *See ibid.*, Art. 27(4).
648. *See ibid.*, Art. 27(5).

420. The price of compulsory insurance depends on multiple factors: the type of motor vehicle, the power of the vehicle, its technical characteristics, intended use, past record regarding adverse events, etc.

421. Indemnity in the case of death, physical injury and material damage caused in traffic accidents in B&H, when the person responsible is unknown or uninsured as well as in the situation of special liquidation due to the bankruptcy or withdrawal of authorization of the insurer, is paid by the Protection Fund of FB&H.[649] A similar provision is contained in the LCIT RS in Article 33(1). After the payment of the indemnity, the Protective Fund assumes all rights arising from the accident towards the person liable for the damage or his/her insurer as well as towards the funds of the company that is in the process of special liquidation.[650] The Protective Fund is financed by the contributions of its members (insurance companies performing the compulsory insurance of motor vehicles on the territory of the Entities), and contributions, from which damages are financed for the purpose of fulfilling obligations from Article 66 of the LICT FB&H.[651]

422. A driver who crossed the B&H border on the territory of the FB&H with a foreign-registered vehicle is obliged to have and, at the request of an authorized person in the Federation, to provide for inspection an international certificate of automobile liability insurance valid in the territory of the Member States of the Green Card System or an automobile liability insurance policy. The registration plate of a vehicle that is normally located on the territory of the signatory states of the Multilateral Agreement is also considered an international certificate of automobile liability insurance, provided that a Multilateral Agreement has been signed with B&H. A driver of a foreign-registered vehicle who does not possess an international certificate of motor vehicle liability insurance cannot use the vehicle on the territory of the Entity if he/she does not have a motor vehicle liability insurance policy, the validity period of which cannot be shorter than seven days longer than ninety days.[652]

§2. Motor Hull Insurance

423. Motor hull insurance is voluntary insurance regulated by the insurance contract concluded between the insurer and the insured. Therefore, unlike compulsory motor vehicle insurance, the existence of the motor hull insurance contract is dependent on the will of the parties and it is contracted by a separate contract. Motor hull insurance concerns primarily all types of motor vehicles and their components. The components of a vehicle are considered to be: the tools, accessories and spare parts that are standardly delivered for that type of vehicle; the radio installed in the

649. *See* the LICT FB&H, Art. 66(1).
650. *See ibid.*, Art. 69(2).
651. *See ibid.*, Art. 60(2).
652. *See ibid.*, Arts 47,48 and the LCIT RS, Art. 35.

vehicle by the manufacturer; the device for insurance against theft, fire extinguisher, safety triangle, safety belts, tachograph, rope, or drawbar, equipment for first aid, spare bulbs, additional exterior and interior mirrors and the lamp-turn signal for marking the vehicle stopped at night and halogen lights, fog lights, rear window heater, rear window wiper, headrest and snow chains.

424. In insurance practice in B&H, motor hull insurance is voluntary insurance of motor vehicles with the purpose of indemnity for the damage on the vehicle caused by an accident even when the driver is liable for it. Motor hull insurance covers the majority of damages caused to the motor vehicle while driving, at a standstill or in the parking lot. Besides insurance of a motor vehicle and its standard equipment, if specially contracted and paid, insurance may cover the driver and the passengers from the consequences of accidents, additional equipment, luggage, travel collections, samples of goods, tools, etc. However, according to the general conditions of motor hull insurance in practice, the insurer is not obliged to indemnify the damage and expenditures which are not caused by the risks covered by the contract, or the damage and expenditures due to: damages caused by driving; damages due to the freezing of liquids in the refrigerator or the engine block; the loss of driving material due to the occurrence of the insured event, etc.; a cargo transported by the vehicle; putting the vehicle in operation before the final repair; technical malfunction of a vehicle; during the transport of vehicles by another means of transport; the damage incurred because of the reduced value of a vehicle as a result of repair; war, invasion or similar operations, sabotage or terrorism; damage caused during the mobilization of the vehicle; damage caused while the vehicle was governed by the person that is not considered to be co-insured. Moreover, unless otherwise agreed, the insurer is not obliged to provide indemnification of damage caused by the participation of a vehicle at racing competitions, rallies or practice drives including the official preparation; damages incurred outside Europe.

425. Insurance conditions usually stipulate that the insured loses his/her insurance rights when the vehicle is operated by a driver without a valid licence for that type of vehicle; if the driver is under the influence of alcohol, drugs or other narcotics; if the damage is caused deliberately or fraudulently by the driver, the policyholder, the insured or members of their close family who live in the same household.

426. When the insured is a natural person, co-insured persons are: persons whom the insured left in control of the vehicle, provided that he/she notified the insurer in writing and that the insurer agreed in the form of a written confirmation or by entering the person's name on the insurance policy; persons who live in the same household with the insured; close relatives of the insured (siblings, parents, offspring) even if they do not live in the same household. If the insured is a legal person, co-insured persons are employees of the insured. Knowledge and behaviour of co-insured persons are observed as knowledge and behaviour of the insured.

427. The notion of motor hull insurance usually includes two basic types of insurance: full and partial motor hull insurance. Full insurance covers risks of collision, theft, robbery, damage in the parking lot, impact of objects, storm, fire, explosion, flood, malicious acts of third parties, damage incurred in manifestations, demonstrations, damage to the upholstery of vehicles, earthquakes, damage and glass breakage, etc. Partial motor hull insurance covers only a part of the risk and is contracted with a lower premium. In insurance practice in B&H, motor hull insurance may be concluded with limited duration, for a period of one year or shorter (short-term insurance), limited duration, for a period of over one year or more (perennial insurance), indefinite duration, when insurance continues year after year.

428. According to insurance conditions, the change of the holder of the right to use or ownership right on the insured vehicle results in the termination of the insurance contract on the twenty-fourth hour of the day when the new user or owner has acquired the vehicle. The previous user or owner is entitled to reimbursement of the premium for the unused period of insurance if the insured event had not occurred in the previous period. But, at the explicit written request of the insured, the rights and obligations from the insurance contract can be transferred to a new owner and they last until the expiry of the current insurance period, as decided by the insurer. If there is a change of ownership on the basis of inheritance, the insurance contract does not change.

429. Insurance conditions also stipulate that after the occurrence of the insured event and following the payment of indemnity from insurance, in the case of vehicle damage (partial damage), the vehicle stays insured for the amount of its value. Insurance terminates in the case of vehicle destruction (total loss).

430. Insurance conditions prescribe that agreements relating to the content of the insurance contract are valid only if they are concluded in writing. Furthermore, all notifications and statements that are given under the provisions of the insurance contract must be in written form. However, if the insurer changes the insurance conditions or the premium system, he/she must inform the policyholder in writing, or alternatively through newspapers, radio or television. If the policyholder does not cancel the contract within thirty days, the new insurance conditions or the premium system apply at the beginning of the next insurance period. If the policyholder cancels the contract, the insurance contract becomes invalid upon expiry of the year in which the insurer received cancellation.

431. The purchase price of a new vehicle is relevant for the determination of the premium at the time of contract conclusion. As for subsequent insurance periods (one year), the purchase price is relevant on the date the insurance was issued unless stated otherwise.

432. Upon the occurrence of the insured event resulting in a total loss, the indemnity is determined in a way that the purchase price on the day of determination is reduced to the amount of amortization of the vehicle and the estimated amount of value of the remains. In the case of partial damage, the amount of repair expenditures will be reduced to the market value of the remaining parts that are being replaced. Repair expenditures include the cost of dismantling, installation and transport. If the value of the vehicle is reduced because the value of the remains of the vehicle is lower than repair expenditures, the vehicle is declared destroyed and the damage is calculated as total loss.

433. Generally, motor hull insurance is valid while the vehicle is on the territory of B&H and other European countries members of the green card systems unless otherwise stated.

§3. OTHER TYPES OF MOTOR VEHICLE INSURANCE

434. The insurance of drivers against accidents is voluntary insurance in addition to compulsory motor vehicle liability insurance. It covers damage caused by the use of a motor vehicle, insured under the policy of motor vehicle liability insurance and incurred by the authorized driver due to his/her own fault. It is usually contracted on the policy of motor vehicle liability insurance during vehicle registration. This insurance usually gives coverage for bodily injuries and all legally recognized types of intangible damage. It also covers death and intangible damage, material expenditures of the funeral, headstone and gravesite. The insured sum is autonomous and independent from the insured sum of motor vehicle liability.

435. Roadside assistance insurance represents a special type of protection for the driver and passengers. Namely, it allows the insured to request help in case of malfunctions, accidents and other problems on the roads of B&H and Europe. Roadside assistance in case of accident or malfunction includes the provision of technical assistance, purchase of spare parts, towing service to the nearest workshop, transport of vehicles at home and abroad, and delivery of lost keys. In the case of an adverse event, the insurer covers the expenditures for car rental, continuance of travel or return, overnight accommodation, mediation in contact with court interpreters, lawyers and experts; costs of disposal, transportation and safekeeping of vehicles.

436. Insurance of persons against consequences of accidents in motor vehicles is insurance of the driver and passengers against risks of death or permanent disability as consequences of accidents while driving. Insurance of the driver and passengers from consequences of accidents in motor vehicles is also voluntary insurance, which may be contracted and enclosed with the policies of compulsory insurance and motor hull insurance.

437. Legal aid insurance covers the costs of representation in criminal proceedings and in administrative proceedings. It also covers the costs related to the indemnity claim realization in connection with the traffic accident and costs of defence in relation to the claims for indemnity from other persons. Insurance of legal aid covers besides the insured and the vehicle owner, the driver and passengers in the insured vehicle.

438. Insurance of treatment after injuries in traffic accidents covers all passengers in the vehicle in case they need treatment in a medical institution after injuries sustained in a traffic accident. It also covers accommodation services and meals for up to ten days in a contractual medical institution. This type of motor vehicle insurance may be arranged when concluding the policy of compulsory motor liability insurance.

Part V. Insurance of the Persons

Chapter 1. Workers' Compensation and Occupational Hazards

439. In B&H workers' compensation, insurance policy is not compulsory for employers and injuries, and professional illnesses of workers that occur in the course of their work are primarily covered within the scheme of social security by the compulsory health insurance organized on the level of the Entities (Federation of B&H and the Republic of Srpska) and Brcko District of B&H (BD B&H).[653] However, due to the minimal character of compulsory health insurance, negative effects of workplace injuries or illness may also be covered by voluntary health insurance and private accident insurance.

440. The rights from compulsory health insurance comprise different entitlements depending on the level of government. Thus, compulsory health insurance provides the right to health protection, compensation of salary during the temporary inability to work, reimbursement of travel expenses resulting from the use of health protection and reimbursement of funeral expenses in the Federation of B&H (FB&H) and BD B&H.[654] Compulsory health insurance in the Republic of Srpska (RS) provides rights to health protection and compensation of salary during the worker's temporary inability to work.[655] The ability to exercise the rights of compulsory health protection is conditioned on the payment of contributions by the employer and employees, as they are the main source of their financing.[656] The resources for the realization of rights from compulsory health insurance are also provided from the budget and personal participation of the insured. The funds for health insurance are established at the level of the Entity of RS and Brcko District B&H, and in the FB&H at the level of cantons.

441. Within the complex institutional framework, health insurance is implemented by the Federal Health Insurance and Reinsurance Institute, which controls

653. *See*: the Law on Health Insurance in FB&H, (OJ FB&H, 30/1997, 7/2002, 70/2008, 48/2011, 100/2014 – Decision of Constitutional Court, 36/2018, 61/2022), the Law on Compulsory Health Insurance in RS, (OJ RS, 93/2022, 132/2022), and the Law on Health Insurance in BD B&H, (OJ BD B&H, 19/2020).
654. *See* the Law on Health insurance in FB&H, Arts 31–52 and the Law on Health Insurance in BD B&H, Arts 20–43.
655. *See* the Law on Health Insurance in RS, Art. 3.
656. *See*: the Law on Contributions in FB&H, (OJ FB&H, 35/1998, 54/2000, 16/2001, 37/2001, 1/2002, 17/2006, 14/2008, 91/2015); and Law on contributions in RS (OJ RS, 116/2012, 103/2015).

and monitors ten cantonal health insurance institutes, the Fund of Health Insurance of the RS and by the Fund of Health Insurance of the BD B&H.

442. In insurance practice, private accident insurance is usually offered in the form of collective insurance of workers against consequences of accidents. The employer may conclude a contract of insurance covering: death caused by accident, death caused by disease, permanent disability (permanent loss of general ability to work partial or complete), daily compensation (impermanent disability for work due to an accident), medical and rehabilitation costs, daily compensation of staying in hospital, etc. This insurance may be contracted in two forms: twenty-four-hour insurance, when workers are insured both at work and outside the workplace or in leisure time, and insurance during working hours (it may also cover the time while travelling to work and home from work, business travels, etc.). The premium of collective accident insurance of workers directly depends on the number of workers, work conditions, activities of particular groups of workers and generally the type of activity performed by the company.

Chapter 2. Bodily Injuries

443. In the legal system of B&H, bodily injury insurance is a type of insurance where the insurer is obliged to pay the insured sum or its part to the insured or beneficiary upon the occurrence of a future, uncertain insured event independent of the exclusive will of the insured and which results in one of the contracted forms of insurance in the case of death of the insured due to an accident, complete or partial permanent disability due to an accident, health impairment that results in a temporary inability to work, hospital treatment and/or costs of treatment.

444. The notion of accident is not defined in the relevant insurance legislation but in the insurance conditions. An accident in the general conditions of insurance of B&H's insurers is defined as any sudden, unforeseen event independent of the will of the insured, which suddenly and mainly from the outside impacts the body of the insured resulting in death or bodily injury (complete or permanent disability) of the insured, or a health impairment with temporary inability to work that requires hospital treatment and/or medical costs. In order to consider a certain event as an accident it must be: sudden, independent of the will of the insured and external (outside the body of the insured), abrupt and with the consequence of death, or health complications of the insured (disability).[657] In the context of the above-mentioned definition, the following events are considered accidents: crashes, the impact of an object on the insured, trampling on the insured, an electric shock or being struck by lightning, falls, slips or tumbles, wounds from weapons or other items, stabbings, animal blows or bites, and insect bites except when such stings cause infectious diseases. An accident is also considered to be: food poisoning or poisoning with chemicals due to the insured's ignorance, infection of a wound caused by an accident, poisoning due to the inhalation of gasses or toxic fumes, burns by fire or electricity, hot objects, liquids or steams, acids, alkalis and similar, strangulation or drowning, choking, effects of X-rays or radiation if the insured is exposed suddenly and unexpectedly, except occupational diseases, etc.

445. The LO FB&H/LO RS provides that the insurer is freed from the obligation of the accident insurance contract if the accident was intentionally caused by the insured,[658] or if the accident was caused by war operations.[659] Besides the exclusions stipulated by the LO FB&H/LO RS, insurance conditions usually prescribe exclusion of the following accidents from insurance coverage: accidents intentionally caused by the insured or beneficiary, accidents that occur as a result of suicide or attempted suicide of the insured for any reason, accidents during the preparation, attempt or execution of criminal offences with premeditation or escape upon such actions, accidents caused by the active participation in physical confrontations

657. *See* Curković, Marijan. *Ugovor o osiguranju osoba: život – nezgoda – zdravstveno* (*Contract of Insurance of Persons: Life – Accident – Health*). Zagreb: Inženjerski biro, 2009, 174–175.
658. *See* the LO FB&H/LO RS, Art. 951.
659. *See ibid.*, Art. 952(2).

(except in proven cases of self-defence), accidents caused as a result of bodily injuries at the time of medical treatments or procedures undertaken by the insured, accidents as a result of the beneficiary deliberately causing the death of the insured, accidents as direct or indirect consequences of war operations or events that are consequences of war, invasion, civil war, rebellion, revolution, uprising or similar events as well as a result of acts of terrorism, accidents due to the active participation in armed actions, earthquakes, direct or indirect exposure to ionizing radiation or radioactive contamination.

446. Unless it is specified and the corresponding premium is paid, insurance does not cover consequences of accidents resulting from the steering and driving of aircraft and vessels of all types (except passengers in public transport), recreational parachute jumps, performing professions of dismantling mines, grenades and other explosive devices and mining, training and participation in public sports competitions. The insurer is not obliged to indemnify damages if the insured refuses medical examination by a doctor chosen by the insurer for which the insurer bears all expenses. If an accident occurs as a result of the use of the aircraft, marine vessels, motor and other vehicles without a valid licence or when the insured allows minors or persons without a proper statutory licence to operate a motor vehicle, proven causal link between the intoxication with alcohol, drugs or other intoxicants or medicines and the occurrence of the accident. The insurance beneficiary loses the rights from insurance if the insured's death occurs as a result of disease (heart attack, stroke, liver disease or kidney disease, HIV infection, etc.), diagnosed as a pre-existing condition before the start of the insurance.

447. Upon the occurrence of the insured event, the insurer is obliged to pay the sums agreed in the insurance contract: the total insured sum in the event of death or disability of the insured due to an accident, percentage of the insured sum that corresponds to the percentage of partial disability if partial disability occurred due to an accident, a daily allowance if the insured is temporarily incapable to perform regular work tasks due to an occupational accident, a daily allowance for hospital stay because of treatment of consequences of the accident, and reimbursement of costs of treatment. The amount of the insured sum and allowances are determined by agreement between the insurer and the policyholder and recorded in the insurance policy. The insured sums in the event of death and permanent disability cannot be cumulated. However, the agreed amount for the daily allowances and reimbursement of costs may be combined with the insured sum in the event of death or disability of the insured.

448. Generally, in insurance practice in B&H, persons aged 14 to 65 may be insured against consequences of accidents. Persons younger than 14 years and older than 65 years may be insured only if some special or additional conditions provide that possibility. Persons with a permanent disability resulting from a certain serious disease or persons whose work capacity decreased due to severe illness, serious physical defect or deficiencies, as well as persons with severe physical disabilities or defects are insured upon the payment of increased premiums. Mentally ill persons and persons deprived of the capacity to exercise rights and working ability are in any case excluded from insurance. However, this exclusion is not applicable when they are passengers on public transport. If during the insurance period the insured gains the status of a person that may not be insured, his/her insurance protection ceases immediately and thus the insurance contract is terminated. Insurance in the case of death due to disease may be contracted only for healthy persons.

449. In addition to individual accident insurance, B&H's insurers also offer collective accident insurance of persons (e.g., employees, members of organized groups and associations). This type of insurance may be contracted as twenty-four-hour Insurance and as insurance during working hours only. In the first case, insurance provides coverage during working hours but also outside the workplace and during leisure time. The second type of insurance covers the insured only in a certain capacity (e.g., as employees) or within a certain period of time and during specified activities at the workplace, on the way to work or from work to home, business trips, etc.).

450. The compulsory form of accident insurance is prescribed by the Law on Compulsory Insurances in Traffic (LCIT FB&H)[660] and the Law on Compulsory Insurances in Traffic (LCIT RS).[661] Owners of vehicles used for the public transport of passengers must conclude a contract of insurance of passengers against consequences of accidents except for passengers in air traffic.[662] The laws define notions of passenger and the minimum insured sum. Passengers are defined as persons travelling by means of public transport, regardless of whether they have a ticket or not, including the persons entitled to a free ride. Persons located in stations or docks or in the immediate vicinity of any means of transport are also considered passengers. However, persons to whom the means of transport are a place of work and who are on duty during transport are not considered to be passengers. The minimum insured sums per passenger are stipulated separately for death, permanent loss of general ability to work and the necessary costs of medical treatment in case of temporary inability to work.

451. The passenger or beneficiary affected by the accident may claim indemnity directly from the insurer with whom the insurance contract is concluded, according to the insurance conditions in the event of the passenger's death.[663] The right of the passenger or beneficiary is independent of the existence of the right to indemnity on the basis of the liability of the transportation vehicle's owner for damages caused to third parties.[664] In the case when the owner of the means of transportation has not concluded an insurance contract, which provides coverage against consequences of accidents, the passenger or insurance beneficiary may request indemnification of

660. OJ FB&H, 57/2020, 103/2021.
661. OJ RS, 82/2015.
662. *See* the LICT FB&H, Art. 18(1) and the LICT RS, Art. 16(1).
663. *See* the LICT FB&H, Art. 21(1) and the LICT RS, Art. 19(1).
664. *See* the LICT FB&H, Art. 21(2) and the LICT RS, Art. 19(2).

damages from the Protection Fund in amounts up to the insured sum prescribed by the legislation. These rights cannot be combined with the rights to indemnification of damage caused by the use of unregistered vehicles or vehicles whose owner did not conclude a contract of motor vehicle liability insurance.[665]

665. *See* the LICT FB&H, Art. 21(4) and the LICT RS, Art. 20(2).

Chapter 3. Private Health Insurance

452. Health insurance in B&H is part of a comprehensive system of social security and is generally available in the form of compulsory insurance. Besides provisions on compulsory health insurance, the legal framework for health insurance in FB&H[666] contains provisions on the voluntary health insurance sector, according to which this category of health insurance provides types of healthcare and rights that are not provided within compulsory and extended health insurance.[667]

453. In the FB&H, the conditions and the manner of exercising rights from voluntary health insurance are determined by the institutions of voluntary health insurance.[668] These institutions are financed from the premiums of voluntary health insurance paid by citizens, companies or other legal entities. Furthermore, the Law provides the possibility to establish one or more institutions of voluntary health insurance or other organizations in order to exercise the rights and ensure means for the voluntary health insurance of citizens.[669]

454. Voluntary health insurance activities in B&H are performed by insurance companies engaged in the field of non-life insurance. The kinds of risks within these types of non-life health insurance are specified as additional insurance, travel health insurance, private health insurance and other voluntary forms of health insurance. The same categorization of types of risks within health insurance is stipulated in Article 2 of the Guidelines for implementation of the Insurance Agency of RS: Decision on the types of insurance.[670]

455. Within the life insurance as risk is singled out additional health insurance that is supplementary to the life insurance.[671] Furthermore, classification of life insurance in the legal framework provides that health insurance (accident, illness) is classified as a type of life insurance when it includes conclusion and implementation of the insurance contract, which provides special compensation in the event that a person becomes handicapped as a result of injuries resulting from an accident, or an incident of a certain type, illness or weakness, provided that these contracts are formulated in a way that they shall last for a period of a minimum of five years, or until the normal period of retirement of the person concerned, or without time limit; or that it cannot be terminated by the insurer, or that they are formulated in a way that they may be terminated only under certain conditions stated in the contract.[672] Regarding the classification of non-life insurance in the RS, it is provided that health

666. The Law on Health Insurance, OJ FB&H, no. 30/1997, 7/2002, 70/2008 and 48/2011 – Decision of the CC, 36/2018, 61/2022 and the Law on Compulsory Health Insurance, OJ RS, 93/2022, 132/2022.
667. *See* the Law on Health Insurance in FB&H, Art. 12.
668. *See ibid.*, Art. 78(2).
669. *See ibid.*, Art. 17.
670. OJ RS, 44/2007.
671. *See* the Decision of the Insurance Supervisory Agency of FB&H on Types of Insurance, Art. 4.
672. *See* the LI FB&H, Art. 9(1) of and Decision of the Insurance Agency of RS on Types of Insurance (OJ RS, 57/2006), Art. 5.

insurance includes fixed monetary compensation, compensation corresponding to the amount of damages and a combination of the previous two.[673]

456. Due to the lack of specific provisions that regulate voluntary health insurance in the current legal system, the general provisions of the LO FB&H/LO RS on insurance contracts are applicable and the main source for this type of insurance are conditions of the voluntary health insurance prepared by insurers.

457. In insurance practice in B&H, insurers adopt conditions on voluntary health insurance that vary in terms of their content. Usually, these insurance conditions carry abbreviated names after offered insurance products or a recognizable code in order to ensure easy recognition in numerous insurance programmes. With regard to natural persons, the contract of voluntary health insurance may be concluded in the form of an individual or family insurance policy. Voluntary health insurance in insurance practice may be contracted for persons from 0–65 years of age. With regard to the duration of such insurance, insurance conditions of B&H's insurers usually stipulate that the insurance contract is concluded for a year with automatic extension. The insurance premium depends on the chosen insurance programme and age at the moment of entry into the insurance contract and may be paid annually, semi-annually, quarterly or monthly. It is common for insurers to offer additional benefits when it comes to health insurance, such as discounts for the conclusion of family insurance, discounts in contractual medical institutions, discounts in contractual pharmacies, the possibility to choose medical institutions and doctors according to the wishes of the insured, etc. Furthermore, voluntary health insurance may be concluded in the form of group insurance for which specific benefits are also usually provided.

458. The travel health insurance policy represents one of the most common types of voluntary health insurance in insurance practice of B&H. Within this policy, the insurer provides coverage of immediate medical help that is the result of the insured's illness while he/she is abroad or a result of an accident suffered during that visit. In insurance conditions, the insured event is defined as a necessary medical treatment of the insured person as a result of illness or as a consequence of an accident. The insurer must reimburse the costs of necessary medical treatment incurred during the temporary visit to foreign countries. That treatment includes out-of-hospital treatment, medicines and bandages, medical devices which are part of the treatment of broken body parts or injuries, as well as aids for walking, costs of transportation to the nearest hospital or doctor that is perceived as an emergency, hospital treatment, emergency surgical operations and related costs, etc. Furthermore, with adequate compensation, the insurer is also required to reimburse the extra costs of medically necessary and prescribed transport from a foreign country to a permanent place of residence of the insured person or to the nearest hospital in the region if it is not possible to guarantee the suitable treatment in the context of the current location of the insured, which may result in endangering his/her health. Also, under certain conditions, the cost of accompaniment may be reimbursed by

673. *See* the Decision of the Insurance Agency of the RS on Types of Insurance, Art. 2.

the insurer. In the case of death, the insurer shall reimburse the extra costs of transportation of remains of the deceased back home or extra costs requested for burial in place of death abroad, but without exceeding the amount specified in the terms of travel insurance.

459. Besides the above-mentioned rules on the scope of coverage and subject of insurance, insurers within their insurance conditions regulate in detail other important aspects of the relationship formed within this type of insurance (rules on contract conclusion, beginning and end of insurance, payment of premium, exclusions, procedures in the case of illness or accident, claims processing, obligations, etc.).

Chapter 4. Life Insurance

460. Within the legal system of B&H, there is no legal definition of life insurance contracts. However, given the general definition of insurance contracts contained in Article 897 of the LO FB&H/LO RS and the main characteristics of life insurance, a life insurance contract can be defined as a contract under which the policyholder undertakes the obligation to pay the insurer the agreed insurance premium, and the insurer undertakes the obligation towards the policyholder to pay the agreed insured sum or annuity to the insured or a person designated by him/her (the insurance beneficiary) in case of occurrence of the agreed insured event (death, survivorship, etc.).

461. Generally, features of contemporary life insurance define its legal nature as a specific legal transaction that is easily distinguished from other insurance legal transactions. This is confirmed by a number of specific legal rules (contained in the substantive provisions and in status-organizational provisions), which provide detailed regulations on life insurance.

§1. Individual Life Insurance

462. Individual life insurance is the type of insurance that gives coverage to one person. Individual life insurance policies are created in accordance with specific interests of clients, and therefore numerous variants of individual life insurance policies appear in insurance practice.

463. With respect to insured risk, life insurance is classified into term life insurance, pure endowment insurance and endowment insurance. In the term life insurance, the insured event is the occurrence of death of the insured person and there are two variants of this insurance in insurance practice: lifelong insurance in the event of a death and life insurance in the event of death within the determined period of time (temporary insurance). While in the first case the concept of savings dominates, the element of uncertainty prevails in the second case. In pure endowment insurance, the occurrence of the insured event is related to the survivorship of certain age of the insured. In this type of life insurance, the obligation of the insurer is to pay the insured sum when the insured survives for a certain period of time. Given that in this type of insurance, the key objective of contract conclusion is to ensure security of the insured in the case of old age and that is the reason why it is frequently agreed that the payment should be in the form of annuity. Endowment insurance policy is a combination of life term insurance and pure endowment insurance, which means that it provides coverage against two different risks. Obligation of the insurer to pay the insured sum occurs upon the death of the insured person (in this case the insured sum is paid to his/her beneficiaries) or upon the survivorship of a certain period of time by the insured. This is the most common type of life insurance in practice since it provides security for old age and in the event of death of the insured, it provides security for the insured's heirs.

464. Forms of life insurance linked to different forms of investment of insurance premiums (such as life insurance contracts connected to the investment funds) are not yet developed in insurance practice in B&H.

465. A life insurance contract is created by the agreement of the contracting parties' wills, i.e., it is concluded through the offer made by the policyholder and its acceptance by the insurer. In the conclusion of life insurance contracts, the general rules of law of obligations[674] apply but specific, imperative rules on the conclusion of the insurance contract are also imposed due to its specificity. These rules regulate the offer to conclude the insurance contract (form of the offer, a deadline for which the offer obliges the offeror, acceptance of the offer by silence and the related moment of contract conclusion). The legal definition of the offer is a proposal to conclude the contract made to a certain person, which includes all essential elements of the contract so that its acceptance means the conclusion of the contract.[675] In the case of life insurance, the contract implies essential elements, such as indications of the contracting parties, the risk, determination of the persons exposed to the risk, the insured sum, premium, the duration of insurance coverage, indication of the general and special insurance conditions, etc.[676] Often the conclusion of a life insurance contract is conditioned by a medical examination of the insured when the insured sum exceeds the amount provided by the insurers' tariff or if the insurer demands it.

466. For formation and validity of a life insurance contract, it is necessary for the agreement of contracting parties to be confirmed with the issuance of the insurance policy or the list of coverage (*ad solemnitatem* form). The insurance policy being a mandatory form of contract conclusion, the life insurance contract falls within the category of formal legal transaction. However, there is an exception to this rule. Namely, when the policyholder made a written offer to the insurer to conclude the insurance contract with all the necessary elements, and the insurer does not refuse within the period between eight or thirty days (if medical examination is necessary), it shall be deemed that the insurer accepted the offer and that the contract is concluded.[677] This exception is provided in the general conditions of insurers as a way of concluding a life insurance contract. Furthermore, the second condition whose fulfilment the insurer requests in order to conclude the contract is payment of a premium in full or its first instalment.

467. The policyholder is obliged to accurately and comprehensively inform the insurer on all circumstances known to him/her present at the moment of contract conclusion, and which are essential for the insurer to assess the risk, i.e., to make the decision on whether and under what conditions the life insurance contract shall

674. *See* the LO FB&H/LO RS, Arts 26–45.
675. *See ibid.*, Art. 32(1).
676. *See* Curković, Marijan. *Ugovor o osiguranju osoba: život – nezgoda – zdravstveno* (*Contract of Insurance of Persons: Life – Accident – Health*). Zagreb: Inženjerski biro, 2009, 47.
677. *See* the LO FB&H/LO RS, Art. 901(2) and (3).

be concluded.[678] It is a pre-contractual obligation of the policyholder whose fulfilment does not necessarily result in contract conclusion because the insurer may refuse the offer when he/she becomes aware of the risk. The circumstances regarded as important for risk assessment depend on the specifics of the case, i.e., the object and type of risk against which insurance is provided. The fulfilment of this obligation of policyholder is facilitated by a questionnaire prepared by the insurer, although the policyholder must also report other circumstances relevant to the risk assessment even though they are not listed in the questionnaire. There are special rules that apply to life insurance in case of the incorrect report of the age of the insured,[679] which differ from the general rules because the distinction between conscientious and unconscientious conduct of the policyholder or the insured is not relevant and the consequence of annulment of an insurance contract is complete restitution for both parties.

468. In B&H's legal system, obligation of the insurer to inform the policyholder was for a long time exclusively included in one phase of contract conclusion and only with regard to general and special insurance conditions that form an integral part of the insurance contract.[680] Furthermore, obligation of the insurer apart from the warning on the insurance conditions included their submission to the insured, except in the case when they are printed on the policy.[681] The change in obligations of the insurer happened in 2005 when in the Entities' laws on insurance companies, provisions from the EU legislation were incorporated that regulate pre-contractual information and information during the insurance period, specifying its manner and content.[682]

469. In insurance practice, the policyholder is obliged to report to the insurer the change in circumstances that may affect the increase of risk after the conclusion of the contract. In insurance conditions, the following increased risks are indicated: change of the insured's occupation, exposure to specific dangers, sports activities of the insured, travel to crisis areas and the insured's addiction to alcohol, drugs, medicaments and nicotine.

---

678. According to the Art. 907 of the LO FB&H/LO RS, the policyholder is obliged to report to the insurer all circumstances relevant for the risk assessment that are known to him/her or could not have remained unknown.
679. The following rules are contained in Art. 944 of the LO FB&H/LO RS: the contract is null and void if the actual age of the insured exceeds the limit up to which the insurer performs life insurance; if the actual age does not exceed this limit the contract is valid and the insured sum is reduced in proportion to the agreed premium and premium that is provided for insurance of persons that are of the insured's age. If the contract is annulled, the insurer must return all received premiums; if the contract is valid, the premium shall be reduced and the insurer is obliged to return the difference between the received premiums and premiums to which he is entitled, if the actual age of the insured is higher than reported.
680. *See* the LO FB&H/LO RS, Art. 902(3).
681. *See ibid.*, Art. 902(4).
682. *See* the LI FB&H, Art. 200, and the LIC RS, Art. 24.

470. Payment of the premium represents one of the basic obligations of the policyholder or the insured from the life insurance contract.[683,684] The premium is agreed upon at the moment of contract conclusion and is usually paid in advance in accordance with the agreed deadlines in the insurance contract. Payment of the premium may be arranged in two ways: as a one-time basis payment and payment in instalments. The specificities of the life insurance are expressed in the case of failure to fulfil the obligation of premium payment. Namely the LO FB&H/LO RS provides specific consequences of non-payment of premium: if the policyholder does not pay the insurance premium upon its maturity, the insurer cannot claim the payment of the premium in the judicial proceedings.[685] In order to ensure that the insurer has some kind of protection, the Law provides the possibility to reduce the insured sum to the amount of surrender value of insurance (provided that at least three annual premiums are paid) or to terminate the contract.[686] In order for these consequences to come to a realization, it is necessary to satisfy certain conditions prescribed by the LO FB&H/LO RS: that the policyholder received an invitation to pay the due premium from the insurer, and that the policyholder (or any other interested person) did not pay within the deadline specified in the letter, which may not be shorter than one month from the day when the letter was delivered to him/her. In insurance practice, in accordance with the rule that deviation from the provision of the LO FB&H/LO RS is allowed when it is in the explicit interest of the insured, the insurer often reduces the requested three annual premiums to two.

471. The obligation of the insurer to pay the insured sum or annuity is formed only in the case of the occurrence of the insured event. However, in the case of particular risks, the LO FB&H/LO RS and insurance conditions provide specific provisions that limit insurance coverage. The LO FB&H/LO RS provides the exclusion of the following risks: suicide of the insured,[687] deliberate murder of the insured,[688] war operations[689] and the possibility to exclude other risks by the contract.[690] Furthermore, insurance conditions usually provide that the obligation of the insurer is completely excluded if the insured event occurred because the accident was intentionally caused by the insured, or if the insured event occurred during the preparation, attempt or execution of a criminal offence. It is common that life insurance contracts exclude or limit risks of particularly dangerous occupations, staying in certain countries, risks that are consequences of previous illnesses or accidents, etc.

472. The insurance contract in the case of the death of a third party who is younger than 14 and a person without the capacity to exercise their rights is legally void and the insurer is obliged to return the premium to the policyholder received

683. *See* the LO FB&H/LO RS, Art. 912(1).
684. However, beside the policyholder and the insured another person may appear as premium debtor or as a person interested in the fulfilment of this obligation.
685. *See* the LO FB&H/LO RS, Art. 945(1).
686. *See ibid.*, Art. 945(2).
687. *See ibid.*, Art. 949.
688. *See ibid.*, Art. 950.
689. *See ibid.*, Art. 952.
690. *See ibid.*, Art. 953.

on the basis of such a contract.[691] If a third person is older than 14 but has not reached 18 years of age, in case of the death of that person the insurance contract requires in addition to his/her written consent, the written consent of his/her legal representative.[692]

473. The LO FB&H/LO RS provides special rights to the policyholder of life insurance before the occurrence of the insured event: the right to request the redemption of the insurance policy, the right to request the advance payment and the right to pledge the insurance policy. At the request of the policyholder of life insurance concluded for the lifetime of the insured, the insurer is obliged to pay him/her the surrender value of the insurance policy if at least three annual premiums are previously paid.[693] The policy must state the conditions under which the policyholder may request the payment of its surrender value and the manner in which that value is calculated in accordance with insurance conditions.[694] Under case law in the FB&H the policyholder may not request the surrender value of the insurance policy without the knowledge and consent of the insured if determination of the beneficiary becomes irrevocable, and it is irrelevant from whose funds premiums are paid.[695] According to the LO FB&H/LO RS, the right to request surrender cannot be exercised by the creditors of the policyholder or the insurance beneficiary, but the surrender value must be paid to the beneficiary at his request if determination of the beneficiary is irrevocable.[696] The exception to this rule exists in the case of creditors to whom the insurance policy is pledged, who may request the surrender of the insurance policy if the debt secured by the pledge is not settled on its maturity.[697]

474. At the request of the policyholder of life insurance concluded for the lifetime of the insured, the insurer may pay him/her in advance part of the insured sum up to the surrender value of the insurance policy, which the policyholder may return at a later date.[698] The policyholder is obliged to pay a certain interest rate on the received advance payments.[699] If the policyholder is late with a payment of the due interest rate, the same procedure as in the case of the request of the surrender applies.[700] The insurance policy may stipulate conditions for, the possibility that the sum received in advance is returned to the insurer, the level of interest rate, consequences of non-payment of due interest rate, as specified in the insurance conditions.[701]

691. *See ibid.*, Art. 947(1).
692. *See ibid.*, Art. 947(2).
693. *See ibid.*, Art. 954(1).
694. *See ibid.*, Art. 954(2).
695. HC FB&H, no: 070-0-Rev-07-001079, from 11 Sep. 2008. Report HC FB&H, 2/2008, para. 14 and DSP 33/2009, pp. 31–32.
696. *See* the LO FB&H/LO RS, Art. 954(3).
697. *See ibid.*, Art. 954(1).
698. *See ibid.*, Art. 955(1).
699. *See ibid.*, Art. 955(2).
700. *See ibid.*, Art. 955(3).
701. *See ibid.*, Art. 955(4).

475. Life insurance policies may be pledged.[702] Pledging the insurance policy has an effect towards the insurer only if he/she is informed in writing that the policy is pledged to a certain creditor.[703] When the policy states per order, pledging is performed by means of endorsement.[704]

476. The policyholder determines the insurance beneficiary in the insurance contract, in a later legal transaction (e.g., transfer or intercession) and with a testament. The policyholder has the right to change or revoke the predetermined beneficiary, but that must be done in writing in the form of the insurer that is verified by the public notary. Creditors of the policyholder and the insured are not entitled to the insured sum contracted for the beneficiary unless the policyholder in accordance with the rules changes or revokes the beneficiary.

§2. Group Life Insurance

477. In addition to individual life insurance, there is group life insurance wherein insurance coverage is provided to a certain group of persons. Each insurer determines the highest or lowest number of the insured. Usually, insured persons belong to a particular community (company, association, trade union, etc.) that allows the insurer to balance the risk. Although general rules of the LO FB&H/LO RS apply to group life insurance, there are certain exceptions to the rule (e.g., medical examination is not required).

478. In insurance practice, group life insurance usually provides insurance coverage in the event of a death and survivorship and it is concluded by the same policyholder for the members of a certain group who are connected through some common interest besides the insurance (e.g., the employer for employees, the association for its members). Group life insurance policies are offered in the same form as individual insurance (term life insurance, endowment insurance and pure endowment insurance). The most common form of group life insurance is endowment insurance.

479. Group life insurance is made of multiple insurance contracts and the insurer issues every insured with an individual policy given the rules contained in Article 946(3) of the LO FB&H/LO RS on the validity of the insurance contract concluded for the case of death of a person other than the policyholder. Namely, in order to achieve validity of such an insurance contract it is prescribed that the prior written consent of the insured person is necessary, which is given on the policy or in a separate letter at the moment of signing the insurance policy with an indication of the insured sum.

---

702. *See ibid.*, Art. 956(1).
703. *See ibid.*, Art. 956(2).
704. *See ibid.*, Art. 956(3).

480. Usually, the insured sum is paid upon the expiry of the insurance period, and in the case of the insured's death, the corresponding part of the insured sum is paid. Coverage of group life insurance generally remains in force during the employment/membership period with the policyholder. Group life insurance also offers the possibility of subsequent insurance of new members of a certain community and the substitution of insured persons during the insurance coverage. Premium payment is the obligation of the policyholder, and it may be fulfilled from their own assets or the insured's assets.

Chapter 5. Pension Funds

481. Compulsory public pension schemes are established at the Entities' level as subsystems of the system of social security. Therefore, there are two pension funds regulated by separate laws.[705] Public funds within the compulsory schemes for pension and disability insurance are established as organizations responsible for securing and exercising rights from the pension and disability insurance – rights for old age, reduction and loss of working capacity and death of the insured in order to ensure social security of the insured persons and members of their family.

482. Voluntary pension funds were primarily established only in the RS. The adoption of new legislation in FB&H in 2016[706] was supposed to allow the emergence of voluntary pension funds as the next phase in the development of the pension system and capital markets in the FB&H. Adoption of the new Law on Voluntary Pension Funds (LVPF FB&H)[707] was prompted by problems in the pension system such as limited coverage and low level of compliance with legal obligations, inadequate level of pensions, financial unsustainability of the current pension system, limited administrative capacity and poor management of the institutions within the social security system.

483. The legal framework for the voluntary investment funds in the RS is established by the Law on Voluntary Pension Funds and Pension Plans (LVPFPP).[708]

484. A voluntary pension fund is defined as a collective investment institution within which voluntary pension contributions are collected from the members of the fund and invested in different types of assets in order to generate revenue and reduce the risk of investment. The principles underlying the voluntary pension funds are voluntary membership, equality of members, distribution of the investment risk, transparency, accumulation and investment of funds. The voluntary investment funds may be organized as open or closed voluntary pension funds. The open voluntary pension fund is a collective investment institution that does not have restrictions on membership, other than those prescribed by the Law. However, a closed voluntary pension fund accepts membership requests only from persons who are employed by the employer or members of trade unions or other associations of independent activities.

485. A voluntary pension fund is organized for the purpose of collecting financial assets through voluntary payment of pension contributions from its members

705. The FB&H Law on the Pension and Disability Insurance, OJ FB&H, 29/1998, 49/2000, 32/01, 73/2005 and 59/2006 – replaced with the Law on the Pension and Disability Insurance, OJ FB&H, 13/2018, 93/2019 – Decision of the CC, 90/2021, 19/2022; and the RS Law on the Pension and Disability Insurance, OJ RS, 134/2011, 82/2013 – Decision of the CC, 103/2015, 15/2022, 132/2022.
706. The Law on Voluntary Pension Funds FB&H.
707. OJ FB&H 104/2016.
708. OJ RS, 13/2009/2005, 107/2019.

and investment of these assets in order to increase the value of assets of the voluntary pension fund. A voluntary pension fund is a special kind of fund without the status of a legal person, i.e., the sum of the assets from voluntary contributions and yields from invested assets reduced for the fees charged to the voluntary pension fund. The members of the voluntary pension fund are its owners.

486. Voluntary pension funds are managed by the company for the management of voluntary pension funds (management company) that have the legal form of a closed joint-stock company that may be established by domestic and foreign, natural and legal persons. Nevertheless, natural persons may have only an unqualified share. Provisions of the law that regulate commercial companies in the RS[709] and FB&H are also applicable to the management companies, but they have a subsidiary nature in comparison to the provision of the LVPFPP RS and the LVPF FB&H.[710]

487. One or more financial institutions must own the majority stake in the share capital of the management company. The management company may not issue preferred shares. The initial capital of the management company during the establishment must be at least BAM 2,000,000.00 in the RS/BAM 3,000,000.00 in FB&H and must be paid in full, into a bank account before entering before entering of the management company in the register of business entities. The initial capital of the management company may not originate from loans or credits or be encumbered in any way. The management company can organize and manage multiple open and closed voluntary pension funds. The LVPFPP RS imposes limitations on the operations of the management companies in a way that prescribes that the management company may not have more than 10% of shares in the capital and governance of other legal entities. The management company must inform the Insurance Agency of the RS on the acquisition of such shares. The management company may not be a creditor or assume the obligations under the contract of guarantee. The LVPF FB&H forbids management company from:[711] performing mediation activities in the acquisition and selling of financial instruments; acquiring or selling assets of the funds it manages for its own account or the account of relevant persons; purchasing property with the funds of the fund or enter into legal transactions not provided for by the LVPF FB&H; performing transactions that violate the provisions of the LVPF FB&H, regulations adopted on the basis of the LVPF FB&H and the fund's brochure, including provisions on investment restrictions; disposing of the fund's assets without imbursement; acquiring or disposing of the assets of the funds it manages at a price less favourable than its fair value; directly or indirectly, simultaneously or with a delay, arranging the sale, purchase or transfer of assets between two funds managed by the same management company under conditions different from market conditions or conditions that put one fund in a more favourable position compared to the other; assuming the obligations in connection with assets that are not

709. *See* the RS Company Law (OJ RS, 127/2008, 58/2009, 100/2011).
710. The legal status of the companies managing the voluntary pension funds is regulated in the Arts 4–27 and 61–64 of the LVPFPP RS and Arts 4–41 of the LVPF FB&H.
711. *See* Art. 32 of the LVPF FB&H.

owned by the fund at the time of assuming these obligations, with the exception of: transactions with financial instruments performed on a regulated market or another market whose rules enable the delivery of financial instruments with simultaneous payment; and transactions for which simultaneous delivery of financial instruments is not possible or are not normally performed through the settlement system with simultaneous payment, whereby the management company must establish appropriate procedures, procedures and measures for the purpose of controlling settlement risk.

488. The Insurance Agency of the RS issues licences for the operations of the management company and organization and management of the fund in accordance with the conditions prescribed by Articles 9–13 of the LVPFPP RS. However, in FB&H, Securities Commission issues authorization for operations of the management company as well as for organization and management of the fund on the basis of requirements prescribed in Articles 11–15 of the LVPF FB&H.

489. The assets of voluntary pension funds are owned by their members in proportion to their share of the assets and are completely separate from the assets of the management company that manages that fund. The voluntary fund's assets must be kept in an account of the custodian bank. The assets of the voluntary pension funds may not be subject to forced collection, a pledge, or mortgage, may not be included in the liquidation or bankruptcy estate of the management company or be used for the payment of the voluntary fund's obligations to third parties.

490. The rules on the investment of assets of the voluntary investment funds (the investment principle, investment policy, modes and amounts of investment, limitations of investment, etc.) are contained in Articles 41–47 of the LVPFPP RS and in Articles 45–57 of the LVPF FB&H.

491. Domestic and foreign natural persons may be members of one or more voluntary pension funds. In order to join an open, voluntary pension fund, a person must conclude a membership contract and sign a statement confirming that he/she fully understands the terms and fees charged. If one person is a member of several voluntary pension funds, he/she must conclude a special membership contract for every voluntary pension fund. Membership of a voluntary pension fund is not conditioned by the payment of contributions, and he/she remains a member even if they stop making payments. The management company has the discretion to refuse membership to the voluntary pension fund that it manages except when a person joins the voluntary pension fund by accession to the pension plan or closed voluntary pension fund.

492. Pension contribution in the voluntary pension fund may be paid by: a natural person or another person on behalf of a natural person, the organizer in their name and on behalf of the employee or a member of the trade union, and the employer in the name and on behalf of the employee, in accordance with the membership contract concluded between the member of the voluntary pension fund and the management company. The total value of all accounting units (investment units in FB&H) of the voluntary pension fund is equal to the net asset value of the voluntary pension fund. The paid pension funds are converted into accounting (investment) units on the same day when they are paid by recording the unit on the individual account of the voluntary pension fund's member. The accounting (investment) units may be expressed in parts.

493. On the basis of the acquired accounting (investment) units, a member of the voluntary pension fund has the following rights: the right to withdraw and dispose of accumulated funds, the right to a proportional part of the yield from the investment, the right to a proportional part of the assets of the voluntary pension fund in the case of the dissolution of the fund and other rights in accordance with the Entities' laws. A member of the voluntary pension fund does not have the right to vote on the basis of the accounting (investment) unit. The accounting (investment) unit is documented on the individual account of a member in the form of electronic recording in the information system of the management company. The management company publishes the value of the accounting (investment) units on its or voluntary pension fund's website on a daily basis and at least once a month in a newspaper distributed in the entire territory of the Entity/B&H.

494. According to the provisions of the LVPFPP RS, a member of the voluntary pension fund is entitled to withdraw and dispose of the accumulated assets (supplementary pension) at the age of 58 years regardless of the period of accumulation or at the age of 53 and at least five years of accumulation in continuity or sixty monthly payments in the period of the accumulation of assets. However, these conditions for the rights to withdrawal and disposal of the accumulated assets do not apply in the case of extraordinary medical expenses or permanent inability to work when assets may be withdrawn and disposed of earlier. However, a member must begin to withdraw and dispose of the accumulated assets no later than the age of 70. Accumulated assets may be withdrawn by a lump sum payment, scheduled payment, purchase of the annuity or by a combination of both methods. Scheduled payments are executed on the basis of the contract concluded between the management company and the member of the voluntary pension fund, in the standardized form prescribed by the Agency. This kind of payment ceases when the entire amount accumulated on the account of the member is paid. The management company, acting on behalf and for the account of the member of a voluntary pension fund transfers his/her assets to the insurance company and purchases the annuity while withdrawing and disposing of accumulated assets through the purchase of annuities. In the event of the death of a member of the voluntary pension fund, assets on his/her account shall be transferred in accordance with the legislation on inheritance.

495. Correspondingly, the LVPF FB&H also prescribes that fund members can exercise rights from voluntary pension insurance (exercise of the right to pension) the earliest at the age of 58. Exceptionally, the right to a pension can be realized even earlier in case of death, under the conditions of the contract from Article 65 and Article 92 of the LVPF FB&H. In the event of the death of a member of the fund before retirement, the funds accumulated in his/her account will be distributed according to the written statement of the member of the pension fund in accordance with the membership agreement. In the absence of a written statement, the funds accumulated in the account will be subject to inheritance proceedings. By exercising the right to pension the fund member chooses the method of pension payment, which can be: temporary or lifelong. An insurance company that disburses pensions under voluntary pension insurance is required to offer a lifetime age pension, and may also offer temporary age pension, variable pension, partial lump sum payments and other types of pensions under its pension scheme.[712] An insurance company that pays pensions within the framework of voluntary pension insurance is obliged to conclude a written pension contract with each member of the voluntary pension fund who chooses that insurance company.

496. An employer, association of employers, professional association and trade union may organize a pension plan (i.e., programme in FB&H) and conclude a contract with one or more management companies, under which they are obliged to make payments of pension contributions on behalf of employees or members of trade unions or associations. An employer can organize a pension programme only for its employees. The management company is obliged to invest the collected funds and allow the withdrawal and disposal of accumulated assets to the members of the plan (programme). According to the LVPFPP RS, a pension plan is an integral part of an open voluntary pension fund managed by the management company with whom the contract on accession to the voluntary pension fund is concluded. A member of the pension plan is also a member of the open voluntary pension fund, with the rights and obligations stipulated by law and the contract on the organization of the pension plan. The conditions and the procedure for the organization and functioning of pension plans are determined by the Minister of Social and Labour Affairs of the RS. The LVPF FB&H stipulates the possibility of establishment of a voluntary pension fund as a closed voluntary fund, and in this case, it can accept applications for membership only from persons who are: employees of an employer who sponsors a voluntary pension fund, or members of the trade union sponsoring the voluntary pension fund.

497. The Insurance Agency of RS is authorized for the supervision of implementation of the Law on the Voluntary Pension Funds and Pension Plans as well as for the adoption of by-laws and governing relevant registries (registry of management companies and registry of voluntary pension funds). Furthermore, the Agency protects interests of the members of the voluntary pension funds, educates the public and improves voluntary pension insurance. The Insurance Agency of the RS is also authorized to issue and revoke licenses for the performance of voluntary pension insurance, to exercise control and supervision of the legality of the management companies and to perform other activities and measures in accordance with the Law.

498. In the FB&H, the Securities Commission has the authority to oversee implementation of the Law, adopt by-laws and govern the Register of Voluntary

712. *See* Art. 104(2)–(5) of the LVPF FB&H.

Pension Funds.[713] However, supervision of insurance companies[714] in the context of payment of the fund member's pension[715] is carried out by the Insurance Supervision Agency of the FB&H in accordance with the LVPF FB&H and the LI FB&H and other by-laws governing the field of insurance.[716]

499. Securities Commission's oversight is performed through indirect control, i.e., by collecting, monitoring and verifying the reports and notifications submitted to the Commission in accordance with the LVPF FB&H, and direct control.[717]

500. If during oversight the Securities Commission determines that there are legal entities, which perform the activities of a management company or operate as voluntary pension funds, without authorization or registration on the basis of the LVPF FB&H, it will prohibit their activities and take other measures,[718] such as issuance of a written warning or order for the elimination of established irregularities, and withdrawal of permission to the appointment of a member of the executive board of the management company.[719] Exceptionally, if during the course of performing direct or indirect control, the Commission assesses that the management company has committed serious irregularities, i.e., that its financial condition or the financial condition of the voluntary pension fund has significantly deteriorated, or that there is this possibility for that as well as the possibility of a significant deterioration of their liquidity, or when it ascertains that this is necessary for the protection of the assets of the members of the voluntary pension fund, it will order the management company to undertake one or more activities from Article 115 of the LVPF FB&H.[720,721] When performing oversight, the Commission has the right to inspect the business books and other documentation of legal entities that are related parties to the management company subjected to oversight and may require those persons to provide it with other information of importance for oversight.[722]

713. *See* Art. 110(1) of the LVPF FB&H.
714. The pension is paid by an insurance company that has the authorization of the Agency for the performance of life insurance business operations and that has consent to perform a part of the operations in the field of voluntary pensions. *See* Art. 103(3) of the LVPF FB&H.
715. *See* Art. 103 of the LVPF FB&H.
716. *See* Art. 118 of the LVPF FB&H.
717. *See* Art. 111(1) of the LVPF FB&H.
718. *See* Art. 111(2) of the LVPF FB&H.
719. *See* Art. 112(1) of the LVPF FB&H.
720. Namely without the prior consent of the Commission, management company does not manage the assets of the voluntary pension fund or dispose of its assets; temporary suspension of the conclusion of new contracts on membership i.e., the pension program; temporary suspension the collection of compensations; suspension of the implementation of the decisions of the executive board and the assembly of the management company without the approval of the Commission; suspension of the receipt of new payments based on already concluded contracts; suspension of receipt of new payments on the basis of already concluded contracts.
721. *See* Art. 113 of the LVPF FB&H.
722. *See* Art. 111(5) of the LVPF FB&H.

Part VI. Social Security

501. In general terms, the term 'social security' in B&H's law refers to the wider area otherwise identified as social insurance, representing efforts to extend social insurance coverage, as a general system set up through legislation that provides compulsory material protection and security for the employees and the other insured persons, as well as members of their families in cases provided for by the social insurance regulations, to the largest possible number of the insureds and to broaden the social insurance payments in certain areas of social insurance.[723] The social security system is financed by contributions from wages and paid by both employees and employers, as part of different insurance programmes and using different rates in the FB&H, the RS and the BD B&H.

502. The FB&H Law on Contributions[724] sets up a system of compulsory contributions, as the basic instruments for financing the compulsory: pension and disability insurance, health insurance and unemployment insurance, as well as the ceiling for contribution rates in the FB&H.[725] However, the RS Law on Contributions[726] regulates the system of compulsory contributions which are also used to fund child protection payments, in addition to pension and disability insurance, health insurance and unemployment insurance.[727]

503. In the FB&H, the contribution rate amounts to 42.5% in total, taking into account both contributions paid by employees (31.03%) and employers (11.5%). In the RS, the contribution rate amounts to 33% and is in full paid by the employees. Depending on the health insurance programme chosen by an employee in the BD B&H, the contribution rate can amount to either 37.5% or 32% in total. In addition, the personal income tax rate is 10% in both the FB&H and the RS.[728]

723. *See*: Sead Dedić, *Socijalno pravo (Social security Law)* (Sarajevo: Pravni fakultet Univerziteta u Sarajevu, 2003), 54 and 56.
724. OJ FB&H, 35/1998, 54/2000, 16/2001, 37/2001, 1/2002, 17/2006, 14/2008, 91/2015, 104/2016, 34/2018, 99/2019, 4/2021, 6/2023.
725. *See* the Law on Contributions, Art. 1(1).
726. OJ RS, 114/2017, 112/2019, 49/2021, 119/2021, 56/2022, 132/2022.
727. *See* the Law on Contributions RS, Art. 1.
728. *See* the Law on Personal Income Tax (OJ FB&H, 10/2008, 9/2010, 44/2011, 7/2013 and 65/2013), Art. 9, and the Law on Income Tax (OJ RS, 60/2015, 66/2018, 105/2019, 123/2020, 49/2021, 119/2021, 56/22.), Art. 4.

§1. UNEMPLOYMENT INSURANCE

504. In terms of the unemployment insurance system in B&H, all eligible insured persons who are unemployed are entitled to unemployment compensation in the form of pecuniary payment by the Employment Bureau, i.e., Services, as well as payment of the contributions for the health and pension insurances on their behalf.[729]

505. In the FB&H, the system of unemployment insurance was set up by the Law on Mediation in Employment and Social Security of Unemployed Persons in the FB&H (LMESSUP FB&H).[730] The Ministry of Labour and Social Policy is responsible for formulating policies related to unemployment compensations, while the Federal Employment Bureau and Cantonal Employment Services implement activities. The unemployment insurance compensations in the FB&H amount to 0.5% for employers and 1.5% for employees.[731]

506. All employed persons who had been paying contributions for unemployment insurance prior to employment termination are entitled to unemployment compensation. An unemployed person is a person who is able to work and is not employed, and who: has no enterprise or other legal entity registered to his/her name, i.e., not earning a dividend based on shares in an enterprise or other legal entity; has no crafts registered; is not engaged in agricultural activity; does not have a pension in line with regulation on pension and disability insurance; is not a regular high school or university student; has no income from any source; and is actively looking for work.[732] According to the provision from Article 3.a. of the LMESSUP FB&H, an unemployed person is deemed to be actively looking for work, if he/she: regularly reports to the employment service; sends applications for work to employers or issues advertisements and responds to advertisements and vacancies; and follows the programme of professional orientation, training and re-qualification.

507. In addition to the previously listed requirements, in order for the unemployed person to be entitled to pecuniary compensation while unemployed, he/she is required also to have had at least eight months of uninterrupted employment or eight months intermittently during the period of the last eighteen months at the moment of employment termination.[733]

508. Those unemployed who meet the above-listed requirements are eligible for pecuniary unemployment compensation, proportionate to their length of service. An unemployed person acquires the right to pecuniary compensation if he/she reports and files a request within thirty days from employment termination, i.e., from the

729. UNICEF, *Analiza nedostataka u oblasti politika socijalne zaštite i inkluzije u BiH (Analysis of the Shortcomings in the Area of Social Protection and Inclusion Policies in B&H)*, http://www.unicef.org/bih/ba/GAPanaliza.pdf (accessed 15 Sep. 2015), 45.
730. OJ FB&H, 55/2000, 41/2001, 22/2005, 09/2008.
731. *See* the Law on Contributions FB&H, Art. 10(1).
732. *See* the LMESSUP FB&H, Art. 3(1).
733. *See ibid.*, Art. 29(1).

day of discontinuing craft or business activity.[734] The compensations paid amount to 40% of the average monthly wage earned in the FB&H, over the previous three months. The periods during which pecuniary compensation is received vary depending on the length of service and are stipulated in Article 30(2) of the LMESSUP FB&H. The compensation is paid monthly. Unemployed person eligible for pecuniary compensation may, at his/her own request, receive one-off compensation, depending on established length of the compensation right in line with Article 30 of the LMESSUP FB&H, on account of wanting to set up, independently or in partnership with another person, an enterprise, shop or perform some other activity as a self-employed person.[735]

509. In the RS, the Ministry of Labour and War Veterans and Disabled Persons' Protection is in charge of the unemployment system, and the RS Employment Bureau is the key institution in terms of the implementation of the unemployment insurance system. The legislative framework for unemployment insurance in RS consists of the provisions from the RS Law on Employment Mediation and Rights During Unemployment (LEMRDU RS)[736] and the Law on Professional Rehabilitation, Training and Employment of Disabled Persons.[737] Contributions for unemployment insurance are paid in the amount of 1% by employees[738,739] while employers do not pay this contribution at all.[740]

510. All employed persons who had been paying contributions for unemployment insurance are eligible for unemployment compensation, provided they meet certain requirements.[741] Unemployed persons, for the purpose of this Law, are identified as persons registered with the Unemployment Bureau, aged 15–65, with full or limited ability to work, who are not employed or exercising in some other way the right to labour.[742] Furthermore, the given person must be actively looking for work and be available for work.[743] Pupils, full-time students, pensioners, holders of commercial agricultural households, in line with the Law on Agriculture[744] and persons with inactive employment rights, are not considered unemployed persons for the purpose of this Law.[745]

511. In addition to the above-outlined requirements, the beneficiary must also have been paying the unemployment insurance contributions over the period of

734. *See ibid.*, Art. 33(1).
735. *See ibid.*, Art. 30.a.
736. OJ RS, 30/2010, 102/2012, 94/2019.
737. *Ibid.*, 37/2012.
738. *See* the Law on contributions RS, Art. 8.
739. OJ RS, 116/12.
740. *See* the Law on Contributions RS, Art. 4.
741. *See* the LEMRDU RS, Arts 34–36.
742. *See ibid.*, Art. 4(1).
743. *See ibid.*, Art. 4(2).
744. OJ RS, 70/2006, 20/2007, 86/2007, 71/2009.
745. *See* the LEMRDU RS, Art. 4(5).

eight months unintermitted over the past twelve months or for at least twelve months intermittently over the period of the last eighteen months prior to employment termination.[746]

512. In the RS, the compensation is paid after a thirty-day period of waiting from the day of employment termination. The amount of pecuniary compensation depends on the length of service insurance of the compensation beneficiary.[747] According to Article 47(1) of the LEMRDU RS, pecuniary compensation is paid monthly in the amount that equals 35% of the average wage which the person earned over the last three months for persons with a record of up to fifteen years of the length of service insurance, or 40% of the average wage for those with over fifteen years of the length of service insurance. The amount of pecuniary compensation may not be under 20% of the average wage paid in the RS, in the previous quarter, in line with data from the Agency for Statistics, nor higher than the amount of one average wage paid in the RS.[748] The period during which pecuniary compensation is paid varies depending on the length of service insurance and may be paid for a minimum of one and a maximum of twelve months.[749]

513. The system of unemployment insurance has also been set up in the area of the BD B&H. The legislative framework for unemployment insurance in the BD B&H is set up by the Law on Employment and Rights During Unemployment (LERDU BD B&H).[750] The amount of contributions in the BD B&H is 1.5% of the gross salary of the employed persons; this is covered by the employer.

514. In line with the LERDU BD B&H, each person registered with the BD B&H Employment Bureau for the purpose of looking for work is entitled to be informed on the possibilities and requirements for employment, mediation for the purpose of obtaining employment, advice on the choice of profession and professional orientation, skilled qualification, training and preparation for employment.[751] In addition to the above-listed rights, the unemployed person whose employment for the purpose of labour regulation terminated without his/her own request, agreement or fault, or whose insurance terminated in a different way, with at least eight months of continuous insurance payment during the past twelve months, or twelve months with interruptions during the past eighteen months, has the right to pecuniary compensation, health insurance, and pension and disability insurance.[752] The unemployed exercise their right to pecuniary compensation at the Employment Bureau, while the rights to health, pension and disability insurance are regulated by the relevant public fund in line with regulations of the BD B&H.

746. *See ibid.*, Art. 36.
747. *See ibid.*, Art. 38(3).
748. *See ibid.*, Art. 47(2).
749. *See ibid.*, Art. 39(1).
750. OJ BD B&H, 33/2004, 19/2007, 25/2008.
751. *See* the LERDU BD B&H, Art. 26.
752. *See ibid.*, Art. 27(1).

515. The rights of unemployed persons stipulated in Article 27 of the LERDU BD B&H are conditioned by the payment of unemployment contribution by the employer, during the minimum prescribed length of service insurance.[753] Furthermore, all employees who have been making unemployment contributions have the right to unemployment compensation, provided they meet certain conditions: the beneficiary must be over 15 years of age, i.e., able to work and be eligible for employment in line with labour legislation, be unemployed and actively seek employment, be registered with the unemployment register maintained by the BD B&H Employment Bureau, not be engaged in independent professional business or enterprise and not be a full-time student or pensioner.[754] A person who is actively seeking employment is identified as a person who, in line with the deadlines stipulated by the general acts of the Employment Bureau, reports to the professional service of the Bureau to obtain information on employment opportunities and communicates to employers and employment agencies on his/her own.[755]

516. Pecuniary compensations are paid after a waiting period of fifteen days following the employment termination. The compensation amount depends on the beneficiary's length of service insurance, and it is paid in the amount of 35% of the average wage which the person earned for those persons with up to ten years of length of service insurance or 40% of the average wage for those with over ten years of the length of service insurance.[756] The amount of monthly compensation cannot be set to be lower than 20% of the average salary in the BD B&H, nor higher than the amount of one average wage in the BD B&H.[757]

517. Those persons without compulsory unemployment insurance may obtain voluntary insurance, under conditions stipulated by the Employment Bureau. However, a person with voluntary insurance may not have a larger volume of rights than the rights provided to persons with compulsory insurance, in line with the LERDU BD B&H.[758]

§2. Health Insurance

518. The health system in B&H is based on the principles of social insurance financed by health insurance contributions of the employed and the public employment services, on behalf of the unemployed, and Bureau or the Pension Fund on behalf of the retired persons.[759] The Health Insurance Funds have been established at the Entity level in the RS and in the BD B&H, and at the level of Cantons in the FB&H.

753. *See ibid.*, Art. 28.
754. *See ibid.*, Art. 4(1) and (3).
755. *See ibid.*, Art. 4(2).
756. *See ibid.*, Art. 36.
757. *See ibid.*, Art. 36(2).
758. *See ibid.*, Art. 25.
759. UNICEF, *Analiza nedostataka u oblasti politika socijalne zaštite i inkluzije u BiH (Analysis of the Shortcomings in the Area of Social Protection and Inclusion Policies in B&H)*, 54.

519. In the FB&H, the legislative framework for health insurance consists of the provisions contained in: the Law on Health Insurance FB&H (LHI FB&H),[760] the Law on Health Protection FB&H (LHP FB&H),[761] the Decision on establishment of the basic package of health rights[762] and the Decision on maximum amounts of direct participation of insured persons in the costs of using certain types of health protection in the basic package of health rights.[763]

520. Health protection encompasses a system of social, group and individual measures, services and activities for the preservation and improvement of health, disease prevention, early detection, timely treatment and healthcare and rehabilitation, as well as the application of health technologies.[764] Each person in the FB&H has the right to health protection and the possibility of exercising the highest level of health, in line with provisions of the LHP FB&H and the LHI FB&H, as well as regulation adopted based on these laws. In the FB&H, health protection is provided and implemented by health institutions, private practice offices, Health Insurance Institutes, Agency for quality and accreditation in health in the FB&H, health chambers, employers and other institutions, humanitarian, religious, sports and other organizations, associations, families and citizens.[765]

521. The health protection programme is funded by revenues collected on account of health insurance contributions, the FB&H budget, cantonal budgets, participation of the health protection beneficiaries in covering some or total costs of the health protection, and other sources in a manner and under conditions stipulated by legislation.

522. According to the LHI FB&H, health insurance as a part of the social insurance of citizens, makes up a single system within which citizens invest funds, based on principles of reciprocity and solidarity, obligatorily in the Cantons ensure exercising of their rights to health protection and other forms of insurance in the way that has been stipulated by the Law, other legislation and other regulation passed based on the Law.[766]

523. Under the conditions stipulated in the Law and other legislation and regulation adopted based on the Law, citizens of the FB&H have the right to health insurance which includes: compulsory health insurance, extended health insurance and voluntary health insurance.[767] Employed persons and other persons performing certain business or having particular capacity, have the right to compulsory health insurance covered under this Law.[768] The right to compulsory health insurance is

760. OJ FB&H, 30/1997, 7/2002, 70/2008, 48/2011, 100/2014 – Decision of CC, 36/2018, 61/2022.
761. OJ FB&H, 46/2010, 75/2013.
762. OJ FB&H, 21/2009.
763. *Ibid.*
764. *See* the LHP FB&H, Art. 2(1).
765. *See ibid.* Art. 4.
766. *See* the LHI FB&H, Art. 1.
767. *See ibid.*, Art. 2.
768. *See ibid.*, Art. 3.

also provided to family members of the insured, in cases stipulated by this Law.[769] Compulsory health insurance ensures the insured and their family members (insured persons) the right to use health protection and the right to pecuniary compensation and assistance in line with this Law.

524. The compulsory health insurance is based on the principles of reciprocity and solidarity of the insured primarily at the Cantonal level,[770] and at the level of two or more Cantons in FB&H, in cases and under conditions stipulated by the Law.[771] The rights enjoyed by the insured in line with this Law cannot be changed through a contract, transferred to other persons, or inherited.[772] Exception from the above stated are pecuniary compensations from compulsory health insurance which are due for payment but remained unpaid due to the death of the insured person and may be subject to inheritance.[773] For the purpose of ensuring the rights related to health protection, i.e., the scope of rights not covered by compulsory health insurance, the Cantonal legislative body may introduce extended health insurance.[774]

525. The rights from compulsory health insurance are financed by the Fund for Compulsory Health Insurance, if their use is in line with what is stipulated in the Law and regulations adopted based on the Law.[775]

526. Citizens may obtain types of health protection and the rights not provided through compulsory and extended health insurance *via* voluntary health insurance.[776]

527. In terms of the institutional framework for health insurance, the Federal Institute of Health Insurance and Re-Insurance controls and oversees the work of ten cantonal health insurance institutes.[777] The responsibility for health protection policy has been decentralized to ten cantonal health ministries.

528. In the FB&H, payment of health insurance contributions and payment of expenditures for health protection is done at the cantonal level. The employees make payments for health insurance based on the amount they receive as wage. The Employment Services make health insurance payments for persons registered as unemployed.

529. Funds for exercising of the rights guaranteed under compulsory health insurance are provided through contributions which are used to set up Health

769. *See ibid.*, Art. 4.
770. *See ibid.*, Art. 6(1).
771. *See ibid.*, Art. 6(2).
772. *See ibid.*, Art. 7(1).
773. *See ibid.*, Art. 7(2).
774. *See ibid.*, Art. 8.
775. *See ibid.*, Art. 9.
776. *See ibid.*, Art. 12.
777. *See ibid.*, Arts 15–16 and 18.

Insurance Funds under the Cantonal Health Insurance Institutes.[778] Funds for exercising rights guaranteed under the extended health insurance are provided through additional contributions in line with Cantonal regulations.[779] Funds for voluntary health insurance are provided by citizens themselves or through companies, institutions or in another way in which they decide on their own to join funds for this type of insurance.[780]

530. In line with the LHI FB&H, compulsory health insurance covers the following categories of insured persons: the insured (groups of the insured are specified in Article 19), members of the families of the insured[781,782] as well as other persons insured under certain circumstances.[783,784]

531. Compulsory health insurance, in cases and under conditions stipulated in the LHI FB&H, provides the insured with the following: health protection, compensation for salaries and travel costs related to health protection use; to members of the family of the insured: health protection and compensation of costs related to use of health protection.[785]

532. The right to compulsory health insurance may be exercised only by the person with the established capacity of the insured person.[786] The capacity of the insured person is established by the cantonal insurance institute, and verified by special accreditation.[787]

533. Money for financing of the rights related to compulsory health insurance is provided from different sources, listed in Article 80 of the LHI FB&H and may be in general terms classified as contributions, budget funds and personal participation of the insured.

534. Through voluntary health insurance insured citizens may secure, for themselves and their family members, additional rights related to health protection,

778. *See ibid.*, Art. 13(1).
779. *See ibid.*, Art. 13(2).
780. *See ibid.*, Art. 13(3).
781. These are: spouse, children, parents, if dependants, grandchildren, brothers, sisters, grandfather and grandmother, if unable to live and work independently and if without means to secure own livelihood, so they are taken care of by the insured. The above-listed family members acquire the right to compulsory health insurance based on this Law, provided they do not exercise the same right based on employment or engagement of business or non-business activity, personal engagement or agriculture (*See* the LHI FB&H, Art. 19(2)).
782. *See* the LHI FB&H, Art. 20.
783. These are: persons engaged in organized public works in the territory of FB&H; persons under compulsory civil protection service or monitoring and information service; persons who perform tasks related to regulation on fire protection, as part of the operational teams of voluntary firemen organizations.
784. *See* the LHI FB&H, Art. 24.
785. *See ibid.*, Art. 31.
786. *See ibid.*, Art. 53(1).
787. *See ibid.*, Art. 53(2).

which are not included under the compulsory health insurance.[788] The conditions and manner of use of the rights from voluntary health insurance are established by the institutes of voluntary health insurance,[789] funded by the voluntary health insurance premiums paid by the citizens, enterprises or other legal entities.[790]

535. Patients participate in costs of all health protection services, including the hospitals, at an average rate of 10%–20%, depending on the type of health service prescribed by the insurance and in line with the Decision on maximum amounts of direct participation of insured persons in the costs of using certain types of health protection in the basic package of the health rights.

536. Furthermore, compulsory health reinsurance has also been organized and implemented in the FB&H.[791] Risks subject to compulsory reinsurance are risks emerging as a result of natural disasters (floods, earthquakes, and fires) and wide-scope epidemics.[792] From the funds earned from reinsurance premiums, the Federation Institute of Insurance and Reinsurance establishes a fund of health reinsurance for the Federation.[793]

537. Similarly, to the FB&H, the RS has a separate legislative and institutional framework of health protection, which unlike the one in the FB&H has set up a centralized system of health protection. The RS Ministry of Health and Social Welfare is in charge of the health protection system in the RS. The legislative framework for health insurance in the RS consists of the RS Law on Compulsory Health Insurance (LCHI RS)[794] and the RS Law on Health Protection (LHP RS).[795]

538. Health protection represents a group of services and activities for the improvement and preservation of the health of people, prevention of diseases and injuries, early detection of diseases, timely treatment and rehabilitation.[796] Health protection is provided at the level of the RS, units of local self-governance and employers *via* the undertaking of specific activities related to the promotion of health, prevention and treatment of diseases and conditions, rehabilitation of the diseased and injured, provision of drugs and medical agents, protection of living and working environment and other specific activities.[797] At the level of the RS, health protection is provided under equal terms, to population and nosological groups of particular social and medical importance.[798] Foreign nationals or persons without citizenship status enjoy the right to health protection in line with provisions of the

788. *See ibid.*, Art. 78(1).
789. *See ibid.*, Art. 78(2).
790. *See ibid.*, Art. 79.
791. *See ibid.*, Art. 91.
792. *See ibid.*, Art. 92(2).
793. *See ibid.*, Art. 93(1).
794. OJ RS, 93/2022, 132/2022.
795. *Ibid.*, 57/2022.
796. *See* the LHP RS, Art. 2(2).
797. *See ibid.*, Art. 25.
798. *See ibid.*, Art. 28(1).

LHP, international agreements and other regulations regulating this area.[799] Health protection is exercised at primary, secondary and tertiary levels.[800] A special form of population health protection is exercised through the organization of the public health system.[801] The health protection is partly financed by the Health Insurance Fund, and partly by the municipality.

539. The LHI RS stipulates that all citizens are covered by compulsory health insurance.[802] The principle of obligation implies that all citizens must have registered health insurance, based on one of the cases stipulated by the LHI RS. The rights related to health insurance include health protection, compensation of wages for the duration of temporary work inability, and the other rights as set forth in the law and acts of the Fund.[803] The rights related to health insurance cannot be transferred to other persons, changed through a contract or inherited.[804] Exercising the rights from compulsory health insurance is conditioned by payment of the health insurance contributions, with the exceptions stipulated in the Article 20 of the LCHI RS. These categories of citizens are able to exercise the rights from compulsory health insurance even if the payment of contributions has not been made, provided that they are registered for health insurance.

540. The insureds, covered by compulsory health insurance, are divided into several groups. The first group consists of the insured, i.e., persons in whose name the contribution for compulsory health insurance is paid.[805] The second group consists of family members of the insured, who have insurance via the insurance holder (the insured) and no health insurance contribution is paid for them.[806] The third group consists of persons insured only for cases of occupational illness and injury at work.[807] The fourth group consists of the other persons covered with compulsory health insurance (a child up to the age of 18, school children and students until the end of their schooling until the age of 26; a woman in the process of family planning, during pregnancy, childbirth and maternity up to twelve months after childbirth, that is, for twins, or the third and every subsequent child up to eighteen months after childbirth; a person older than 65 years; a person with a disability etc.).[808] The fifth group includes foreign nationals whose coverage is insured via signed international agreements on social insurance.[809]

799. *See ibid.*, Art. 55.
800. *See ibid.*, Art. 35(1).
801. *See ibid.*, Art. 35(2).
802. *See* the LCHI RS, Art. 2.
803. *See ibid.*, Art. 4(1).
804. *See ibid.*, Art. 4(2).
805. *See ibid.*, Arts 15–21.
806. *See ibid.*, Art. 19.
807. *See ibid.*, Art. 17.
808. *See ibid.*, Art. 20.
809. *See ibid.*, Art. 21.

541. Health insurance contributions are paid by employees, i.e., employment bureaus in case of unemployed persons, war veterans and disabled war veterans and civilian victims of war.

542. In the area of the BD B&H, a separate legislative framework has been set up for the purposes of health insurance. Two laws are applied: the LHP BD B&H[810] and the Law on Health Insurance BD B&H (LHI BD B6H).[811] In line with the LHP BD B&H, health protection includes a system of social, group and individual measures, services and activities aimed at improving and preserving the health of people, preventing diseases and injuries, early detection of diseases, timely treatment, healthcare and rehabilitation, as well as application of health technologies.[812] Health protection is provided at the level of the BD B&H and employers, by undertaking specific activities related to the promotion of health, prevention and treatment of diseases and conditions, rehabilitation of the diseased and injured, provision of medicines and medicinal agents, protection of living and working environment, as well as other specific activities.[813]

543. In line with the principle of comprehensiveness, the system of health protection includes all citizens of the BD B&H in terms of the application of unified measures and procedures of health protection. It covers promotion of health, disease prevention at all levels, early diagnosis, treatment and rehabilitation.[814] The LHP BD B&H follows along the lines of solutions provided by relevant regulation in the FB&H and the RS, stipulating the right to health protection for each citizen in line with provisions of the LHP BD B&H and the LHI BD B&H, while foreign nationals and persons without citizenship have the right to health protection, in line with provisions of the above-mentioned laws and international agreements and other regulations in the area.[815]

544. Health insurance, as part of the social security of citizens, is a single system in which the citizens – through investing the funds based on the principles of reciprocity and solidarity, in the BD B&H, ensure the exercising of the right to health protection and other rights stemming from health insurance as stipulated under the LHI RS and regulations adopted based on that Law, providing that the required contribution has been paid. Compulsory insurance is identified as a type of insurance which is compulsory for all employed persons and other persons identified in the LHI BD B&H; after paying the required contributions, these persons are provided with the basic health protection service package, as well as other rights stipulated in the LHI BD B&H.[816] Extended health insurance is a type of additional

810. OJ BD B&H, 02/2001, 19/2007, 28/2008.
811. *Ibid.*, 01/2002, 07/2002,34/2008.
812. *See* the LHP BD B&H, Art. 3(1).
813. *See ibid.*, Art. 6.
814. *See ibid.*, Art. 16.
815. *See ibid.*, Arts 21 and 22.
816. *See* the LHI BD B&H, Art. 2(1).

insurance related to services outside of the basic package of services, provided through the Health Insurance Fund of the BD B&H.[817]

545. The right to compulsory health insurance is enjoyed by all employed persons and other persons performing certain activities or in a certain capacity, as stipulated under this Law.[818] Compulsory health insurance is provided to all the insured (listed in Article 18 of the LHI BD B&H), and the right to compulsory health insurance is also provided to the family members of the insured.[819] Compulsory health insurance provides the right to health protection and the right to pecuniary compensation and assistance stipulated under this Law, to the insured and their family members, under conditions prescribed in this law.[820]

546. In line with the LHI BD B&H, persons without a clearly established insurance category are provided with services identical to the services of compulsory health insurance, through voluntary health insurance, as a special type of insurance.[821]

547. Funds for exercising the rights under compulsory health insurance are provided from contributions, which are used to set up the funds of the Health Insurance Fund, in line with this Law and regulations adopted on the basis of this Law. The funds may be obtained from other sources as well, as identified under the law and other regulations adopted based on the law (taxes, premiums, payables, budget funds of the BD B&H).[822] Funds for exercising the rights under the extended health insurance are provided from the additional contributions of the insured,[823] and funds for voluntary health insurance are provided by citizens themselves or through companies, institutions or in some other way in which they decide to bring funds for this type of insurance together.[824]

§3. Pension and Disability Insurance

548. In line with the Constitution of B&H, the system of pension and disability insurance is under competency of the Entities' authorities. In line with the above, each of the Entities has its separate legislation regulating the area of pension and disability insurance. Pension and disability insurance are one of the most significant and at the same time one of the most efficient forms of organized protection of workers and their families, which enables them to exercise certain social services in case of insured risk.[825]

817. *See ibid.*, Art. 2(1).
818. *See ibid.*, Art. 6.
819. *See ibid.*, Art. 6(2).
820. *See ibid.*, Art. 7(1).
821. *See ibid.*, Art. 2(1) point 3.
822. *See ibid.*, Art. 12(1).
823. *See ibid.*, Art. 7(2).
824. *See ibid.*, Art. 3.
825. Dedić, *Socijalno pravo (Social Security Law)*, 129.

549. The LPDI FB&H[826] is based on the principles of reciprocity, solidarity between generations and obligation to have a pension and disability insurance. In line with the LPDI FB&H, compulsory pension and disability insurance ensures to the insured rights in case of disability, death or old age.[827] Voluntary pension and disability insurance may be provided to persons who do not have coverage of compulsory insurance. The rights from the pension and disability insurance include the right to old-age pension, disability pension, family pension, the right of the insured with altered work capacity and the right based on physical disability.[828]

550. According to the LPDI FB&H, the insured are identified as two big groups: insured and the insured persons, in a narrow sense.[829] The insured group includes several specific subgroups, specifically listed in Articles 10–16 of the LPDI FB&H. The persons who are insured based on the provisions from Article 17 of the LPDI FB&H, while in the following circumstances: (i) during participation in the action of rescue or defence against natural disasters (fire, flood, earthquake and other disasters caused by force majeure) on the territory of the FB&H or in an action undertaken to save the lives of citizens or eliminate material damage to property; (ii) during the provision of assistance to authorities at their request; (iii) pupil or student during practical classes, i.e., during professional practice at the employer; (iv) during the performance of compulsory work while serving a prison sentence, juvenile prison and during the execution of an educational measure in an educational institution, re-education institution or a special educational institution; during re-qualification or additional qualification; while working for the employer without establishing an employment relationship (volunteer work); during the performance of temporary and occasional jobs through youth cooperatives until the age of 26 if is in regular education; during the performance of certain public functions or civic duties at the invitation of the competent authorities and authorities of the local self-government unit; a person with developmental disabilities during professional training, after completing basic education; during participation in organized sports competitions. In order to obtain the status of insured for the aforementioned person, the person responsible for the payment of contributions is obliged to submit the application of the person who is in these circumstances to the Unified System of Registration, Control and Collection of Contributions of the Tax Administration of the FB&H.[830]

551. Rights from pension and disability insurance in accordance with the LPDI FB&H are:[831] *in the event of old age* – old age pension; *in the event of disability* – insured persons with the I. category of disability – loss of working ability are provided with a disability pension and insured persons with the II. category of disability – changed working ability, the right to be assigned to another appropriate workplace, i.e., the right to appropriate employment, retraining or retraining, as well

826. OJ FB&H, 13/2018, 93/2019 – Decision of the CC, 90/2021, 19/2022.
827. *See* the LPDI FB&H, Art. 2.
828. *See ibid.*, Art. 4(1).
829. *See ibid.*, Art. 2.
830. *See ibid.*, Art. 18.
831. *See ibid.*, Art. 39.

as the right to appropriate financial compensation in connection with the use of these rights, is ensured; *in the event of the death of the insured person, that is, of a beneficiary of an old age or disability pension* – a family pension and the right to compensation for funeral expenses in accordance with the LPDI FB&H; in the *event of physical disability* – compensation for physical disability.

552. The B&H citizens who are not covered by compulsory pension and disability insurance may provide for themselves and members of their families through voluntary insurance the rights from pension and disability insurance.[832] Voluntary insurance is available to those persons who are 15 years old (until the age of 65) and possess general health capacity.[833] Persons who are full-time students or a person who has attained the right to a pension cannot obtain insurance via the voluntary insurance option.[834] Disability, as the basis for acquiring the right in voluntary insurance, exists when it is established that the insured due to permanent changes in the state of health, which cannot be eliminated by treatment or medical rehabilitation, has complete inability to earn.[835]

553. The retirement pension as one of the types of pension provided for by the LPDI FB&H is a permanent social welfare payment to which the insured are entitled as the basic right from the pension and disability insurance based on the old age risk. The right to retirement pension is acquired by the insured in case of old age, specifically: when they turn 65 years of age and at least fifteen years of pensionable service, i.e., when they turn forty years of pensionable service, regardless of the age.[836] The procedure for establishing the old age-based pension is stipulated in detail in Articles 41–47 of the LPDI FB&H.

554. The categories of guaranteed and lowest pension have been introduced to the pension and disability system of FB&H, aiming to provide social security for the insured.[837] The lowest amount of pension belongs to the beneficiary of old-age, family or disability pension, whose pension is determined in a smaller amount than the pension[838] paid for December 2016 in the FB&H, adjusted for all corresponding increases on the day of exercise of rights, and further adjusted in accordance with Article 79(1) of the LPDI FB&H[839].[840] Exceptionally, if financially possible, the

832. *See ibid.*, Art. 19.
833. *See ibid.*, Art. 19(1).
834. *See ibid.*, Art. 20.
835. *See ibid.*, Art. 48(6).
836. *See ibid.*, Art. 40.
837. *See ibid.*, Art. 81.
838. *See ibid.*, Art. 81(1).
839. Which stipulates that pensions are adjusted on 15 Apr. of each year in such a way that the adjustment is made in the amount of the sum of 50% of the increase in consumer prices and 50% of the increase in GDP in the FB&H in the previous year, and according to the data of the Federal Bureau of Statistics, except for pensions realized in the year in which adjustment is made, and at most up to the growth rate of the gross domestic product in the previous year. Exceptionally, the maximum pension will not be adjusted/increased until the lowest amount of pension n reaches 1/5 (one fifth) of the amount of the highest pension realized in accordance with the previous regulations in the amount of 2,174.48 KM.

Government of the FB&H can with special decision determine an increase in the amount of the lowest pension in a higher percentage and at most up to the growth rate of the real gross domestic product in the previous year.[841] The guaranteed amount of the pension belongs to the insured person who has achieved the right to a pension with forty years of pensionable service, and to whom the pension was determined in a smaller amount than the guaranteed pension paid for December 2016 in the FB&H, adjusted for all corresponding increases on the day of exercise of rights, and further adjusted in accordance with Article 79(1) of the LPDI FB&H.[842] Exceptions to the lowest pension are prescribed in Article 82 of the LPDI FB&H.

555. The right to disability pension is acquired by those insured who have been identified with category I disability, under the following conditions: if the disability was caused by injury at work or occupational disease, regardless of the length of pensionable service; if the disability was caused by injury or disease outside the workplace, under the condition that prior to the occurrence of the disability, the person had pensionable service which covers at least one-third of the period between 20 years of age and the occurrence of disability, with calculation of the working life based on full years.[843] The insured with category I disability established by the age of 30 will acquire the right to disability pensions if the disability was caused by injury outside work or disease, provided that prior to occurrence of the disability, he/she had full pensionable service which covers at least one-third of the working life, as well as at least one year of insurance.[844] Establishment of the disability pension is regulated by the provisions of Articles 59–66 of the LPDI FB&H.

556. Exercising the right to family pension is conditioned by general and specific conditions related to the insured and a member of the insured's family. Namely, family members (identified under Article 69 of the LPDI FB&H) acquire the right to family pension if the deceased insured fulfil one of the following conditions: met conditions for retirement pension; based on the length of service, fulfilled conditions for disability pension; was beneficiary of retirement or disability pension.[845] Under the LPDI FB&H, meeting of the specific conditions is provided for family members of the deceased insured and they are related to certain characteristics: kin, age, capacity to earn money to sustain themselves, parenting duties, etc.[846] The family pension is set based on the retirement or disability pension that the insured would have been entitled to at the moment of death, i.e., pension that pension beneficiary would get at the moment of death. Also, the pension ceiling is determined based on the indicated amount of pension depending on the number of family members who

840. *See* the LPDI FB&H, Art. 81(2).
841. *See ibid.*, Art. 81(3).
842. *See ibid.*, Art. 81(4).
843. *See ibid.*, Art. 52.
844. *See ibid.*, Art. 58(1).
845. *See ibid.*, Art. 68.
846. *See ibid.*, Arts 70–74.

are entitled to the pension, and it amounts: for one family member 70%, for two 80%, and for three 90%, for four and more family members 100% of the basis.[847]

557. The right to pecuniary compensation for physical disability is acquired by the insured whose physical disability in the amount of at least 30% resulted from an injury at work or occupational disease.[848] Physical disability exists when the insured has suffered a loss, a serious injury or significant incapacitation of an organ or parts of the body, which worsens the natural activity of the body and requires greater effort in meeting the needs of living, regardless of whether the disability was caused in that way or not. The basis for pecuniary compensation for physical incapacitation is the lowest pension amount.[849]

558. The funds for pension and disability insurance, in line with the LPDI FB&H and separate regulations, are provided from contributions for pension and disability insurance, budget of FB&H and other sources.[850] In line with the Law on Contributions, the contribution rate for pension and disability insurance amounts to 17% paid by the insured and 7% paid by the employer, i.e., a total of 24% paid against the wage. The Federal Fund for Pension and Disability Insurance operates as a single provider of such type of insurance in line with the LPDI FB&H insurance.

559. In the RS, the LPDI RS[851] establishes compulsory pension and disability insurance based on intergeneration solidarity and sets forth the rights and obligations in the scope of that insurance, as well as the option of voluntary insurance for persons who are not covered by compulsory insurance.[852] Compulsory and voluntary insurance, based on the principles of reciprocity and solidarity, provide to the insured the rights in case of old age and disability, and in case of the death of the insured, i.e., pension beneficiary, the right is provided to the members of their families.[853] The rights from the pension and disability insurance are exercised and used only under conditions stipulated by the Law.[854] The scope of rights depends on the length of pension service of the insured and the wages ceiling and insurance base against which the pension and disability insurance was paid for.[855] According to the LPDI RS, the insured is a person who has compulsory pension and disability insurance and a person with voluntary pension and invalid insurance.[856] The LPDI RS includes the following as the insured covered by compulsory insurance: insured

847. *See ibid.*, Art. 76(1).
848. *See ibid.*, Art. 67(2).
849. *See ibid.*, Art. 67(4).
850. *See ibid.*, Art. 124(1).
851. OJ RS, 134/2011, 134/2011, 82/2013, 96/2013 – Decision of the CC, 103/2015, 111/2021, 15/2022, 132/2022.
852. *See* the LPDI RS, Art. 1.
853. *See ibid.*, Art. 2.
854. *See ibid.*, Art. 3(1).
855. *See ibid.*, Art. 3(2).
856. *See ibid.*, Art. 9.

workers, insured religious officials and insured farmers.[857] The LPDI RS further divides the given categories of the insured into subcategories described in Articles 11–14. Compulsory insurance also considers the insured the person who is the beneficiary of the pecuniary compensation due to unemployment while receiving the compensation against which the pension and disability insurance compensation has been paid.[858]

560. The person who is not an insured one in the compulsory insurance is able to obtain voluntary insurance under conditions, in the scope and in the way provided for in the LPDI RS, if they have a residence in the territory of the RS or the BD B&H, general health capacity and are older than 15 years of age.[859] A person who is a regular high school or university student cannot be an insured party under the voluntary insurance scheme.[860] The length of service for retirement, on which the rights from pension and disability insurance are exercised, includes the length of insurance service as well as the specific length of service[861, 862]

561. The rights from the pension and disability insurance include: in case of old age – retirement pension, in case of disability – reassignment to another post, re-qualification or additional qualification, pecuniary compensation in relation to the reduced work capacity, disability pension, and in case of the insured's death, i.e., beneficiary of the retirement or disability pension – family pension.[863]

562. The insured has the right to a retirement pension when they turn 65 years of life and at least fifteen years of insurance.[864] The insured under 65 years of age has the right to retirement pension once they turn 60 years of age and forty years of pensionable service.[865] The LPDI RS differentiates between men and women and stipulates a separate rule which says that insured women even if under 65 years of age have the right to retirement pension once they turn 58 years of age and thirty-five years of insurance.[866] The ceiling of retirement pension is set by multiplying the personal score of the insured with the value of the general score on the day of exercising the right.[867]

563. In terms of the rights based on the disability, the insured with established reduced work capacity has the right to: be reassigned to another post, get

857. *See ibid.*, Art. 10.
858. *See ibid.*, Art. 15.
859. *See ibid.*, Art. 19.
860. *See ibid.*, Art. 20.
861. *See ibid.*, Art. 22.
862. For more information on the length of insurance and particular length of service, *see*: the LPDI RS, Arts 23–36 and Arts 37–39.
863. *See* the LPDI RS, Art. 40.
864. *See ibid.*, Art. 41.
865. *See ibid.*, Art. 42(1).
866. *See ibid.*, Art. 42(2).
867. For more details, *see* the LPDI RS, Arts 45–48.

re-qualified or obtain additional qualification and be awarded pecuniary compensation in relation to the reduced work capacity.[868] The employer provides the above-listed rights to the insured.[869]

564. The insured whose loss of work capacity was caused by an injury outside of the workplace or by disease, that occurred prior to meeting the conditions of age pension, has the right to disability pension, provided that up until the disability occurred this person had acquired five years of insurance service or ten years of pensionable service.[870] Provided that up until the disability occurred the insured has had two years of work service, this person has the right to claim disability pension until they are 35 years old. The insured who after 58 years of age has been identified with the reduced work capacity, has the right to disability pension with the right to re-qualify or obtain additional qualifications, provided that up until the occurrence of disability he/she has had five years of insurance service or ten years of pensionable service, and the insured person who has lost the work capacity as a result of injury at work or occupational disease, has the right to disability pension regardless of the years of pensionable service.[871] Disability pension is set in the same manner as the retirement pension.[872] For the insured with less than fifteen years of work service, the disability pension is set for the insurance service of fifteen years.[873] For the insured whose disability was caused by injury at work or occupational disease, the disability pension is set for the insurance service of forty years.[874]

565. Through the LPDI RS, the most significant changes to the system of pension and disability insurance were made, i.e., pecuniary compensations were removed for cases of physical disability and assistance and care for third persons, as well as stricter criteria introduced for acquiring the right to retirement pension, and the identification of the pension base is done using an average wage of the insured.[875]

566. The right to family pension belongs to all the family members of the deceased insured who on the day of death met the criteria for invalid pension and the family members of the deceased beneficiary of the retirement pension or disability pension.[876] Family members listed in Article 70 of the LPDI RS have the right to family pension, provided they meet a series of specific conditions.[877] The family pension after the death of the insured, i.e., beneficiary of the retirement or disability pension, is set based on the disability pension that he would be receiving

868. *See* the LPDI RS, Art. 54(1).
869. For more information on the right to reassignment to another work post, re-qualification or additional qualification also, *see* the LPDI RS, Arts 55–59.
870. *See* the LPDI RS, Art. 60(1).
871. *See ibid.*, Art. 60(2) and (3).
872. *See ibid.*, Art. 61.
873. *See ibid.*, Art. 62.
874. *See ibid.*, Art. 63.
875. For more information on amounts of disability pension, please *see* the LPDI RS, Arts 64–68.
876. *See* the LPDI RS, Art. 69.
877. *See ibid.*, Arts 71–77.

on the day of his/her death, and in the percentage identified based on the number of family members entitled to the pension.[878] The pensions acquired by 31 December of the previous year, are harmonized on 1 January each year, as of 2013, in line with the percentage representing one-half of the sum of the percentage of change of the average net wage and the percentage of change of the consumer prices at the annual level in RS in the previous year.[879]

567. According to the LPDI RS, the beneficiary to whom the pension was set in the amount which is smaller than the lowest amount of pension, as stipulated in the Law, will be paid the lowest pension, which cannot be lower than 50% of the average pension paid against the RS budget in December of the previous year.[880] The lowest age and invalid pension paid from the RS budget depends on the length of pension service and is set in the percentage of average pension in December of the previous year.[881]

568. The Fund for Pension and Disability Insurance was set up in the RS to exercise the rights of pension and disability insurance and to identify needs and interests in this area of insurance.[882, 883] Finances for exercising the rights from pension and disability insurance and the work of the Fund are provided from: contributions, budget of the RS, profit from the RS Reserve Pension Fund and other sources.[884]

569. In the context of social policy in B&H, special attention is devoted to the protection of war veterans and family members of the killed and social protection. These segments include regulation at the Entity level, characterized by a complex legislative and institutional framework.[885]

---

878. *See ibid.*, Arts 79(1) and (2) and 80.
879. *See ibid.*, Art. 83.
880. *See ibid.*, Art. 85(1)(2).
881. *See ibid.*, Art. 85(3).
882. *See ibid.*, Art. 97.
883. For more information on the RS Fund for Pension and Disability insurance, *see* the LPDI RS, Arts 98–112.
884. *See* the LPDI RS, Art. 152.
885. The following regulation is applied: the Law on the Rights of Defenders and Members of Their Families (OJ FB&H, 33/2004, 56/2005 and 70/2007, 9/2010, 90/2017, 29/22), the Law on Early Favourable Retirement of Defenders from the Defensive-liberating War (OJ FB&H, 43/2013), the Law on the Special Rights ff The Holders ff The War Rewards and Medals and Members of Their Families (OJ FB&H, 70/2005, 70/2006, 9/2010, 90/2017, 29/22), the Law on the Rights of Demobilized Soldiers and Their Family Members (OJ 41/2019), Law on the Rights of Soldiers, Disabled Soldiers and Families of the Killed Soldiers from the Defensive-Fatherland War in RS (OJ RS, 134/11, 09/12, 40/12), Law on Protection of Civil Victims of War (OJ RS, 24/2010), Law on the Base of Social Protection, Protection of Civilian Victims of War and Protection of Families with Children (OJ FB&H, 36/99, 54/04, 39/06, 14/09, 7/2014 – Decision of the CC, 45/2016, 19/2017, 40/2018), Cantonal laws on social protection of civilian victims of war and protection of families with children, the Law on Social Protection in RS (OJ RS, 37/12), Law on Child Protection in RS (OJ RS, 4/2002, 17/2008, 1/2009), the Law on Social Protection in the BD B&H, (OJ BD B&H, 1/2003, 4/2004, 19/2007, 2/2008, 21/2018, 32/2019, 5/2022), the Law on Child Protection (OJ BD B&H, 18/2020, 29/2020, 41/2020, 13/2021) and numerous by-laws passed based on the aforementioned laws.

Part VII. Insurance Intermediaries

570. Insurance mediation activity in B&H, as in the rest of the insurance area, is regulated at the Entity level with specific laws: the Law on Mediation in Private Insurance (LIM FB&H)[886] and the Law on Insurance Mediation (LIM RS),[887] which prescribe in detail the requirements for carrying out insurance mediation activities and their supervision. Even though both of these laws adopted in 2005 were products of legislation reform conducted for the purpose of harmonization with EU legislation, their content was not identical. Differences between Entities' laws have become even more conspicuous after their uneven amendments in 2009[888] and 2010.[889] However, after adoption of new legislation on insurance mediation in the RS in 2017 (the Law on Representation and Mediation in Insurance and Reinsurance [LRMIR RS]),[890] differences became blatant.

571. Contractual relations in the context of insurance mediation are regulated by provisions of the Entities' laws on obligations[891] (LO FB&H/LO RS)[892] on agency activities (Articles 84–98) and brokerage activities (Articles 813–826) in general and provisions which stipulate specific rules on insurance agents (Article 906).

886. OJ FB&H, 22/2005, 8/2010, 30/2016.
887. OJ RS, 17/2005.
888. The Law on Amendments to the LRMIR RS, OJ RS, 106/2009.
889. The Law on Amendments to the LIM FB&H, OJ FB&H, 8/2010.
890. OJ RS, 47/2017.
891. Regarding the area of insurance, both of these laws have provisions of identical content.
892. OJ SFRY, 29/1978, 39/1985, 45/1989 and 57/1989; OJ RB&H, 2/1992, 13/1993, 13/1994; OJ RS, 17/93, 3/1996.

Chapter 1. Law of Establishment and Supervision

§1. General Introduction

572. The conclusion of a contract between the insurer and the insured in the insurance markets in B&H is conducted more and more frequently through the engagement of third parties – insurance intermediaries. According to the provisions of the Entities' laws, there are two categories of intermediaries: insurance agents and insurance brokers.

573. *Insurance agents* carry out the activity of insurance mediation on behalf and for the account of one or more insurance companies based on one or more contracts or authorizations.[893] In the RS, insurance agents may concurrently carry out operations or activities of the insurance agency on behalf and for the account of several insurers at the same time in different types of insurance.[894] Exceptionally, they may represent several insurance companies at the same time in the same types of insurance, but only with written consent of the represented insurance companies.[895]

574. The second category of insurance intermediaries in B&H's law is the *insurance broker,* which independently performs the activity of mediation with the sole aim of establishing a connection between the persons seeking insurance or reinsurance and insurers or reinsurers.[896] The insurance broker assumes the activity concerning the insurance or reinsurance of risk in the name of the insured. Furthermore, the broker also accepts the obligation to do preparatory work for the conclusion of insurance or reinsurance contracts. If explicitly stipulated in the contract, the broker helps with its handling and enforcement, especially in cases involving compensation claims.[897] The insurance mediation laws prescribe key obligations of the insurance broker in Article 10 of the LIM FB&H and Article 20 of the LRMIR RS.

575. The supervision of insurance intermediaries' activities is performed by the competent Entities' insurance agencies (Agency for insurance supervision of FB&H[898] and Insurance Agency of RS[899]).[900] The relevant laws contain provisions on supervision and establishment of special authorities of the competent agencies in that regard (in Article 13 of the LIM FB&H and Article 35 of the LRMIR RS). Within the implementation of insurance intermediaries' supervision, the Entities' agencies stipulate conditions for acquiring and verifying expert knowledge required for carrying out insurance mediation activities, as well as the rules on keeping the

893. *See* the LIM FB&H, Art. 6(1) and the LRMIR RS, Art. 4(1).
894. *See* the LRMIR RS, Art. 10(1).
895. *See ibid.*, Art. 10(2).
896. *See* the LIM FB&H, Art. 8(2) and the LRMIR RS, Art. 15(1).
897. *Ibid.*
898. *See* http://www.nados.ba/eng/index.html.
899. *See* http://www.azors.rs.ba/azors/lat/index.html.
900. *See* the LIM FB&H, Art. 12 and the LRMIR RS, Art. 35.

register, recording data in those registers and the means of public access to the registers.[901]

576. Even though both laws provide for the possibility of withdrawing the authorization to perform activities from insurance intermediaries, the situations in which the competent agencies may proceed differ. The Insurance Agency of the RS differentiates between withdrawal of authority to represent and mediate and withdrawal of authorization to represent and mediate in insurance depending on the fact if the intermediary is a natural or legal person.

577. In the first case, Agency will withdraw of authority to represent and mediate when: establishes that the data on which authority was granted was untrue and when the insurance intermediary (agent or broker natural person) ceases to meet the requirements for performing insurance representation or insurance mediation.[902] Furthermore, the Agency may withdraw authorization for representation or authorization for mediation in the following cases: when the insurance representative, i.e., insurance agent or the insurance broker, a natural person, does not act according to the order issued by the Agency; if the insurance representative, i.e., insurance agent or the insurance broker, a natural person, within a period of two years, commits a restitution offence prescribed in Article 45 of the LRMIR RS.[903] In case of withdrawal of authorization for representation or authorization for mediation, a natural person whose authorization has been revoked cannot submit a request for re-issuance of authorization before the expiration of one year from the date of finality of the Agency's decision by which the authorization was revoked.[904]

578. Correspondingly, in the second case, the Agency will withdraw the authorization for representation or mediation given to the company: when it determines that the data on the basis of which the licence was issued was untrue; if the company for insurance representation, an entrepreneur for insurance representation or insurance brokerage ceases to meet the requirements for performing the activity of insurance representation/insurance mediation prescribed by the LRMIR RS; and when the Agency issues consent for voluntary liquidation.[905] The Agency may withdraw the authorization for representation, i.e., the authorization for mediation in the following cases: if the insurance representation company, the insurance representation entrepreneur or the insurance brokerage company do not act according to the order issued by the Agency; if the representation company in insurance, an entrepreneur for insurance representation or an insurance brokerage company have been legally declared accountable for the criminal offences of money laundering and/or financing of terrorist activities or have been declared accountable for a serious violation of the provisions regulating the prevention of money laundering and financing of terrorist activities; and if the company for representation in insurance, an

901. *See* the LIM FB&H, Art. 11 and the LRMIR RS, Arts 5, 16, 19, 23, 28, 29.
902. The LRMIR RS, Art. 38(1).
903. The *ibid.*, Art. 38(2).
904. The *ibid.*, Art. 38(3).
905. The *ibid.*, Art. 39(1).

entrepreneur or insurance brokerage company, within a period of two years, commits a misdemeanour in restitution prescribed in Article 41 of the LRMIR RS.[906] In case of revocation of the licence for representation, i.e., the licence for mediation, the person whose licence was revoked cannot submit a request for re-issuance of the licence before the expiration of one year from the date of finality of the decision of the Agency by which the licence was revoked.[907]

579. The Agency for Supervision of Insurance in the FB&H may cancel its decisions on the authorization of an insurance agent or insurance broker when the insurance intermediary registered for carrying out insurance mediation activities ceases to meet one of the requirements prescribed in provisions of Articles 7 and 9 of the LIM FB&H as well as in the case when the interest of the insured is endangered or when the insurance intermediary's failure to comply with laws and other regulations is established.[908]

580. Decisions of the agencies in the FB&H and the RS are final and represent the basis for initiation of the administrative dispute before the competent courts. The breaches of the rules stipulated by laws are sanctioned. While the LRMIR RS prescribes fines for commitment of offences,[909] the LIM FB&H in addition to fines prescribes prison sentences.[910]

§2. Registration

581. According to B&H law, in order to carry out a mediation activity in the insurance and reinsurance sector, intermediaries must be registered in special registers kept by the competent insurance agencies. Insurance agencies keep different registers for insurance agents and insurance brokers, for natural and legal persons. The Insurance intermediaries' registration performed by the competent Entities' agency is valid for the entire territory of B&H. However, an insurance intermediary registered in one Entity (FB&H or RS) may provide insurance mediation services on the territory of the other solely via their organizational units in that Entity.[911] Special rules apply when an insurance intermediary registered in one Entity intends to perform activities for the first time in the other through its organizational units, which, *inter alia*, instruct: the notification of the competent agencies, the information exchange between the agencies and fixed deadlines after which the intermediary may start operating through their organizational unit.[912] The organizational unit

906. The *ibid.*, Art. 39(2).
907. The *ibid.*, Art. 39(3).
908. *See* the LIM FB&H, Art. 14.
909. *See* the LRMIR RS, Art. 40.
910. *See* the LIM FB&H, Art. 23.
911. *See ibid.*, Art. 3(2) and the LRMIR RS, Art. 25(1).
912. *See* the LIM FB&H, Arts 4 and 5 and the LRMIR RS, Arts 26 and 27.

of the insurance intermediary must be established in accordance with the provisions of the legislation on companies effective in the Entity in which that unit intends to operate.[913]

582. According to the Entities' legislation, insurance intermediaries may be natural or legal persons that must fulfil a number of different conditions in order to be registered. Among other conditions (stipulated in Article 7 of the LIM FB&H and Articles 5 and 16 of the LRMIR RS), a natural person has to pass a professional exam of knowledge and competence in order to carry out activities of insurance mediation. Namely, a natural person – as an insurance intermediary has to prove possession of professional knowledge and professional skills. If the insurance intermediary is a legal person (insurance agency or brokerage company), the laws prescribe mandatory forms for its establishment as a joint-stock company or a limited liability company in accordance with the Entities' legislation on companies.[914]

583. Carrying out insurance mediation activities in insurance and reinsurance is conditioned with specific requirements stipulated for the two main categories of insurance intermediaries – insurance agents and insurance brokers. In addition to the application for obtaining authorization from the competent Agency, an insurance agent must submit a number of documents clearly indicated in Article 7 of the LIM FB&H and Articles 5 and 7 of the LRMIR RS in order to be registered. Registration of the insurance broker also requires submission of extensive documentation prescribed in Article 7 of the LIM FB&H and Articles 16 and 18 of the LRMIR RS with the application for registration. However, an insurance broker must also fulfil other specific conditions. If the broker is a natural person, the LIM RFB&H prescribes that they must have blocked assets in the amount of BAM 200,000.00 in order to ensure the execution of activities and must have a valid professional liability insurance in the event of a fault or negligence.[915] Policyholders have priority over blocked assets in comparison to any other general or specific priority.[916] When it comes to the brokerage company in FB&H, the applicant must have deposited funds in the amount of BAM 200,000.00 for the purpose of successful performance of the activity and must be assured against professional liability in the event of an error or omission with minimum coverage in the amount of BAM 400,000.00, and this insurance contract must cover a period equal to the period of registration of an insurance brokerage plus one month.[917] In the RS, after amendments to the LRMIR RS, previously mentioned conditions for registration have been modified. Presently, according to the provisions of the LRMIR RS, brokerage company in addition to fulfilling the conditions of personnel and technical competence, must have insurance coverage for the liability from activities and from professional negligence in the amount of the insured sum, which may not be less than BAM 600,000.00 for

913. *See* the LIM FB&H, Arts 4(4) and 5(4) and LRMIR RS, Art. 3(2).
914. *See* the LIM FB&H, Arts 7(1) and 8(1) and the LRMIR RS, Arts 7(1) and 18(1).
915. *See* the LIM FB&H, Art. 9(6).
916. *See ibid.*, Art. 9(8).
917. *See ibid.*, Art. 9(3).

each claim, or BAM 960,000.00 for all claims in one year,[918] and a brokerage company must ensure that the cash portion of net capital is at a level not less than the amount of BAM 50,000.00.[919]

584. Registration is obtained for a period of two (FB&H) and four years (RS), and the insurance broker is required to resubmit all the documents necessary for registration within thirty days before the expiration of the two-year period for which it is registered. Registration remains valid with the exception of the following cases: when the insurance broker fails to resubmit the documents and when the submitted documents show that the applicant is not a person eligible to act as an insurance broker.[920]

585. Within thirty days from the date of submission of the insurance intermediaries' registration application and prescribed documents, the competent Agency delivers a decision on the application or requests a correction or amendment of that application. The competent Agency's decision on registration of a company for insurance mediation (insurance agency or brokerage company) is a precondition for registration of that company in the court register.

586. According to B&H insurance law, various mediation activities can be carried out not only by the insurance agency and insurance brokerage companies but also by other types of legal persons involved in other actions. However, in such cases, solutions contained in the legislation on insurance mediation in force in the Entities differ. Amendments to the LRMIR RS in 2009 have allowed banks, microcredit institutions and RS's postal services enterprises, which have obtained authorization from the Agency of RS in accordance with provisions of the LRMIR RS, to carry out mediation, i.e., representation in insurance and reinsurance.[921] When it comes to insurance agency activities, provisions of the LRMIR RS and regulations of the Agency of RS apply to the microcredit institutions and postal services enterprises as well as special secondary legislation that stipulates detailed rules for performing insurance agency operations by those legal entities.[922]

587. However, in the FB&H in 2010, the Law on amendments of the LIM FB&H introduced a provision allowing public corporations such as postal operators to perform the operations of the insurance agency. The public corporations' performance of these services is conditioned by authorization from the Agency for

918. *See* the LRMIR RS, Art. 18(4).
919. *See ibid.*, Art. 18(2).
920. *See* the LIM FB&H, Arts 7(9) and 9(6).
921. *See* the LRMIR RS, Art. 2(5) of LRMIR RS. Correspondingly, the LRMIR also allows insurance representation to be performed by a bank, a microcredit organization and the Postal Service Company of the RS in form of joint company seated in Banja Luka, which have received a licence for representation and who entered the activity of insurance representation in the register of business entities. *See*: the LRMIR RS, Arts 4(1) and 8.
922. *See* the LRMIR RS, Arts 4(1) and 8.

Supervision of Insurance in the FB&H and the registration of natural persons, which may act as insurance agents within those public corporations, in the Registry of the Agency.[923]

923. *See* the LIM FB&H, Art. 6(2).

Chapter 2. Insurance Intermediaries and the Insurance Contract

588. The role of the insurance intermediary in the process of conclusion of the insurance contract is only partly regulated by the provisions of the Entities' legislation on insurance intermediaries and to a much larger extent by the provisions of laws on obligation (LO FB&H/LO RS), which contain general rules on agency and brokerage activities as well as specific provisions on insurance agents.

589. It should be noted that the sole purpose of the insurance agent is to initiate, propose and execute preparatory work prior to the conclusion of the contract or to conclude a specific insurance contract.[924] The role of the insurance agent is not necessarily limited to the conclusion of the contract – he or she may be obliged to assist in the implementation or execution of concluded contracts, especially in damage claims cases, as well as to offer consulting services during the period of insurance coverage in accordance with specific provisions of an individual contract with the insured.[925] However, according to the LRMIR RS during the course of the contract, the insurance agent is not entitled to collect premiums from the policyholder or the insured.[926] In the RS, the insurance agent is liable for the activities performed on behalf of the insurer, on whose account the insurance contract is concluded.[927] The relationship between the insurer and insurance agent is based on a written contract, and a copy of that contract (insurance agency contract) must be submitted to the competent Agency (in the FB&H or the RS).[928]

590. In addition to the general rules on agency that apply to issues, such as the possibility of agency,[929] the effects of agency,[930] authorization's delegation,[931] excess of the authorization's limits,[932] conclusion of contract by an unauthorized person,[933] etc., the LO FB&H/LO RS also contains specific rules on insurance agents. Those rules regulate in more detail the relationship between the insurer and the insurance agent with respect to the authorizations conferred to the agent to act on behalf and for the account of the insurer. The insurer can restrict the scope of the insurance agent's authorizations, and those restrictions have an effect on the policyholder only if they were known to him/her.[934] If the insurer has not specified the scope of the insurance agent's authorizations, the agent is entitled to conclude the insurance contract on behalf and for the account of the insurer, negotiate and

924. *See ibid.*, Art. 6(1) and LRMIRRS, Art. 2(2).
925. *Ibid.*
926. *See* the LRMIR RS, Art. 13(3).
927. *See ibid.*, Arts 11 and 13(1).
928. *See* the LIM FB&H, Art. 6(3) and the LRMIR RS, Art. 11(2).
929. *See* the LO FB&H/LO RS, Art. 84.
930. *See ibid.*, Art. 85.
931. *See ibid.*, Art. 86.
932. *See ibid.*, Art. 87.
933. *See ibid.*, Art. 88.
934. *See ibid.*, Art. 906(2).

stipulate modifications of the contracts or extension of their validity, issue the insurance policy, collect insurance premium payments and accept statements addressed to the insurer.[935]

591. The insurer on whose behalf and for whose account the insurance contract is concluded pays the insurance agent's commission. The LRMIR RS stipulates provision that the Agency will adopt a document prescribing the limit of the amount of the insurance agents' commission when the financial position and financial discipline of insurance companies and the smooth functioning of the insurance market are threatened in the long term due to the contracted commission of the insurance agents, as well as a document on regulation other mutual relations of insurance agents with the insurance company or parties related to the insurance companies.[936] This provision is not contained in the LIM FB&H.

592. The insurance contract is increasingly concluded through insurance brokers in the insurance markets of B&H. Entities' legislation on insurance mediation was adopted in 2005 when only a couple of rules governed the relationship between brokers and policyholders or the insured. It was the provision that provided for the obligation of the insurance broker to inform the person seeking the insurance or reinsurance on any legal or financial dependence of the insurer or reinsurer including any possession of shares or stocks in those legal entities, which could affect the broker's freedom of choice of the insurer or reinsurer for placing risk.[937]

593. After the changes in 2009, provisions were introduced in the LRMIR RS that defined the responsibilities of the broker towards the policyholder or the insured, especially in the pre-contract phase that aimed at the protection of their interests. These responsibilities included providing information, explanations and advice to the insured or insurance contractor on all circumstances relevant to the decision of the policyholder or the insured to conclude the insurance contract with a particular insurance company.[938] In order to fulfil this duty towards the policyholder or insured person, the insurance broker must prepare adequate risk analysis and adequate coverage; draft an assessment of financial capacity of the insurance company to cover the risks on the basis of available professional information; mediate at the request of the policyholder or the insured in the conclusion of insurance contracts, which, in any particular case provides the highest level of security (this responsibility of the broker may be limited to certain insurance operations, provided that the broker explicitly has informed the policyholder/insured about it); deliver the contract with insurance conditions to the policyholder/insured and provide information to him/her on the methods of premium calculation; and check the contents of the insurance policy.[939] The aforementioned provisions are contained in

935. *See ibid.*, Art. 906(1).
936. *See* the LRMIR RS, Art. 13(4).
937. *See* the LIM FB&H, Art. 10(1)(t) and the LRMIR RS, Art. 18(1)(c).
938. *See* the LRMIR RS, Art. 16(1).
939. *See ibid.*, Art. 16(3).

the new LRMIR RS as well.[940] In the course of the contractual relationship, the broker has to continuously monitor the insurance contracts concluded through his/her mediation and has the obligation to propose amendments to the contract (if it is in the best interests of the insured). The broker also has to provide assistance for the duration of the insurance contract and in the occurrence of the insured event, to make sure that the insured takes all legal actions necessary for the protection and implementation of his/her rights stipulated in the insurance contract within the deadlines prescribed for these legal actions.[941] Furthermore, the broker has to make transparent all legal and economic ties, including the contracted commission, with a certain insurance company.[942]

594. The aforementioned broker obligations towards the policyholder or the insured are not included in the LIM FB&H; thus, there are significant differences between Entities' regulations on insurance brokerage with regard to broker obligations.

595. The Entities' legislation on insurance mediation contains several legal provisions that define the relationship between the insurance broker and the insurer. Namely, the insurance broker has complete freedom to choose the insurer and is legally and economically independent from the insurer.[943] Amendments to the LRMIR RS introduced additional responsibilities for the insurance broker towards the insurer which require the broker: to inform the insurer about the offer to conclude a contract of the insured, that is, the policyholder;[944] to protect the interests of the insurer to the extent that this obligation also exists towards the insured; and to notify the insurer about all the risks that are known to them or should be known to them.[945] The LRMIR RS also prescribes the same obligations of the insurance broker towards the insurer.[946]

596. As already indicated, the LO FB&H/LO RS contains general rules on brokerage, which can apply to the relationship between the insurance broker and its principal. Under the brokerage contract, the broker assumes the obligation to try to find and connect persons seeking insurance (or reinsurance) with insurers or reinsurers who are willing to negotiate the conclusion of a specific insurance (or reinsurance) contract.[947] The broker is primarily obliged to carry out preparatory work for the conclusion of the insurance or reinsurance contract, i.e., to seek the possibility of the conclusion of a specific contract with the attention of a prudent businessman and point out such a possibility to the principal.[948] At any time, the principal may revoke the brokerage order (unless he/she renounced this possibility),

940. *See* the LRMIR RS, Art. 20.
941. *See ibid.*, Art. 20(8).
942. *See ibid.*, Art. 20(7).
943. LIM FB&H, Art. 10(1)(3) and LRMIR RS, Art. 12(2) and (3).
944. *See* LRMIR RS, Art. 16(4).
945. *Ibid.*
946. *See*, the LRMIR RS, Art. 21.
947. *See* LO FB&H/LO RS, Art. 813.
948. *See ibid.*, Art. 818(1).

and under the condition, that revocation is not contrary to conscientiousness.[949] The general rule of brokerage is that the principal does not have to enter into negotiations for the contract conclusion with the insurer found by the broker nor does he/she have to conclude the contract with that insurer under the conditions specified to the broker, but he/she is liable for damages if he/she acted contrary to the conscientiousness.[950] The broker is obliged to mediate in the course of negotiations and to strive to achieve the conclusion of the contract if such obligation is expressly agreed, but the broker shall not be liable if despite all the due diligence his/her endeavour is unsuccessful.[951] The broker must inform the principal about any circumstances relevant to the intended business activity that are known to him/her or that had to be known to him/her.[952] The contract may also specify the obligation of the broker to assist in the processing and execution of the contract whose conclusion had been negotiated by the broker, particularly in the case of damage claims.

597. According to the general rules of contract law regarding the brokers' liability, the broker is liable for the loss that might be sustained by either party involved in the process of his/her mediation, which may occur if the broker mediates on behalf of a person without sufficient business capacity whose lack of capacity was known or should have been known to him/her, or if the broker mediates on behalf of a person whose incapacity to fulfil his/her contractual obligations was known or should have been known to him/her, and generally shall be liable for any loss caused by his/her fault.[953] Furthermore, the broker is liable for the loss sustained by the principal due to the broker's disclosure of information on the content of the brokerage order, negotiations or conditions and terms of the concluded contract to the third party without permission of the principal.[954]

598. Even though general rules of the law of obligation provide that the intermediary, i.e., broker is entitled to certain compensation by the principal if the contract whose conclusion he/she mediated is concluded,[955] the laws stipulate an exception to this rule. The insurance broker does not have the right to request payment of commission or any other payment from the policyholder or the insured (unless expressly agreed in writing)[956] if they receive a commission from the insurer.[957] However, if the contract with the insured, i.e., policyholder, has an explicit written clause that the insurance broker has the right to a commission or any other payment, the insurance broker has no right to request a commission or any other payment from the insurer on the basis of that contract.[958]

949. *See ibid.*, Art. 816.
950. *See ibid.*, Art. 817.
951. *See ibid.*, Art. 818(2) and (3).
952. *See ibid.*, Art. 819.
953. *See* the LO FB&H/LO RS, Art. 820(1).
954. *See ibid.*, Art. 820(2).
955. *See ibid.*, Art. 813 LO.
956. *See* the LRMIR RS, Art. 24(1).
957. *See* the LIM FB&H, Art. 8(2) and the LRMIR RS, Art. 24(1).
958. *See* the LRMIR RS, Art. 24(2).

599. The LO FB&H/LO RS prescribes that the broker is entitled to compensation even if it is not explicitly contracted[959] and acquires the right to remuneration at the moment of the conclusion of contract he/she mediated unless something else is contracted.[960] Regarding the reimbursement of costs incurred during the execution of the brokerage order, the general rule on brokerage is that the broker is not entitled to reimbursement of these costs unless this possibility is stipulated in the contract, and in that case, the broker is entitled to such reimbursement even if the insurance contract is not concluded.[961]

600. The recently adopted LRMIR RS stipulates obligations of insurance agent and insurance broker to provide information to insured and/or insurance contractor, before conclusion of insurance contract, about:[962] their business names and seats; entry in the Agency's register and method of examination of the entry; names of the insurance companies with which it has concluded contracts; any legal or financial dependence of that insurance intermediary, i.e., insurance agent or broker on the insurer with whom the insurance contract will be concluded, including any direct or indirect ownership of 10% and more percentages of capital or voting rights in the insurer, which could affect the freedom of choice of the insurer; any legal or financial dependence of the insurer, with whom the insurance or reinsurance contract will be concluded, from that insurance mediation company (insurance agent or broker), including any direct or indirect ownership of 10% or more of capital or voting rights in that insurance mediation company; and the methods of protection of their rights and interests. Moreover, the insurance agent and broker are obliged to inform the insured and/or insurance contractor, before concluding the insurance contract, whether they are contractually obliged to one or more insurers, and at the request of the insured and/or insurance contractor, they have to provide information on the names of those insurers.[963] The aforementioned information should be provided: in physical or electronic form; in accessible manner for the insured and/or insurance contractor; in a clear and accurate way that is understandable to the insured and/or insurance contractor; and in one of the languages that are in official use in the Entity of RS.[964] Exceptionally, information may be provided verbally at the request of the insured and/or insurance contractor or when risk coverage is instantly needed.[965] In this case, information must be provided in a regular manner (written physical or electronic form, accessible manner, clear and accurate etc.) immediately after the conclusion of the insurance contract.[966]

601. With regard to consumer protection, the LRMIR RS lays down the following obligations of insurance intermediaries: obligation to ensure the protection of the rights and interests of the insured and/or insurance contractor, in accordance

959. *See* the LO FB&H/LO RS, Art. 822(1).
960. *See ibid.*, Art. 823(1).
961. *See ibid.*, Art. 824.
962. *See* the LRMIR RS, Art. 31.
963. *See ibid.*, Art. 31(2).
964. *See ibid.*, Art. 31(3).
965. *See ibid.*, Art. 31(4).
966. *See ibid.*, Art. 31(5).

with regulations, rules of the profession and good business practices; obligation to provide a procedure that enables the insured and/or insurance contractor to submit a complaint; and obligation to provide information on the possibility, method and deadline for submission of a complaint; the required content of the complaint; the address, fax number or e-mail address for receiving complaints and the deadline for submitting a response to the complaint.[967] Insurance intermediaries are obliged to respond to every received, written complaint within thirty days and notify the complainant of the right to: initiate proceedings with the Insurance Ombudsman for the purpose of out-of-court dispute resolution and file a lawsuit.[968]

602. Furthermore, in the context of consumer protection the LRMIR RS prescribes: that the insurance broker is obliged to inform the insured and/or insurance contractor about possibility to conclude an insurance mediation contract with several insurance brokers;[969] the insured and/or insurance contractor have the right to choose one or more insurance intermediaries;[970] and that insurance intermediaries are obliged to inform the insured and/or insurance contractor, that they have the possibility to conclude an insurance contract with one or more insurers.[971]

967. *See ibid.*, Art. 33(1).
968. *See ibid.*, Art. 33(2).
969. *See ibid.*, Art. 33(3).
970. *See ibid.*, Art. 33(4).
971. *See ibid.*, Art. 33(5).

Part VIII. Reinsurance and Co-insurance

603. A limited number of legal norms in B&H's legal framework in the insurance sector directly regulate reinsurance and co-insurance as risk-levelling methods. Specific provisions governing the area of reinsurance are contained in the Entities' legislation on insurance and insurance companies.[972] Insurance contract law provides only one provision dedicated to reinsurance contained in the Entities' laws on obligations (the LO FB&H and LO RS).[973] This provision exempts reinsurance from regulations applicable to the insurance contract.[974] Likewise, only one provision of the LO FB&H/LO RS refers to co-insurance and stipulates the fundamental principle of legal relations established by co-insurance.[975]

604. Reinsurance represents a special system of insurance operations that exists concurrently with operations of direct insurance in the insurance markets of B&H. The Entities' laws on insurance companies contain two similar definitions of reinsurance. While the LI FB&H describes reinsurance as a company's activity of conclusion and execution of contracts on reinsurance of the insured excess risk of insurer with reinsurer,[976] the LIC RS defines reinsurance as the company's activity that covers the entire or part of the risk taken by the insurer (reinsured) or another reinsurer.[977]

605. Reinsurance operations are the conclusion and fulfilment of reinsurance contracts[978] as well as the processing of claims and payments of indemnity arising from the contract.[979] In B&H's law, all direct insurance companies, except companies for mutual insurance, can perform reinsurance operations with permission of competent agencies in the Entities.[980] Agencies in the Entities supervise the reinsurance operations performed by companies under their jurisdiction, with a special

972. *See* for example: the LI FB&H, Arts 61(4), 62(1), 70, 71, 72, 79, 99, 100, 101, 102 and the LIC RS, Arts 2(1), 3, 17, 35, 49(2), 53(2).
973. OJ SFRY, 29/1978, 39/1985, 45/1989, 57/1989; OJ RB&H, 2/1992, 13/1993, 13/1994; and OJ RS, 17/1993, 3/1996.
974. *See* the LO FB&H/LO RS, Art. 899(2).
975. *See ibid.*, Art. 935.
976. *See* the LI FB&H, Art. 3(3).
977. *See* the LIC RS, Art. 2(1).
978. *See* the LI FB&H, Art. 3(3).
979. *See* the LIC RS, Art. 2(1).
980. *See* the LI FB&H, Art. 12(7) and the LIC RS, Art. 3(3).

focus on their solvency and financial capacity to assume risks. Furthermore, agencies have the authority to prohibit a company from taking the reinsurance risk for which it does not have sufficient financial potential.[981]

606. According to the provisions of the Entities' legislation on insurance companies, every joint-stock company that pursues or plans to pursue reinsurance activities must first obtain a special permit from the competent agency, which covers all types of reinsurance.[982] The reinsurance company must be established in the form of a joint-stock company that performs reinsurance operations as the sole object of its activity.[983] The company can perform reinsurance related to the risks of life and non-life insurance.

607. The competent Entities' agencies (the Agency for Supervision of Insurance in the FB&H and the Insurance Agency of the RS) supervise reinsurance operations in the insurance market in B&H.[984] The Entities' laws on insurance companies prohibit insurance companies operating in the Entities to conclude reinsurance contracts with reinsurance companies that do not have a licence issued in B&H, without prior permission of the competent agencies. However, the LIC RS provides that competent Agency in the Entity of RS may not reject the licensing of reinsurance companies that meet the internationally acceptable standards for solid performance of reinsurance operations.[985] The mentioned restrictions do not apply to reinsurance companies that have the authorization of activities issued in B&H.[986]

608. A company licensed by the Agency in the RS or the FB&H can provide reinsurance coverage in the entire territory of B&H.[987]

609. In general, provisions of the LIC FB&H and the LIC RS applicable to insurance companies also apply to reinsurance companies, except when reinsurance companies are expressly exempt or when those rules are contrary to reinsurance operations.[988] The minimum capital and guarantee fund may not be less than BAM 6,000,000.00 if a company exclusively performs reinsurance activities.[989] The reinsurance company's assets of the share capital may not originate from loans or credits or be encumbered in any way.[990]

981. *See* the LIC RS, Art. 3(3).
982. *See* the LI FB&H, Art. 12(7) and the LIC RS, Art. 3(4).
983. *See* the LI FB&H, Art. 12(8) and the LIC RS, Art. 3(4).
984. *See* the LI FB&H, Art. 12(9) and the LIC RS, Art. 3(4).
985. *See* the LIC RS, Art. 3(5). This provision was contained in previous law LIC FB&H in Art. 3(6). However, it is no longer contained in new LI FB&H.
986. *See* the LIC RS, Art. 3(5).
987. *See* the LI FB&H, Art. 12(10) and the LIC RS, Art. 3(6).
988. *See* the LI FB&H, Art. 12(11) and the LIC RS, Art. 3(7).
989. *See* the LI FB&H, Arts 25(1) and the LIC RS, Arts 49(2) and 53(2).
990. *See* the LI FB&H, Arts 25(2).

610. Both laws prescribe the application of particular rules on reinsurance companies:[991] reinsurance companies are exempt from the application of provisions on granting approval for the performance of certain types of insurance;[992] reinsurance companies must have the highest solvency margin required for insurance companies; reinsurance companies can form technical reserves in cooperation with the direct insurer in order to avoid the double formation of technical reserves; provisions on consumer protection enshrined in the LIC F&B and the LIC RS are not applicable to reinsurance.

611. With regard to reinsurance obligation, the LI FB&H prescribes that the insurance company must cover with reinsurance part of the insured assumed risks which exceed the maximum of self-retention according to the tables of maximum coverage.[993] According to the assessment of each individual risk or portfolio, the self-retention of the insurance company may be lower than in the maximum coverage tables.[994]

612. For every business year insurance company must accept the programme of planned reinsurance,[995] which must contain: calculated own shares in accordance with individual types of insurance; the table of maximum coverage compiled on the basis of the calculation of the own shares; procedures, bases and benchmarks for determining the highest possible damage for individual insured risks; opinion of the authorized actuary of the insurance company or reinsurance company on the programme of planned reinsurance or retrocession.[996] With regard to calculation of own shares, insurance company primarily takes into account: amount of capital, overall scope of work, amount of insurance premium in groups and types of insurance, and shares of insurance according to individual types of insurance on the bases of the overall scope of work and amount of insurance premium in groups and types of insurance, and corrections due to deviations in certain types of insurance.[997] The supervisory agency prescribes additional elements, which should be included in the calculation of the planned reinsurance[998] through the adoption of specific by-laws.[999]

613. A reinsurance contract is a contract under which one contracting party (the reinsured) cedes a part of its obligation to another contracting party (the reinsurer) in its coverage and pays for that reinsurance premium. In essence, the part of risk exceeding the self-retention (or own retention) is reinsured.[1000] Contracting parties

991. *See ibid.*, Art. 12(12) and (13) and the LIC RS, Art. 3(8).
992. *See* the LIC FB&H, Art. 3(10) and the LIC RS, Art. 3(9).
993. *See* the LI FB&H, Art. 99(1).
994. *See ibid.*, Art. 99(2).
995. *See ibid.*, Art. 100(1).
996. *See ibid.*, Art. 100(2).
997. *See ibid.*, Art. 100(3).
998. *See ibid.*, Art. 100(4).
999. *See* Rulebook on additional elements to be included in the calculation of planned reinsurance in FB&H, OJ 84/2017.
1000. *See* the LI FB&H, Art. 3(3) and the LIC RS, Art. 2(1).

in the reinsurance relationship are the insurer and the reinsurer, and the directly insured is left out of this contractual relationship. Thus, in the case of occurrence of the insured event, the insured cannot claim indemnity directly from the reinsurer. Vertical transmission of risk can be further continued in a manner that the reinsurer may acquire reinsurance coverage from another reinsurance company and transfer to it part of the risk accepted into reinsurance. In literature and insurance practice, the insurance of reinsurer is called retrocession.

614. The direct insurance contract forms the basis for assumption of obligations by the reinsurer and thus the reinsurance relationship represents a kind of upgrade of the direct insurance relationship. The existence of a valid insurance contract is a precondition for the conclusion of a valid reinsurance contract, and any change or termination of the direct insurance contract is reflected in the reinsurance relationship arising from that contract.

615. The conclusion of reinsurance contracts and their content are not regulated by national sources of law. As previously mentioned, reinsurance relationships are explicitly exempt from the application of provisions of the LO FB&H/LO RS containing the rules on insurance contract law.[1001] Given this regulative void, it is left to the contracting parties to stipulate a number of contract elements, such as risk, premium, commission, deposit, etc. As a result, different solutions regarding the procedure of conclusion of the reinsurance contract and its content appear in practice and are developed under strong influence of foreign markets and foreign partners. This is particularly apparent in the form and substance of the offer. Submission of the offer is preceded by the supply of information that represents the basis for preparation of the content of the offer. The reinsurer usually submits the reinsurance offer in the form of the so-called slip (i.e., information about the risk) that includes basic contract elements and contract provisions eligible for further negotiation. Even though it is possible for the insurance company to offer the prepared slip to the reinsurer, it is not common in practice. The type of reinsurance contract (e.g., whether it is proportional or non-proportional, obligatory or facultative) determines the type of offer. Such a reinsurance contract usually lacks a framework contract.

616. Negotiation and the signing of the slip would normally precede the conclusion of the reinsurance contract in insurance practice in B&H. Under the influence of changes in the reinsurance market, this approach has been modified, and in current practice, it is usual to offer reinsurance in the form of a slip and framework contract contained in a single document. While legislation in force does not explicitly prescribe the form of reinsurance contracts, the interpretation of the provisions contained in Articles 3, 79 and 135 of the LI FB&H and Article 35 of the LIC RS shows that a reinsurance contract should be concluded in written form. Due to the underdevelopment of B&H's insurance markets with a small number of reinsurers and insurance brokers, reinsurance contracts are concluded directly.

1001. *See* the LO FB&H/LO RS, Art. 989(2).

617. Reinsurance contracts concluded by insurance companies are under supervision of competent insurance agencies in the FB&H and the RS. They examine the identity of the reinsurer, control conditions and provisions under which reinsurance is concluded and control the proportion of ceded risk.[1002] Also, LIC RS stipulates obligations of insurance companies to submit to the competent agency all copies of the reinsurance contract within three months from the issuing of the decision on authorization for work.[1003] Moreover, for the purpose of supervision of insurance companies, agencies can also require all other documents on reinsurance.

618. Although different divisions of reinsurance exist (facultative, obligatory and facultative obligatory; complete and partial; active and passive), the most important division is based on the manner in which responsibilities are shared between the reinsurer and the insurer: contracts in which the obligation of the reinsurer is defined in relation to the risk covered by the insurer (quota and exceeding reinsurance) and contracts in which the obligation of the reinsurer is defined with regard to the insured sum or indemnity that the insurer should pay to the insured (contract of excess of loss reinsurance and stop loss treaty).

619. Under the *contract on reinsurance of proportional part of risk* (quota share reinsurance), the insurer cedes a certain percentage of all risks covered by reinsurance to the reinsurer. The reinsurer assumes liability to pay to the reinsured indemnity as a certain percentage that is owed to the insured, and the reinsured assumes liability to pay the reinsurer, the same percentage, in the form of the premiums collected from the policyholders (the insured). *Reinsurance of excess risk* (exceeding reinsurance), unlike *reinsurance of proportional part of risk,* covers only damages for risks whose sum exceeds a certain limit, i.e., self-retention of the insurer. The insurer has access to the excess of loss reinsurance when it wants to cover losses for a predetermined sum (so-called priority losses) and beyond that, losses are assumed by the reinsurer. The stop loss treaty forms the obligation of the reinsurer to cover part of the losses, i.e., loss incurred in one type of insurance in a certain period, most often a year. Obligations of the reinsurer in this form of non-proportional reinsurance are determined only at the end of the reinsurance period based on the comparison of the amount of premiums collected and damages paid within this period.

620. In B&H's insurance practice, proportional contracts that cover entire portfolios prevail in terms of the volume of premiums. Numerically, facultative contracts dominate, within which there are predominantly proportional (quota) contracts, but there are also non-proportional contracts XL, i.e., reinsurance of excess loss.

621. Co-insurance represents one of the modes of levelling insurance risk, but in comparison to reinsurance, it is less used in practice. Legal relations of co-insurance are usually created when one insurer cannot entirely cover certain risks

1002. *See* the LI FB&H, Art. 135 and the LIC RS, Art. 17.
1003. *See* the LIC RS, Art. 35.

and for that reason shares that risk with other insurers (so-called horizontal dispersion of risk among the insurers). The essence of co-insurance is embodied in an insurance contract concluded with several insurers who have agreed on covering and sharing of the risk.[1004] Every insurer (co-insurer) that participates in sharing of the same risk assumes its share of risk in accordance with the established part (quota) of the insured sum or insured value. The total sum of coverage of insurers participating in co-insurance may not exceed the insured value. Correspondingly, LI FB&H defines co-insurance business operations as conclusion and execution of insurance contracts with several insurance companies that have agreed on the joint cover and distribution of risks, where each insurance company specified in the insurance policy is responsible to the insured for full compensation.[1005]

622. According to the LI FB&H, insurance company, together with one or more insurance companies, may co-insure risks from the types of insurance for which it has received approval to perform insurance operations.[1006] However, insurance company may not co-insure risks in an amount that exceeds its own shares according to certain types of insurance in accordance with the tables of maximum coverage from Article 100 of the LI FB&H.

623. The process of establishment and implementation of co-insurance relations is simplified in practice through the establishment of the lead or main co-insurer which is usually authorized to perform operations such as issuance of policy, collection and allocation of premiums, processing of damages and so on. A characteristic of co-insurance is that issued policy (i.e., collective policy) in addition to standard elements specified in Article 902(1) of the LO FB&H/LO RS always contains a list of all co-insurers and their shares in the coverage of risks, and the co-insurance policy must be signed by all the co-insurers.[1007]

624. The relationship between the insured and the insurer in co-insurance can be established on two principles: the principle of joint liability and the principle of shared liability. According to the first principle, co-insurers are liable to the insured as joint debtors for the total amount of damages regardless of the size of their single share or according to the LO FB&H/LO RS 'every insurer indicated in the insurance policy is responsible to the insured for the entire indemnity'.[1008] The principle of joint liability provides a more favourable position for the insured in a complex legal relationship of co-insurance, particularly in the case of impossibility of the one co-insurer to fulfil their obligation (e.g., in the case of bankruptcy). Application of the principle of joint liability in the relationship of co-insurance prevails in B&H law. If the relationship between the insured and the insurer is based on the principle of shared liability, the insured may demand from each co-insurer only indemnification of the part of damages in proportion to their share in coverage of the risk.

1004. *See* the LO FB&H/LO RS, Art. 935.
1005. *See* the LI FB&H, Art. 4.
1006. *See ibid.*, Art. 101(1).
1007. Curak, Marijana & Jakovčević, Drago. *Osiguranje i rizici* (*Insurance and Risks*), Zagreb: RRIF Plus, (2007), 270.
1008. *See* the LO FB&H/LO RS, Art. 935.

Part IX. Taxation of Insurance

§1. Taxation of the Company

625. B&H has a complex tax system that is the reflexion of a specific state organization. While the system of direct taxation is composed of three separate tax subsystems: FB&H, RS and Brcko District of B&H (BD B&H), the indirect taxation system is established at the state level.

I. Corporate Income Tax

626. Insurance companies and other legal entities performing an independent, permanent economic activity through the sales of products and provision of services on the market for the purpose of generating an income, are considered taxpayers when it comes to corporate income tax. As a direct tax, income tax is regulated at the Entities' level by the Law on Corporate Income Tax of the FB&H (LCIT FB&H)[1009] and the Law on Corporate Income Tax of RS (LCIT RS)[1010] and by the Law on Corporate Income Tax at the level of BD B&H (LCIT BD B&H).[1011]

627. In the FB&H, the corporate income tax is determined and reported on the basis of data presented in the business books and records kept in accordance with the accounting regulations and IAS/IFRS, as well as data from the records and corrections which are prescribed by the LCIT FB&H and the Rulebook on the Implementation of the LCIT FB&H.[1012]

628. Corporate income tax is paid at the rate of 10% on the determined tax basis on the tax balance.[1013]

629. Taxpayers are insurance and reinsurance companies which generate income – on the market in FB&H, RS BD B&H or on the foreign market.[1014] Taxpayers in

1009. OJ FB&H, 15/2016, 15/2020.
1010. OJ RS, 94/2015, 1/2017, 58/2019.
1011. OJ BD B&H, 17/2022, 38/2022.
1012. OJ FB&H, 88/2016, 11/2017, 96/2017, 94/19, 87/2020.
1013. *See* the LCIT FB&H, Art. 31.
1014. *See ibid.*, Art. 3(1).

the context of the company income tax are also non-resident insurance and reinsurance companies when they generate income from a resident of FB&H.[1015] Resident companies, in terms of the LCIT FB&H, are those insurance and reinsurance companies whose head office (registration) is entered in the court register of business entities in the FB&H or companies whose actual management and supervision over the business operations are based in the FB&H.[1016] A non-resident company is a company established outside the territory of B&H whose head office or actual management and supervision over business activities also lies outside the territory of B&H.[1017]

630. The period in which the corporate income tax is determined is a calendar year, but this period may be even shorter in the case of cessation of business before the end of the calendar year; commencement of business operations during the year; status changes, etc. A taxpayer is obliged to submit a correctly and accurately filled out tax declaration with the tax balance, to the competent branch office of the Tax Administration: for the tax period ending with 31 December, that is, by the end of the year. A tax declaration with a tax balance and other supplements must be submitted to the competent tax office within a maximum of thirty days upon the end of the deadline prescribed for the submission of annual financial reports – that is, by 30 March of the current year for the previous year. As for the tax period ending in the course of the calendar year (cessation of business, status changes, etc.), the tax declaration with the tax balance and other supplements is submitted to the competent tax office within a maximum of ninety days from the last day of such tax period. In the second case, in accordance with the provisions of the LCIT FB&H, regulations on registration and all other regulations related to the business operations of legal entity, the only valid date is the date of the status change from the court registry.

631. The tax basis of corporate income tax is determined in the tax balance by harmonizing expenditures and income and capital gains/losses declared in the financial statements in the manner as prescribed by the LCIT FB&H.[1018] The tax basis is calculated as the profit declared in the financial statement increased by tax–unrecognized expenditures and other tax-unrecognized items and reduced by non-taxable items in accordance with the LCIT FB&H.[1019] Every income and capital gain realized by a taxpayer is included in the tax basis, except for items that, in accordance with the LCIT FB&H, are not included.[1020] The amount of corporate income tax is calculated by multiplying the tax basis with the income tax rate.[1021] Pursuant to Article 8 of the LCIT FB&H, to determine the tax basis, all expenditures, income

1015. *See ibid.*, Art. 3(4).
1016. *See ibid.*, Art. 5(1).
1017. *See ibid.*, Art. 5(2).
1018. *See ibid.*, Art. 7(1).
1019. *See ibid.*, Art. 7(2).
1020. *See ibid.*, Art. 7(3).
1021. *See ibid.*, Art. 7(4).

and capital gain/loss are recognized in the amounts declared in the business books, which are in accordance with the accounting regulations, unless otherwise prescribed by the LCIT FB&H.

632. According to the LCIT FB&H, expenditures for the formation of mathematical reserves, if they are formed in accordance with the regulations of the competent Agency, are recognized as tax–permissible to the insurance and reinsurance companies.[1022] Furthermore, expenditures for the formation of technical insurance reserves are also recognized as tax-permissible (except for mathematical reserves), under the following conditions: (a) that they are formed in accordance with the regulations of the competent insurance Agency; (b) that the amount of increase in the reserve in the current balance sheet compared to the previous period does not exceed 20%.[1023] Expenditures that exceed the amounts previously mentioned are not tax deductible expenditures and cannot be conveyed to a future tax period.[1024]

633. According to the provisions of the LCIT FB&H (Articles 36–37), tax incentives are prescribed only in cases of relatively significant investments[1025] and new employment. Regarding the latter, the taxpayer has the right to a tax-recognized expenditure in the amount of twofold sum of the gross salary paid to newly hired employees if it meets the following conditions: (a) the duration of the employment contract must be at least twelve months full-time and (b) the newly hired employee was not employed by taxpayer or related person in the previous five years.[1026]

634. When a taxpayer generates revenue or income through business activities performed outside the territory of B&H (directly or through its business unit) and pays corporate income tax on them, the tax paid abroad is incorporated into the paid tax, up to the amount of corporate income tax that would have been paid in the Federation on such income, with the obligation of the taxpayer to provide Tax Administration with evidence on payment of tax abroad for recognition of tax paid abroad.[1027] Ratified treaties (agreements, conventions) on avoidance of double taxation, signed by B&H are implemented when taxing non-residents and prevail over the provisions of the LCITFB&H.[1028]

635. Pursuant to the LCIT FB&H, the withholding or retention tax represents a type of tax that is calculated on revenue that has been realized by the non-resident in the territory of the Federation.[1029] The withholding tax is calculated and paid by the payer at the payment of the income. The payer is obliged to file the report on calculated and paid withholding tax to the Tax Administration within ten days of the

1022. *See ibid.*, Art. 16(3).
1023. *See ibid.*, Art. 16(4).
1024. *See ibid.*, Art. 16(5).
1025. *See ibid.*, Art. 36.
1026. *See ibid.*, Art. 37(1).
1027. *See ibid.*, Arts 32 and 33.
1028. *See ibid.*, Art. 35.
1029. *See ibid.*, Art. 38(1).

day of payment.[1030] The basis for calculation of the withholding tax is the gross amount paid by the resident of the Federation to the non-resident on the basis, *inter alia*, insurance premiums for insurance or reinsurance of risk in the Federation.[1031] The withholding tax is paid at the rate of 10% (and on dividends at the rate of 5%).[1032]

636. The LCIT FB&H and the Rulebook for the Implementation of the LCIT of FB&H prescribe: how to determine this type of tax, the filing of tax declarations, payment of tax obligations and their statute of limitations if they are not timely determined and charged.[1033] Pursuant to the Rulebook on the Implementation of the LCIT FB&H, the corporate income tax is determined after the end of the calendar year or other period for which it was necessary to calculate and state corporate income tax according to the tax basis precisely determined for that period.[1034] Control, determination and collection of corporate income tax are performed in a manner and according to procedures prescribed by the FB&H Law on Tax Administration.[1035]

637. The taxation of income generated by insurance and reinsurance companies as well as income of other legal entities on the territory of the RS is regulated by the LCIT RS which establishes the general legal framework for the taxation of the income of legal persons in the RS and foreign legal persons who generate revenues in the RS.[1036] Pursuant to the LCIT RS, the taxpayers are: a legal person from RS for incomes obtained from any source whether in the RS, FB&H, BD B&H or abroad; a business unit of a legal person with seat in FB&H or BD B&H for income realized in the RS; a foreign legal person carrying out business activity and has a permanent place of business in the RS for the income that relates to that permanent place of business; a foreign legal person obtaining revenue from real estate located in the RS for the income that relates to that real estate and other legal persons specified in Article 3 of the LCIT RS. The business unit of a legal person from the FB&H or the BD B&H is a taxpayer of the corporate income tax in RS for income realized through performance of business activities in the RS.[1037] The income of a foreign legal person is taxable if it is a result of activities performed in the territory of the RS through the permanent place of business of a foreign legal entity.

638. The tax basis of the legal person from the RS is the income generated in the RS and outside its territory, and the tax basis of a foreign legal person that has a permanent place of business in the RS is only the income generated in the RS.

1030. *See ibid.*, Art. 35(5).
1031. *See ibid.*, Art. 38(1).
1032. *See ibid.*, Art. 35(7).
1033. *See ibid.*, Arts 47–57.
1034. *See ibid.*, Art. 47.
1035. OJ FB&H, 33/2002, 28/2004, 57/2009, 40/2010, 27/2012, 7/2013, 71/2014, 91/2015, 44/2022.
1036. *See* the LCIT RS, Art. 1.
1037. *See ibid.*, Art. 3(2).

639. The operating, financial, non-operating and extraordinary revenue and revaluation revenue calculated on the income balance in accordance with the law governing accounting, with the exception of revenue for which the LCIT RS prescribes another method of calculation, are recognized for the determination of tax basis in the tax declaration.

640. Corporate income tax is paid at the rate of 10% for the tax year in both the FB&H and the RS. The tax year for legal persons is the calendar year unless the competent Ministry of Finance determines a different tax year to be used, which is not the calendar year.

641. The tax declaration for a tax year must be submitted no later than ninety days upon the end of the tax year, and in case of a calendar year, no later than 31 March of the current year for the previous year.

642. If a legal person from the RS obtains revenue in a foreign state and the revenue is taxed both in the RS and in that foreign state, whether paid directly or upon deduction by another person, then the tax paid in the foreign state is to be deducted from the RS corporate income tax, unless such legal person from the RS does not choose the foreign tax to be treated as expenditure that is deductible when determining the tax basis for the tax year.[1038]

643. The reduction of corporate income tax for the tax paid abroad for the tax year may not exceed the amount of the corporate income tax calculated by applying the rate of tax of that legal person for that tax year in the RS. In case corporate income tax paid abroad exceeds the amount of tax on income realized in the RS, the excess amount is then transferred within a period of five tax years and is subject to the same limitations for those tax years.[1039]

644. The third corporate income taxation subsystem in B&H is established on the territory of BD B&H. The Law on Corporate Income Tax of BD B&H (LCIT BD) established a general legal framework for the taxation of the income of legal persons based in the BD B&H, the business units of legal persons on the territory of the BD B&H based in the FB&H and the RS and foreign legal persons that generate revenue in the BD B&H.[1040]

645. Correspondingly to the solutions contained in the Entities laws on corporate income tax, the LCIT BD B&H prescribes that the taxpayers are: a legal person from BD B&H for income obtained from any source whether in B&H or abroad; a business unit of a legal person with headquarters in the Entities for the income generated in the BD B&H; a foreign legal person carrying out an economic activity and permanent place of business in the BD B&H for the income that is attributable to

1038. *See ibid.*, Art. 50(1).
1039. *See ibid.*, Art. 50(2).
1040. *See* the LCIT BD B&H, Art. 1.

the permanent place of business; a foreign legal person generating revenue from real estate located in the BD B&H for the income that is attributable to the real estate.[1041]

646. Pursuant to the LCIT BD B&H, the tax basis for the tax year is taxable income determined in the tax balance.[1042] Taxable income is determined by adjusting the revenue and expenditure of the taxpayer stated in the income statement, in accordance with the law, except for revenue and expenditures for which this Law prescribes a different method of calculation.[1043]

647. Taxable revenue with the aim of calculating the tax basis includes all revenue sources, whether in cash or in kind, and regardless of whether that revenue is linked to the operations of a legal person, other than revenue under Article 7 of the LCIT BD B&H.[1044] The calculation of the tax basis, *inter alia*, does not include revenue in the form of interest from the securities that are issued or guaranteed by B&H, BD B&H, the Entities, the Central Bank, enterprises, insurance companies, investment funds and banks or other financial institutions.[1045] When calculating the tax basis from revenue, the deductible expenditures are those directly attributable to the generated revenue.[1046] Expenditures that are recognized and deductible from revenue, among others, are the insurance premiums paid by the employer for personal gain unless those premiums are included in employees' salaries.[1047]

648. Pursuant to the LCIT BD B&H, insurance legal persons, including banks and authorized credit institutions, are not allowed to have a deduction on the basis of written-off suspicious claims that arise in connection with the sale of goods or services, but only if the revenue from the sale was previously included in the tax basis of the legal person.[1048] As for insurance and reinsurance companies, the deduction is allowed to increase reserves as registered in accounting documents in accordance with the law.[1049] For insurance contracts, relating to reinsurance, reserves are reduced to cover only part of the risk borne by the insurance company and may not exceed 20% of the tax basis.

649. For insurance contracts, relating to reinsurance, reserves are reduced to cover only part of the risk borne by the insurance company and are not to be higher than 20% of the tax basis.

650. The income tax in the BD B&H is also paid at the rate of 10% on a tax basis for that tax year.

1041. *Ibid.*
1042. *See* the LCIT BD B&H, Art. 5(1).
1043. *See ibid.*, Art. 5(2).
1044. *See ibid.*, Art. 6.
1045. *See ibid.*, Art. 7.
1046. *See ibid.*, Art. 8(1).
1047. *See ibid.*, Art. 8(2).
1048. *See ibid.*, Art. 10(2).
1049. *See ibid.*, Art. 10(5).

651. The general rule is that the tax year for legal persons is the calendar year – in the case when a legal person becomes a taxpayer during the tax year or ceases to be the taxpayer during the tax year, the tax year is the period in the calendar year when the legal entity was the taxpayer.[1050] The tax declaration for a tax year must be submitted no later than ninety days upon the end of the tax year, and in case of a calendar year, no later than 31 March of the current year for the previous year.[1051]

II. Other Taxes

652. In addition to income tax, insurance and reinsurance companies may be taxpayers when it comes to real estate taxes and property taxes. Real estate tax is regulated in B&H at three levels: in the FB&H at the cantonal level, the level of the RS and the BD B&H. More specifically, in B&H there are currently twelve effective laws on real estate tax: ten effective laws are adopted at the cantonal level in the FB&H, and one law in the RS and in the BD B&H. Also, special taxes on the property have been established by the relevant laws at the cantonal level in the FB&H.

§2. Taxation of Insurance

653. While the LI FB&H doesn't include specific provisions with regard to taxes, the LIC RS stipulates that indirect taxation, as well as fees, duties or other costs arising from insurance contracts, concluded in the territory of one Entity by the insurance company that is based in the other Entity, are subjected to Entity regulations in which they were concluded;[1052] and also that data relating to the collection of indirect taxes for the transaction of insurance in one Entity through the organizational unit of the insurance company from the other Entity of B&H shall be governed by the rules determined by the competent Entity Agency in whose territory the transactions are performed.[1053]

I. Value Added Tax

654. Unlike direct taxes, the obligation to pay the Value Added Tax (VAT) was introduced in B&H, at the state level by the adoption of the Law on Value Added Tax (LVAT).[1054] It is operationalized by the provisions of the Rulebook on the Implementation of the LVAT.[1055] Insurance and reinsurance services, including the

1050. *See ibid.*, Art. 21(1) and (2).
1051. *See ibid.*, Art. 22(1).
1052. *See* the LIC RS, Art. 37(1). Identical provision was contained in Art. 38(1) of the LIC FB&H which is no longer in force.
1053. *See* the LIC RS, Art. 37(3).
1054. OJ B&H, 9/2005, 35/2005, 100/2008, 33/2017.
1055. *Ibid.*, 93/2005, 21/2006, 60/2006, 6/2007, 100/2007, 35/2008, 65/2010, 44/2020, 47/2022, 87/2022.

accompanying services provided by insurance brokers and insurance agents, are exempt from paying the VAT,[1056] which is in accordance with the provisions of the LVAT B&H, paid on goods and services that are performed by the taxpayer in the territory of B&H within its activity for the remuneration, and on the importation of goods into B&H.[1057]

655. If the insurance company is also registered to carry out other activities that result in taxable turnover in the amount higher than BAM 50,000.00, it is obliged to register itself under VAT as a taxpayer. When determining whether or not the threshold of BAM 50,000 is crossed, the trade of related companies and other entities, either through possession of shares or in any other way are under common direct or indirect control of the insurance company, will be taken into account.

II. Personal Income Tax

656. Income taxation, as well as the previously considered case of corporate income tax, is governed by the laws adopted at the Entity level (the FB&H and the RS) and the BD B&H level. The adoption of new laws on income tax in B&H introduced a single method of taxation of natural persons' income. By adopting new legislation on income tax, B&H has moved to the synthetic concept of income taxation based on the assumption that all revenues generated by the taxpayer are to be taxed pursuant to a single, comprehensive tax.

657. The Law on Personal Income Tax (LPIT)[1058] prescribes the method of determination and payment of tax on income of natural persons in the FB&H.[1059] A taxpayer is a resident of the FB&H and a non-resident who generates income, as follows: (1) a resident who generates income in the territory of the FB&H and outside the territory of the FB&H; (2) a non-resident performing self-employed activity through a permanent place of business in the territory of the FB&H; (3) a non-resident performing employment activities in the FB&H; (4) a non-resident who generates revenue on the territory of the FB&H from movable property or real estate, copyrights, patents, licenses, investment capital, or any other activity which results in the realization of revenue that is taxable pursuant to the LPIT FB&H.[1060]

658. Income tax is taxable income earned by taxpayers: from dependent activity, independent activity; property and property rights; capital investment; and participation in competitions and games of chance.[1061] The income tax basis of a resident represents the difference between the total taxable revenues earned in one

---

1056. *See* the LVAT B&H, Art. 25(1).
1057. *See ibid.*, Art. 3.
1058. OJ FB&H, 10/2008, 9/2010, 44/2011, 7/2013, 65/2013. Provisions of the Law are further operationalized through the by-law– Rulebook on the implementation of the LPIT FB&H, (OJ FB&H, 67/2008, 04/2010, 86/2010, 10/2011, 53/2011, 20/2012, 27/2013, 71/2013, 90/2013, 45/2014).
1059. *See* the LPIT FB&H, Art. 1(1).
1060. *See ibid.*, Art. 2(1).
1061. *See ibid.*, Art. 4.

tax period and the total deductions that can be recognized in connection with the acquisition of such revenue (transferred loss, expenditures necessary for the acquisition of that revenue and personal deduction).[1062] The tax basis of the income of the non-resident (from Article 2(1) item 3) and 4) of the LPIT FB&H) is paid income.[1063]

659. Personal income tax is determined and paid for the calendar year. However, the tax period may be shorter than the calendar year in case: when a resident during a calendar year becomes a non-resident and vice versa; and when the capacity of the resident as a taxpayer starts or ceases to exist.[1064] Income tax is paid at a rate of 10%.[1065]

660. It is necessary to note that several specific provisions pertaining to the insurance are contained in the LPIT FB&H, particularly in Articles 5(9), 6(1) item (13), 22(1) item (2), 33(2) and (3) and 24(7). Pursuant to the LPIT FB&H, the insurance or other compensation of damages made to the property, in the amount that is used to replace or repair damaged property represents revenue that is not considered to be income.[1066] Article 6(1) item 13 of the LPIT FB&H provides that the income tax is not paid on the revenue of natural persons realized on the basis of paid life insurance premiums, which have the character of savings and paid revenue from voluntary pension insurance, paid by insurance and reinsurance companies which have their headquarters in the territory of the Federation, arising from paid premiums on which are paid mandatory contributions and income tax. Pursuant to the LPIT FB&H, the revenues generated from the paid-up capital of voluntary additional insurance (life, pension) that is saved from premiums that were subject to deductions are included in the income from investment of taxable capital.[1067] Article 33(2) of the LPIT FB&H and Article 61(1) of the Rules for the implementation of the LPIT FB&H provides that the taxable income in respect of insurance[1068] shall be subject to paying of the withholding tax at the rate of 10%, without the right to a reduction of the basis for personal deductions pursuant to Article 24(7) of the LPIT FB&H.[1069] Accordingly, the paid insured sum is the basis for taxation, on which the tax rate of 10% is applied. The same treatment has the payment of the surrender value of the sum insured, i.e., it will constitute the basis for the calculation of taxes on the occasion of the surrender value payment. The insurer is obligated to deduct the amount of 10% and pay it to the tax office in the area where the insured person lives. Calculated and suspended income tax pursuant to Article 33(2)

1062. *See ibid.*, Art. 7(1).
1063. *See ibid.*, Art. 7(2).
1064. *See ibid.*, Art. 8(2).
1065. *See ibid.*, Art. 9.
1066. *See ibid.*, Art. 5(9).
1067. *See ibid.*, Art. 22(1) item (2).
1068. *Ibid.*
1069. Pursuant to Art. 24(7) of the LPIT FB&H, resident taxpayer may increase personal deduction by annual accounting of the income tax and the premium paid for a life insurance that has the character of savings, and/or paid for voluntary pension insurance, and up to 0.7 of the basic personal deduction for which, pursuant to para. 1 of this Article, for which right he/she qualified himself in the tax period.

of the LPIT FB&H is considered the final tax obligation of the taxpayer, and the taxpayer does not enter this income in the annual tax declaration.

661. The provisions of the LPIT FB&H are also relevant for insurance intermediaries in the case of natural persons. In fact, as already noted, the income from self-employed activity is also taxed. It includes the income that a natural person realizes through the independent permanent activities engaged in as a primary or subsidiary occupation in order to generate income.[1070]

662. In addition to other incomes, the income from self-employment also pertains to the incomes of insurance intermediaries, natural persons – brokers and insurance agents achieved by the performance of independent professional activities.[1071] Self-employment income constitutes the difference between operating revenues and operating expenditures incurred in the tax period, and the tax basis is determined by applying the accounting principle.[1072] Operating incomes for the purposes of the LPIT FB&H are considered all incomes obtained from any source received in cash, goods and services, which have been realized independently or by the joint performance of activities, regardless of whether the natural person is registered or not for this activity.[1073] Operating expenses that are deductible from the income are the costs paid during one tax period that are in full explicitly and directly related to the performance of that independent activity.[1074]

663. Also, in the area of the RS, the income produced by a natural person is subjected to taxation in accordance with the regulations of the income tax. The 2006 Law on Income Tax (LPIT RS)[1075] has been replaced by the new Law on Income Tax,[1076] which has been in force since 1 September 2015.

664. As already noted, the subject of taxation is the income produced by a natural person in the tax period in accordance with the provisions of the LPIT RS.[1077]

665. Personal income tax is calculated and paid on the incomes from personal income, income arising from independent business activity, copyright, rights related to copyright and rights of industrial property, capital, capital deductions and foreign sources of other income.[1078] The income tax shall be paid at the rate of 10%, except for the small business income and income from foreign sources, which are paid in

1070. *See* the LPIT FB&H, Art. 12(1).
1071. *See ibid.*, Art. 12(2).
1072. *See ibid.*, Art. 13.
1073. *See ibid.*, Art. 14(1).
1074. *See ibid.*, Art. 15(1).
1075. OJ RS, 91/2006, 128/2006, 120/2008, 71/2010, 1/2011, 107/2013.
1076. *Ibid.*, 60/2015, 66/2018, 105/2019, 123/2020, 49/2021, 119/2021, 56/22.
1077. *See* the LPIT RS, Art. 2(1).
1078. *See ibid.*, Art. 3(1).

accordance with specific provisions of the LPIT RS.[1079] The income tax is determined and paid for the calendar year, but the tax period may be shorter than the calendar year if: the taxpayer during the calendar year becomes a non-resident; and when a resident acquires or loses the status of the taxpayer.[1080]

666. A taxpayer is a natural person who under the provisions of the LPIT RS realizes taxable income if he/she is a resident of the RS, for income earned in the RS, the FB&H, the BD B&H or another country, or a non-resident for income earned in the RS.[1081] Pursuant to Article 7 of the LPIT RS, personal income tax basis is the difference between the total revenue generated in a one-tax period and the total expenditures recognized in accordance with the LPIT RS.

667. The relevant provisions of the LPIT RS relating to tax exemptions in insurance are the payment of the insured sums from the property insurance and insurance of persons, as well as the payment of the insured sums from the insurance of persons for indemnification of the suffered damage, except for payment of insurance of lost benefit or income; and a final payment of life insurance, other than the amount of paid premium for life insurance up to BAM 1,200 per year.[1082] The new LPIT RS introduced the right to reduce the tax basis of income tax,[1083] in addition to the paid pension contributions for voluntary pension insurance of up to BAM 1,200 per year, also on the ground of paid premium of life insurance at the insurance company that has a licence of the Insurance Agency of RS, up to BAM 1,200 per year.[1084]

668. With regard to the insurance industry in the broad sense including insurance mediation, relevant are provisions of the LPIT RS regulating: income from self-employment – all revenues obtained through any source, received in cash, goods and services, realized through independent or joint performance of activity;[1085] and other income, i.e., all the revenues realized by a natural person on any grounds, except for the income referred to in Article 3 (items 1–6) of the LPIT RS. Specifically, the revenue from self-employment, in addition to the revenues from agriculture, forestry and fisheries, revenues from entrepreneurial activities and self-employment, includes professional activities of natural persons, which are on that basis registered in the appropriate registry[1086] and therefore apply to insurance intermediaries (insurance agents and insurance brokers). It is important to note that a natural person performing professional activity cannot obtain the status of a small business entrepreneur. Furthermore, pursuant to the LPIT RS, other income also

1079. *See ibid.*, Art. 4.
1080. *See ibid.*, Art. 5.
1081. *See ibid.*, Art. 6.
1082. *See ibid.*, Art. 8(3) items 8) and 9).
1083. *See ibid.*, Art. 7.
1084. *See ibid.*, Art. 10(1).
1085. *See ibid.*, Art. 14(1).
1086. *See ibid.*, Art. 14(1) and (3).

includes revenues generated on the basis of contracts, i.e., revenues of agents and collectors who perform these tasks by an order of the payer.[1087]

669. As regards the tax basis for these types of revenues – the RS income tax system, the tax basis for tax on self-employment income is the difference between income and expenses occurring by independent activity within the tax period.[1088] When it comes to the tax basis for these types of revenues – incomes in the tax system of RS, the tax basis for calculation of tax on self-employment income is the difference between revenues and expenditures as a result of performing independent activity within the tax period,[1089] and the tax basis of other income is the difference between the revenue referred to in Article 52 of the LPIT RS and paid contributions.[1090]

670. Under the new LPIT RS, capital income from dividends and shares in the income of legal persons are no longer taxed.[1091] In this way, this taxation is harmonized with the taxation in the FB&H as well as the conditions for doing business in B&H's market.

671. Article 71 of the LPIT RS stipulates that the RS Minister of Finance has to pass six new rulebooks relating to the implementation of the LPIT RS within ninety days from the entry of this Law into force, and by that time the Rulebook on the Implementation of the LPIT RS will apply.[1092]

672. The LPIT BD B&H is applied in the area of BD B&H,[1093] which prescribes the method of determining and paying of tax on personal income of natural persons in the BD B&H. In addition, the revenues from this tax belong to the budget of the BD B&H.[1094] The provisions of the LPIT BD B&H are almost identical to the LPIT FB&H, with minor deviations, and operationalized by the Rulebook on the implementation of the LPIT BD B&H.[1095]

673. The taxpayer in terms of the LPIT BD B&H is a resident of the BD B&H and a non-resident who generates income: resident and non-resident who generates income in the area of the BD B&H and outside the BD B&H; a non-resident performing employment activity through a permanent place of business in the BD B&H; a non-resident performing a self-employed activity in the area of the BD B&H; a non-resident who generates revenue in the BD B&H from movable property and real estate, copyrights, patents, licenses, investment capital, or any other

1087. *See ibid.*, Art. 52 item 5.
1088. *See ibid.*, Art. 15(1). Tax basis shall be determined by applying the principle of accounting (cash), *see* LPIT RS, Art. 15(2).
1089. *See* the LPIT RS, Art. 15(1).
1090. *See ibid.*, Art. 53.
1091. *See ibid.*, Art. 32.
1092. OJ RS, 22/2011, 22/2014, 2/15, 9/2015.
1093. OJ BD B&H, 60/2010, 14/2017, 24/2020, 21/2022.
1094. *See* the LPIT BD B&H, Art. 1.
1095. OJ BD B&H, 6/2011.

activity which results in the generation of revenue that is taxable in accordance with the LPIT BD B&H. Taxable incomes are incomes realized by the taxpayer from employment activity, self-employment activity, property and property rights, capital investments, and participation in games of chance.[1096] The income tax basis of a resident is the difference between the total taxable revenues earned in one tax period and total deductions that can be recognized in connection with the acquisition of such revenue, such as assigned loss, expenditures necessary for the acquisition of that revenue and personal deduction.[1097] The income tax basis of non-residents under Article 3(1) items b), c) and d) of this Law is the difference between the total taxable revenue earned in one tax period and total deductions that can be recognized in connection with the acquisition of such revenue, such as assigned loss and expenditures necessary for the acquisition of that revenue.[1098]

674. Revenues and expenditures on which the taxable income is determined are determined based on the cash method of accounting.[1099] As with the Entities' laws on income tax, the tax period is the calendar year with the possibility that the tax period is shorter in the cases when: a resident during a calendar year becomes a non-resident or vice versa; and when a resident ceases to be a taxpayer.[1100]

675. In the BD B&H, the LPIT BD B&H as well as the LPIT FB&H provides that indemnity from insurance or other compensations of damage made to the property in the amount needed to replace or repair damaged property is revenue that is not considered as income.[1101] The expenditures that are deducted from revenues when determining the income from employment activity are included and paid into compulsory contributions from salaries in accordance with the regulations in force, including the contributions for pension and disability insurance, health insurance, and unemployment insurance.[1102] Pursuant to the LPIT BD B&H, a resident taxpayer may increase personal deduction for paid premium for life insurance that has a character of savings up to 50% of basic personal deduction.[1103]

676. In the BD B&H, the income tax is paid at the rate of 10%.

677. Furthermore, as the Entities' regulations on income tax, the LPIT BD B&H also contains provisions relevant to the insurance intermediaries who are natural persons in the provisions of Articles 13–20.

1096. *See* the LPIT BD B&H, Art. 5.
1097. *See ibid.*, Art. 8(1).
1098. *See ibid.*, Art. 8(2).
1099. *See ibid.*, Art. 8(3).
1100. *See ibid.*, Art. 9.
1101. *See ibid.*, Art. 6(1).
1102. *See ibid.*, Art. 12.
1103. *See ibid.*, Art. 25(4).

Part X. Risk Management and Prevention

678. Risk management generally signifies a variety of measures and procedures for the detection, analysis and control of risk in the insurance sector. In the literature, the main phases of risk management are risk identification, risk assessment, selection of methods for risk management, evaluation, application of selected methods for risk management and review.[1104] Risk avoidance, risk retention, risk transfer, risk sharing and risk reduction signify five basic methods of risk management.[1105] Risk avoidance entails not undertaking activities that are risky. Risk retention, one of the most common methods of risk management, consists of not undertaking activities directed at avoidance, reduction or transfer of risk where risk retention is consciously realized by undertaking predictable and relatively small losses. Risk management through transfer is executed in such a manner that the risk is transferred from one subject to another subject more prepared to bear the risk. Risk sharing is achieved through the distribution of losses and risks that are shared in the majority of cases (insurance is one of the mechanisms designed to regulate risk through distribution). Risk reduction as a manner of management is realized through the prevention and control of risk. Risk prevention in insurance can be defined as the undertaking of measures in order to eliminate and reduce adverse effects of causes that may induce damage.

679. Although risk management has increasingly developed in the last fifteen years, this area in the insurance law of B&H has only gained more attention in the last few years. In the RS, the 2010 changes of the Law on Insurance Companies RS (LIC RS),[1106] *inter alia*, entailed the enactment of provisions directly related to risk management in insurance and which imposed compliance with rules on capital adequacy, liquidity and solvency.[1107] Thus, after amendments, the LIC RS prescribed the obligation of insurance companies to ensure that they always dispose of with sufficient capital in terms of scope and type of insurance activities performed and with regard to risks to which they are exposed to during the performance of

---

1104. *See* Kočović, Jelena & Šulejić, Predrag. *Osiguranje* (*Insurance*), Beograd: Centar za izdavačku delatnost Ekonomskog fakulteta u Beogradu, (2006), 101.
1105. *See* Marović, Boris & Avdalović, Veselin. Osiguranje i upravljanje rizikom (*Insurance and Risk Management*), Subotica: Biografika, (2005), 70–72.
1106. OJ RS, 17/2005, 1/2006, 64/2006, 74/2010, 47/2017, 58/2019.
1107. *See* the LIC RS, Art. 52a(1).

those activities (capital adequacy). Insurance companies are also required to operate in such a manner so that they are able to timely fulfil due obligations (the principle of liquidity) or to ensure that they are permanently able to complete all their obligations (the solvency principle).

680. If an insurance company cannot cover a part of the assumed risk and the risk exceeds the shares in risk compensation, according to the tables of maximum coverage (self-retention), the company is obliged to transfer that part of the risk to reinsurance or to co-insure the risk with one or more insurance companies.[1108] Besides, an insurance company is obliged to manage sources and fund investments in such a way so that it is at all times able to meet due obligations, daily calculate amounts of liquid assets and to adopt and regularly conduct liquidity management policy (rules of liquidity management) for the purpose of ensuring liquidity.

681. Furthermore, with regard to risk management, the LIC RS stipulates limitations to the payment of dividends, i.e., prohibits insurance companies to pay out profit in the form of dividends in cash or to make payments based on participation in the profit to members of the management or employees in the following cases: if the company does not meet the capital adequacy requirements set out in the regulations governing the field of insurance; if it does not meet the requirements of liquidity and solvency, or if payments would jeopardize its liquidity or solvency; and, if the Insurance Agency of RS orders the removal of irregularities and illegalities in the presentation of data in financial reports of insurance companies, due to which the financial reports of companies are not true and accurate, i.e., if the insurance company fails to comply with orders of the Insurance Agency of RS.[1109]

682. According to the LIC RS, without the consent of the Insurance Agency of RS, an insurance company cannot increase share capital and carry out emissions of debt securities and other financial derivatives that represent an item of capital when determining capital adequacy.[1110]

683. Insurance companies must cover accumulated losses from the previous business year in the following year.[1111]

684. If the capital of an insurance company is not sufficient due to the increased solvency margin or other reasons, the management of the insurance company must immediately adopt and implement measures within its competence in order to provide capital or to draft a proposal of measures that are within competence of other bodies of the insurance company in relation to obtaining the necessary capital. The insurance company must notify the Agency of RS within eight days of the adoption of these measures.

1108. *See ibid.*, Art, 52a(2).
1109. *See ibid.*, Art. 52a(3).
1110. *See ibid.*, Art. 52a(6).
1111. *See ibid.*, Art. 52a(1).

685. In the context of risk management, in order to protect policyholders, the LIC RS stipulates that the Insurance Agency of RS may impose certain requirements on insurance companies such as the requirement to have more capital in case a weakened financial position of the insurance company could jeopardize the rights of policyholders. In this situation, the amount of capital is determined in accordance with a financial plan with propositions of measures for the minimum duration of three years. There may be a reduction in the value of the insurance company's assets, including its capital account, or the obligation to cover technical and mathematical reserves and guarantee a fund if there is a change in the market value of those assets; or the need to adjust the calculation of the solvency margin of the insurance company for the amount of reinsurance if the content of the reinsurance contracts in relation to the previous business year is significantly changed, or if the reinsurance contracts do not allow a balanced transfer of risk.[1112]

686. If the Insurance Agency of RS establishes that an insurance company violates risk management rules (rules of liquidity and solvency, capital adequacy requirements, rules on funds formation for coverage of technical and mathematical reserves, reinsurance rules, rules of investment of funds for coverage of technical and mathematical reserves, restrictions in dividend payments, etc.) and rules on the protection of policyholders, it may issue a decision to determine the additional measures against the insurance company, which are prescribed in Article 54(8) of the LIC RS. Furthermore, according to the amendments of the LIC RS, the Insurance Agency of RS may withdraw the licence of the insurance company, if it continues, *inter alia*, to violate the rules of risk management after the decision of the Agency on illegality or irregularity or the decision on taking further measures.[1113]

687. Further regulatory activities undertaken by the Insurance Agency of RS are reflected in the adoption of the subordinate legislation (Rulebook on management in the insurance company RS)[1114] that is dedicated to the establishment of the risk management system[1115] and prescribes the minimum requirements and rules for detecting, measuring, monitoring and assessment of risks to which an insurance company is exposed.[1116] In the Rulebook, risk is defined as the probability of occurrence of events, which may have adverse effects, i.e., lead to negative deviations in relation to the business objectives of insurance companies.[1117] Also, risk is considered to be the inability to achieve business objectives or the danger that events, procedures, unused resources and capacities may have a negative impact on the achievement of business objectives of an insurance company.[1118] Risk management in terms of the Rulebook embraces strategies, policies, procedures and reporting that are necessary for the detection, measurement, risk monitoring (governing and control) and continuous reporting on an individual and group basis on the risk to

1112. *See ibid.*, Art. 52a(9).
1113. *See ibid.*, Art. 29(4).
1114. OJ RS, 107/2015.
1115. *See* the Rulebook on Management in the Insurance Company, Arts 13–26.
1116. *See ibid.*, Art. 1(2).
1117. *See ibid.*, Art. 13(1).
1118. *See ibid.*, Art. 13(2).

which an insurance company is exposed to, or could be exposed to in its operations and on the interdependence of those types of risk.

688. According to the Rulebook, an insurance company is obligated to prescribe, organize and establish comprehensive, reliable, effective and efficient risk management through its internal regulations with the aim to ensure the maintenance of risk exposure at a level that will not threaten the achievement of business goals and assets (funds) of the company (i.e., at a level which will ensure the protection of interests of policyholders, insurance beneficiaries, damaged third parties and other creditors).[1119] The executive board or management of the insurance company is obliged to enact strategies, policies and procedures for risk management and to ensure their implementation as well as to establish and document appropriate processes for risk management.[1120]

689. The objective of risk management is the identification, measurement and control of the exposure to risk by insurance companies for the purpose of more efficient risk management in order to achieve strategic objectives in accordance with legislation and internal regulations of the insurance company.[1121] The Rulebook lists the main types of risks to which insurance companies are exposed to or may be exposed to in their operations, such as insurance risk, market risk, credit risk, operative risk, liquidity risk, risk of exposure concentration, legal risk, strategic risk, reputation risk, etc.[1122] According to the Rulebook, risk management entails the identification of risk, risk measurement, risk monitoring and risk reporting.[1123] The obligation of an insurance company is to submit a report on risk management to ensure all levels of management and leadership obtain the timely, complete and accurate information necessary for making business decisions related to the actual risk profile, to minimize possible losses on the basis of individual types of risk.[1124] This information contains relevant data on the risk profile or changes in the risk profile, measures and activities that should be taken and data on positive and negative changes in performance indicators that suggest or may suggest a change in exposure to the risk.[1125]

690. An internal audit is required at least once a year to assess the appropriateness and effectiveness as well as efficiency of the risk management function in the company.[1126] The executive board of an insurance company is obliged to continuously follow and evaluate risk management and to present a report on risk management as part of an annual report on business activities of the insurance company where it must state the objectives and policies of the company in relation to risk

1119. *See ibid.*, Art. 15(1).
1120. *See ibid.*, Art. 15(2).
1121. *See ibid.*, Art. 14(1).
1122. *See ibid.*, Art. 14(2).
1123. *See ibid.*, Art. 20.
1124. *See ibid.*, Art. 25(1).
1125. *See ibid.*, Art. 25(2).
1126. *See ibid.*, Art. 25(3).

management, the exposure of the insurance company to risk set out in the Article 14(2) and the general assessment of risk management.[1127]

691. Therefore, from the content of the Rulebook, it is evident, that the effort to operationalize provisions of the LIC RS is directed at the modernization and improvement of the efficiency of risk management mechanisms in insurance companies in order to increase the protection of the consumers of insurance services. The new system of management should follow the changes in the risk profile of an insurance company and must be under continuous supervision of the Insurance Agency of RS, which may in the case of established violation of risk management rules determine the additional measures specified in the Article 54(8) of the LIC RS.

692. However, the Rulebook on Management in the Insurance Company in RS was declared null and void in 2016,[1128] after only one year of implementation.

693. The new insurance law, adopted in the FB&H in 2017 (the Law on Insurance [LI FB&H])[1129] in contrast to the previous law regulates risk management in insurance in Chapter III (Articles 60–103) which includes the following sections: section A. General Provisions, Section B. Risk Management, section C. System of Internal Controls, section D. Insurance Company Capital, section E. Capital Adequacy, section F. Liquidity Management, section G. Technical Reserves, section H. Assets for coverage of technical reserves in non-life and life insurance, section I. Reinsurance and co-insurance of risks, and section J. Prevention of money laundering and financing of terrorist activities.

694. According to Article 60(1) of the LI FB&H, the insurance company is required to ensure the existence and functioning of an effective management system that includes risk management, internal control system, internal audit and actuarial activity. This management system should be harmonized with the size and organizational structure of the specific insurance company, the scope of its activities and types of insurance that performs.[1130] The Supervisory Agency prescribes the way of regulating the management system in the insurance company[1131] in the Rulebook on the types and systems of risk management in insurance companies and reinsurance companies.[1132]

695. Insurance companies and reinsurance companies must have in place an effective risk management system that includes strategies, processes and reporting procedures that are necessary for the identification, measurement and monitoring of

1127. *See ibid.*, Art. 26(2).
1128. OJ RS, 50/2016.
1129. OJ FB&H, 23/2017, 103/2021.
1130. *See* the LI FB&H, Art. 60(2).
1131. *See ibid.*, Art. 60(3).
1132. OJ FB&H, 92/2017, 27/2018.

risks, risk management and continuous reporting on an individual and group basis about the risks to which they are exposed or could be exposed, and about the mutual dependence of those risks.[1133]

696. The risk management system should be efficient and well integrated into the organizational structure and decision-making processes of the insurance company or reinsurance company and should take into account the persons who effectively manage the company or have other key functions.[1134]

697. The risk management system covers risks that are included in the calculation of the capital requirement in terms of solvency as well as risks that are not included or not fully included in that calculation.[1135] The risk management system includes: (a) underwriting risks and forming reserves, (b) asset and liability management, (c) investments, especially derivatives and similar liabilities, (d) liquidity and concentration risk management, (e) operational risk management, (f) reinsurance and other risk reduction techniques.[1136] The insurance company's risk management system should at least include the assessment of the following risks: (a) non-life insurance risk, (b) life insurance risk, (c) health insurance risk, (d) market risk, (e) deposit and investment risk, (f) operational risk.[1137] The Rulebook on the types and system of risk management in insurance companies and reinsurance companies in FB&H prescribes that the insurance company is obliged to establish, document and apply written rules related to the risk management system and to ensure that the same rules are implemented, at least in the areas previously referred.[1138] These written rules are adopted by the executive board with the approval of the supervisory board of the insurance company and they should be adjusted in case of any significant change in the management system or in the business area.[1139] These written rules are subject to internal review at least once a year, and they need to be regularly updated.[1140] Within the framework of the risk management system, the company performs its own assessment of risk and solvency, which is an integral part of the business strategy and is taken into account when making strategic decisions for the company.[1141]

698. Furthermore, the company is obliged to ensure a clear division of business functions and prevent conflicts of interest.[1142] This means that powers and responsibilities must be defined in such a way that employees responsible for taking over or managing risks at the operational level cannot be entrusted with supervision and

---

1133. *See* the LI FB&H, Art. 61(1).
1134. *See ibid.*, Art. 61(2).
1135. *See ibid.*, Art. 61(3).
1136. *See ibid.*, Art. 61(4).
1137. *See ibid.*, Art. 61(5).
1138. *See* the Art. 4(3).
1139. *See* the Rulebook on the types and system of risk management in insurance companies and reinsurance companies in FB&H, Art. 4(5).
1140. *See ibid.*, Art. 4(6).
1141. *See ibid.*, Art. 4(4).
1142. *See ibid.*, Art. 4(7).

control at the same time.[1143] In case when complete separation of business functions is not suitable due to the size of the company, then the company is obliged to ensure, in another way, avoidance and management of conflicts of interest.[1144]

699. The executive board of the company (management) has ultimate responsibility for the effectiveness of the entire risk management system and all employees must participate in the operation of the risk management system.[1145] The management of the company must be informed about the risks to which the company is exposed or to which it could be exposed, in such a way so that it can identify them, monitor and assess their impact on the company's operations, and must adopt appropriate measures to manage them.[1146]

700. The entire risk management system must be documented in such a way that the management of the company as well as third parties, can at any time understand the operation of a particular process within the risk management system.[1147]

701. The insurance company is obliged to identify, assess and measure the risks to which it is exposed in its operations and to manage these risks by applying qualitative and quantitative methods of management.[1148] Procedures for identifying, assessing and measuring risks, as well as for risk management should be established in accordance with the regulations, standards and rules of the insurance profession.[1149] The types of risks in the performance of insurance activities, the conditions and methods of identification, measurement and monitoring of these risks and the management of these risks are prescribed by the Rulebook on the types and system of risk management in insurance companies and reinsurance companies.[1150]

702. With regard to risk management function within the insurance company, the company is obliged to establish it as an independent function within the framework of the risk management system in such a way that it facilitates the implementation of the risk management system.[1151] As a part of this function, the company is obliged to ensure the performance of at least the following tasks: identification of risks to which the company is exposed or could be exposed in its operations; analysis and assessment, that is measurement of risks to which the company is exposed or could be exposed in its operations; monitoring the risks to which the company is exposed or could be exposed in its operations; management of risk to which the company is exposed or could be exposed in its operations; monitoring the risks to

1143. *See ibid.*, Art. 4(8).
1144. *See ibid.*, Art. 4(9).
1145. *See ibid.*, Art. 4(10) and (11).
1146. *See ibid.*, Art. 4(12).
1147. *See ibid.*, Art. 4(13).
1148. *See* the LI FB&H, Art. 61(6).
1149. *See ibid.*, Art. 61(7).
1150. *See* the Arts 8, 9, 10 and 11.
1151. *See* the Rulebook on the types and system of risk management in insurance companies and reinsurance companies in FB&H, Art. 5(1).

which the company is exposed or could be exposed in its operations; defining the risk profile of the company, that is, risk tolerance and ability to accept risk, in accordance with strategies, constant monitoring of the company's risk profile, with the establishment of an early warning and risk prevention system, in connection with the fulfilment of the conditions defined by law for the constant maintenance of liquidity and solvency; verification of the application and effectiveness of procedures and measures for managing the risks to which the company is exposed or could be exposed in its operations; reporting to the company's executive board on risk management; participation in the creation, implementation and review of the risk management strategy, as well as other internal acts and procedures and measures from the domain of company risk management; advising the company's executive board regarding the establishment of the company's risk profile, and monitoring the established risk profile; contribute to the establishment of an effective system of internal controls; providing proposals and recommendations for appropriate and effective risk management; carrying out stress resistance testing; and conducting other examinations that are necessary for an effective risk control system.[1152]

703. Essential role in performance of the risk management function within the insurance company belongs to the function holder who must be qualified for the tasks he/she performs[1153] and has appropriate knowledge in the field of insurance or other related financial services, skills and experience in order to be able to perform and explain the methods and manner of performing the delegated tasks.[1154] The holder of the function of risk management is obliged to perform his duties with the attention of a good expert.[1155] The company is obliged to provide the holder of the risk management function with the necessary authority and access to all data essential for the fulfilment of the aforementioned tasks.[1156]

704. Most important rules on risk management are contained in the Article 62 of the LI FB&H. Firstly, according to the Law an insurance company manages risk if in its operations it ensures: (a) share capital at least in the amount prescribed by Article 25 of the LI FB&H, (b) technical reserves in accordance with Article 80 of the LI FB&H, (c) liquidity of the company in accordance with Article 75 of the LI FB&H, (d) timely payment of damages, contracted insurance sums and performance of other obligations from the basis of insurance in accordance with the rules of the insurance profession, good business practices and business ethics, (e) depositing and investing assets of technical and mathematical reserves in accordance with Articles 89 and 93 of the LI FB&H, (f) guarantee fund in accordance with Article 73 of the LI FB&H, (g) solvency margin in accordance with Articles 71 and 72 of

1152. *See ibid.*, Art. 5(2).
1153. The tasks for which the holder of the risk management function is in charge must be documented and transparent. *See* Art. 5(5) of the Rulebook on the types and system of risk management in insurance companies and reinsurance companies in FB&H.
1154. *See* the Rulebook on the types and system of risk management in insurance companies and reinsurance companies in FB&H, Art. 5(4).
1155. *See ibid.*, Art. 5(6).
1156. *See ibid.*, Art. 5(3).

the LI FB&H, (h) co-insurance and reinsurance of risks excess above the maximum self-retention in accordance with Articles 99 and 101 of the LI FB&H, (i) coverage of insurance costs with an overhead allowance, (j) true and objective presentation of financial statements, (k) other activities in order to fulfil the previously stated obligations in points from (a) to (j), as well as other obligations prescribed by the LI FB&H related to risk management.[1157] Secondly, the insurance company is obliged to operate in such a way that the risks to which it is exposed, in individual or all types of insurance operations it performs, do not exceed the values or limits prescribed by the LI FB&H and the regulations adopted on the basis of it.[1158] Thirdly, the insurance company is obliged to operate according to the principles of liquidity and solvency.[1159]

705. The insurance company is obliged to keep statistical data on insurance operations, risks covered by insurance, insured cases and claims records and to process this data by applying the statistical standards for insurance prescribed by the Supervisory Agency.[1160]

1157. *See* the LI FB&H, Art. 62(1).
1158. *See ibid.*, Art. 62(2).
1159. *See ibid.*, Art. 62(3).
1160. *See ibid.*, Art. 63.

Selected Bibliography

Bikić, Abedin, '*Obligaciono pravo – opći dio*' (*Law of Obligations – General Part*). Sarajevo: Pravni fakultet Univerziteta u Sarajevu, 2004.

Blagojević, Milan & Tajić, Haso. 'Građansko i privredno parvo u praksi sudova u Bosni i Hercegovini (Aktuelna sudska praksa 2009–2012.)' (Civil and Commercial Law in practice of courts in Bosnia and Herzegovina – Current Case Law 2009–2012). Sarajevo: Privredna Štampa, 2013.

Blagojević, Milan et al. Odštetno pravo i pravo osiguranja u sudskoj praksi (Indemnity Law and Insurance Law in Case Law). Sarajevo: Privredna Štampa, 2013.

Bukljaš, Ivan & Vizner, Boris. Komentar Zakona o obveznim (obligacionim) odnosima (Commentary to the Law on Obligatiry Relations). Zagreb: Vlastita naklada, 1979.

Čović, Šefkija. *Poslovno pravo* (*Company Law*). Sarajevo: Pravni fakultet Univerziteta u Sarajevu, 2003.

Curak, Marijan & Jakovčević, Drago. *Osiguranje i rizici* (*Insurance and Risks*), Zagreb: RRIF Plus, 2007.

Curković, Marijan. Obvezna osiguranja u prometu (*Compulsory Insurance in Traffic*). Zagreb: Inženjerski biro, 2007.

Curković, Marijan. Ugovor o osiguranju osoba: život – nezgoda – zdravstveno (*Contract of Insurance of Persons: Life – Accident – Health*). Zagreb: Inženjerski biro, 2009.

Dedić, Sead. *Socijalno parvo (Social Security Law)*. Sarajevo: Pravni fakultet Univerziteta u Sarajevu, 2003.

Đorđević, Slavko & Samardžić, Darko. *Njemačko ugovorno parvo osiguranja sa prevodom zakona* (VVG) (*German Contract Law with Translation of the Law – VVG*). Belgrade: IRZ (Deutsche Stiftung für internationale rechtliche Zusammenarbeit e. V.), 2014.

Jankovec, Ivica & Miladinović, Zoran. *Pravo osiguranja* (*Insurance Law*), Niš: Centar za publikacije Pravnog fakulteta u Nišu, 2006.

Kočović, Jelena & Šulejić, Predrag. *Osiguranje* (*Insurance*), Beograd: Centar za izdavačku delatnost Ekonomskog fakulteta u Beogradu, 2006.

Marjanski, Vladimir. *Ugovor o osiguranju* (*Insurance Contract*), Centar za izdavačku djelatnost Pravnog fakulteta u Novom Sadu, Novi Sad, 2007.

Marović, Boris & Avdalović, Veselin. Osiguranje i upravljanje rizikom (*Insurance and Risk Management*), Subotica: Biografika, 2005.

Matijević, Berislav. Osiguranje u praksi – Odabrani radovi (*Insurance in Practice – Selected Papers*). Zadar: Naklada, 2007.

Selected Bibliography

Muminović, Edin. *Međunarodno privatno parvo (International Private Law)*. Sarajevo: Pravni fakultet Univerziteta u Sarajevu, 2006.

Ostojić, Siniša. Osiguranje i upravljanje rizicima (*Insurance and Risk Management*). Beograd: Data Status, 2007.

Pavić, Drago. 'Obveznopravna obilježja ugovora o osiguranju' (*Obligatory-Law Features of Insurance Contract*). Hrvatska pravna revija, 8(2004): 28–35.

Pavić, Drago. 'Osigurljiv interes' (*Insurable Interest*). Svijet osiguranja 6(2004): 39–48.

Pavić, Drago. Ugovorno pravo osiguranja – Komentar zakonskih odredaba (*Contractual Insurance Law – Commentary to the Statutory Provisions*). Zagreb: Tectus, 2009.

Perović, Slobodan. 'Stručno mišljenje o nacrtu zakona o obligacionim odnosima Federacije BiH/Republike Srpske'– knj. I, Opšti deo, sa stanjem 28. januara 2003. Beograd, 15. februar 2003' (An expert's opinion on the draft law on obligations of the Republic of Srpska/Federation of Bosnia and Herzegovina: Volume 1, general part, situation on 28 January 2003. Part II). Anali Pravnog fakulteta u Beogradu, Vol. 51(1–2) (2003): 10–86.

Šulejić, Predrag. '*Pravo osiguranja*' (*Insurance Law*). Belgrade: Pravni fakultet u Beogradu, 2005.

Šulejić, Predrag. 'Zaštita potrošača i ugovor o osiguranju' (*Consumer Protection and Insurance Contract*). Pravni život, 3–4 (2008): 41–49.

Trifković, Miloš & Simić, Milić & Trivun, Veljko. *Poslovno pravo: ugovori, vrijednosni papiri i pravo konkurencije* (*Company Law: Contracts, Securities and Competition Law*), Sarajevo: Ekonomski fakultet u Sarajevu – Izdavačka djelatnost, 2004.

Index

The numbers given here refer to paragraph numbers.

Index

www.ingramcontent.com/pod-product-compliance
Lightning Source LLC
Chambersburg PA
CBHW071436230926
51846CB00001B/257
* 9 7 8 9 4 0 3 5 2 8 0 7 6 *